Mickey Rooney

Mickey Rooney
A Show Business Life

James A. MacEachern

McFarland & Company, Inc., Publishers
Jefferson, North Carolina

LIBRARY OF CONGRESS CATALOGUING-IN-PUBLICATION DATA

Names: MacEachern, James A., 1949– author.
Title: Mickey Rooney : a show business life / James A. MacEachern.
Description: Jefferson, North Carolina : McFarland & Company, Inc., Publishers, 2017 | Includes bibliographical references and index.
Identifiers: LCCN 2017012242 | ISBN 9780786496396 (softcover : acid free paper) ∞
Subjects: LCSH: Rooney, Mickey. | Actors—United States—Biography.
Classification: LCC PN2287.R75 M33 2017 | DDC 791.43028/092 [B] —dc23
LC record available at https://lccn.loc.gov/2017012242

BRITISH LIBRARY CATALOGUING DATA ARE AVAILABLE

ISBN 978-0-7864-9639-6 (print)
ISBN 978-1-4766-2682-6 (ebook)

© 2017 Estate of James A. MacEachern. All rights reserved

No part of this book may be reproduced or transmitted in any form or by any means, electronic or mechanical, including photocopying or recording, or by any information storage and retrieval system, without permission in writing from the publisher.

Front cover image of Mickey Rooney in the 1950s (Photofest)

Printed in the United States of America

*McFarland & Company, Inc., Publishers
Box 611, Jefferson, North Carolina 28640
www.mcfarlandpub.com*

Acknowledgments

My sincerest thanks to the following people for their contributions to this book: Fred Roos, Carroll Ballard, Kelly Reno, Tim Farley, Barry Morrow, Corey Blechman, Lane Wyrick, Roger Corman, and Carl Reiner. I also want to give special thanks to Dick Rockwell for decades of stimulating conversations about movies, and my friend Jelena Krstovic for her encouragement and support.

Table of Contents

Acknowledgments	v
Introduction	1
One. Born in a Trunk	3
Two. Mickey (Himself) McGuire	16
Three. Shakespeare and O'Neill	23
Four. Fame Comes to Andy Hardy	31
Five. Jockeying for Parts	46
Six. Noir Star	59
Seven. Ava, with the Laughing Eyes	82
Eight. The Marrying Kind	93
Nine. Murder, He Wrote	114
Ten. *Sugar Babies*	123
Eleven. *The Black Stallion*	138
Twelve. Small Screen, Big Star	149
Thirteen. *Bill*	167
Fourteen. The Long Exit	176
Appendix A: Those Interviewed for This Book	183
Appendix B: Mickey Rooney's Credits	189
Appendix C: Awards and Honors	201
Bibliography	203
Index	205

Introduction

Much has been made about the extraordinary longevity of Mickey Rooney's career. But it's not just for his endurance that he will be remembered. There is an amazing body of work to be found, if one knows where to look. In some ways Rooney's incredible versatility has made it more difficult to assess his merits as an actor. In fact, most people think of him as primarily a comedian or, more broadly, as an entertainer. His career encompassed every facet of show business, from vaudeville to radio to films, TV, and even nightclubs. He could do so many things well—singing, dancing, playing the drums and piano, doing impressions, playing both comedy and drama—that critics and the audience lost sight of the fact that, at his core, he was, as Laurence Olivier stated, "The greatest actor America has produced." Wonderful performances in 1950s film noirs and supporting roles that saved otherwise routine World War II dramas and service comedies might have gained critical attention earlier if Rooney were not also headlining in Las Vegas or doing *The Mickey Rooney Show* on television, or making headlines by filing for bankruptcy or getting sued for his umpteenth divorce.

Why Mickey Rooney? I've been asked that question many times. I had some personal interest because he reminded me a bit of my dad, who was also of small stature, had a Scottish heritage, and only received a fifth-grade education. (Rooney, of course, had very little formal education and probably never read anything but scripts and the racing form.) When I was growing up, Rooney was always on TV, either in some old movie or doing a guest shot on a game show, a talk show, or as a dramatic actor on many of the top series—everything from *Combat!* to *Wagon Train*.

But as much as he was omnipresent on the tube and as many times as he went on and on about how he had been the number-one box-office star in the world, you never got the feeling of knowing who he really was. His basic life story—about how he had been on the stage since he was a

INTRODUCTION

toddler and was making movies by the time he was six, and how he became a big star working for MGM, and was infamous for his many marriages—was generally known, but the guy who seemed to be everywhere never seemed to be a real human being. He always appeared to be a creation of the movies. He was every bit a fabrication, much like Mickey Mouse, who, Rooney claimed, was named after him. He was always living out some male adolescent fantasy. He married and was divorced by many beautiful women, including Ava Gardner for Chrissake. In what universe does a very short, ordinary-looking, not all that intelligent man end up marrying one of the most beautiful women in the world and then get divorced because *he* was cheating on *her*? It can only happen in the movies, right?

Mickey Rooney is fascinating because he continued to get married, despite the fact that he kept ending up in divorce court. He continued to bet on the horses when he had no money to bet with. He continued to talk nonsense to the press and in TV interviews when anyone could tell him that his best path was to just shut up. And he continued to make bad movies and take part in one misguided play or business venture after another, smiling through it all. And yet, just when everyone had given up on him, he would somehow knock everybody out with a live dramatic performance like *The Comedian*, or surprise us with a hilarious guest shot on a comedy series. He persevered and endured longer than any other performer in the history of show business. It was a shock when he passed away because it didn't seem like he would ever die.

I don't think anyone knew the real Joe Yule, Jr. (Mickey's original name) or Mickey McGuire (his legal name, briefly, in the late 1920s and early '30s), least of all Mickey Rooney. Andy Hardy, Whitey Marsh, Baby Face Nelson, Killer McCoy, Homer Macauley, Mickey Moran, Sammy Hogarth, and Bill Sackter all became real to their audience because of Rooney's genius as a performer. The great actors like Olivier and Brando got to play all the signature roles from Shakespeare to Tennessee Williams to O'Neill but, in the end, even they knew that the acting profession is a child's game and its essence is about pretending to be someone else. One of the greatest filmmakers of all time, Ingmar Bergman, once said, "Actors who don't have a direct connection to their childhood are not good actors. They are boring intellectual actors."

Joe Yule, Jr., Mickey McGuire, and Mickey Rooney were not intellectual actors; they just loved to pretend.

CHAPTER ONE

Born in a Trunk

> Look, I come from vaudeville, I come from burlesque, I come from heartaches, I come from sadness, I come from gladness, I come from work and sweat and respect for the craft.
> —Mickey Rooney, 1998

Mickey Rooney was born into show business, more precisely into the world of vaudeville and burlesque. The entertainment focus in burlesque was much narrower than vaudeville. It was more about the scantily clad girls and lowbrow comics. Burlesque at the time of Rooney's birth was still rather innocent and did not feature the nudity of more recent memory. Still, burlesque was considered to be vaudeville's poor cousin, and many considered it to be about one step above the circus. There were hawkers going through the audience selling candy and Cracker Jack and, if you were lucky, you could even win a prize.

Mickey's father, Joe Ninian Yule, Sr., was born in Edinburgh, Scotland, and immigrated to Brooklyn with his mother and older brother Jim when he was about six years old. Joe's mother died shortly after arriving in America and left him and his brother to fend for themselves. Young Joe found some work as a child actor in stage melodramas like *The Slaves of New York* and *The Volunteer Organist*. He entered the Army in 1917 when the U.S. joined the war against Germany, and fought in France. After the war he got a job in burlesque as a property man for a company called Jack Reid's Record Breakers.

* * *

American burlesque and vaudeville really began with minstrel shows, dating back to 1830. The first producer of such shows was Thomas D. Rice, who put together songs and dances around a unifying theatrical pattern. All the performers in these minstrel shows were white men who applied

Joseph Hart Vaudeville Co. direct from Weber & Fields Music Hall, New York City, 1899.

burnt cork to their faces to simulate Southern blacks during the plantation era. Rice introduced what would become a racial (as opposed to racist) stock character, the eager-to-please, shuffling, childlike negro. This character would endure for another century, not only in minstrel shows but

One. Born in a Trunk

also in vaudeville, on radio and early television, particularly on the enormously popular *Amos 'n' Andy Show*.

There was an established format in minstrel shows. The orchestra was backstage, the blackface performers were upstage, and a whiteface "middleman" or "interlocutor" was in front of the performers. There were six musicians on the side of the stage who were positioned in a semicircle; they played the "bones," which were pieces of wood that, when slapped together, sounded like castanets. These men also played "tams," or the tambourine. The interlocutor would begin the show by saying, "Gentlemen, be seated!" The minstrels would then sit down and the show would begin. The first part of the program consisted of some gags and songs between the interlocutor and the two end performers.

The second part was called the "Olio," which was a condensed variety show of quartet singers, terpsichorean novelties that included soft-shoe and clog dancing, and, on most occasions, a female impersonator. While the stage was being set up for the third act of the program, the orchestra would play. The finale was a song-and-dance routine called a "general ruckus" or "walk-around."

A long line of patrons outside Vaudeville House in January 1912.

As the minstrel shows gained in size and popularity, they became a more lucrative enterprise and these shows would travel from town to town by train, with the names of the troupes emblazoned on the sides of the boxcars. Eventually, Rice took his show to New York, where it was a big hit, spawning more minstrel companies. One of the most famous was Christy's Minstrels, which was very popular in the 1860s and toured the United States. The sounds of the banjo, the tambourine, and the raucous reactions of audiences were familiar to almost everyone in small towns and big cities in America after the Civil War.

The man most responsible for creating what became known as "vaudeville" was Tony Pastor. Pastor was a successful beer hall owner who would occasionally book some variety acts to entertain his customers. They were usually racy female dancers or vulgar male comedians. Pastor soon discontinued this risqué form of entertainment in favor of "clean" variety acts that were suitable for the entire family. This proved to be an immediate success and, before long, fellow impresarios such as Benjamin Franklin Keith and his partner Edward Franklin Albee, and Frederick Freeman Proctor, moved their variety shows into well-equipped, custom-built vaudeville theatres. As the trend increased in popularity, vaudeville "circuits" developed. These were allied networks of theatres that were organized to make booking various acts easier and to keep the performers busy, thus turning it into a full-time occupation. The major vaudeville booking agents were in New York and Chicago. The nationally known acts would play in the top circuits like the Keith-Albee on the East Coast, and the Sullivan-Considine in the West. You might find The Marx Bros. (as they were billed) or Buster Keaton (then a child acrobat appearing with his parents in an act known as The Three Keatons) working these circuits. Newspapers in large towns had listings of who would be playing at the local vaudeville theatres. There was strict regulation regarding performers' conduct, salaries, and material—the phrase "blue material" supposedly originated with the blue envelopes in which Keith managers would send back censored gags, making them hated by many performers.

Rooney's mother, Nell Carter, was born in Arkansas but raised in Kansas City, Missouri, with her sister Edna and brothers Harry and Charlie. She was also orphaned at an early age and had a restless spirit. She left home at fourteen and was hired as a dancer by a traveling show called *Miller's Maidens*. She made all of $1 per week and probably felt that she should never have left home. Carter was not one to stay with some-

One. Born in a Trunk

thing that wasn't working and, before long, she signed with another show, this one featuring a small-time comic named Bobby Barker. Her salary was now $14 a week, but this was hardly commensurate with the arduous work of doing five shows a day, not to mention the brutal traveling conditions. Small-time vaudeville troupes traveled the back roads to small towns in Oklahoma and Nebraska along treacherous dirt roads and stayed in dirty rooming houses. Carter was, by all accounts, a very good dancer, but she was short and was therefore relegated to the pony line in front of the taller chorus girls. Positioned at the end of the line, she was, in the parlance of vaudeville and burlesque, an "end pony." She declared years later that she worked in burlesque when you had to be a good dancer and not just show off your body. She quit playing tank towns when she landed a job with Jack Reid's Record Breakers.

The small-time burlesque performer dreamed of making it rich as a big-time vaudeville performer like Sophie Tucker, Jack Benny, Burns & Allen, Al Jolson, Eddie Cantor, or George Jessel. These well-known entertainers commanded large salaries and only performed two shows a day—a matinee and an evening show. They worked in ornately designed theatres in the big cities and were under contract to the most prestigious circuits. Even those who made their reputations in other fields, including "The Sultan of Swat" Babe Ruth, radical temperance advocate Carrie Nation, and the charismatic evangelist Aimee Semple McPherson, appeared in vaudeville. Will Rogers entertained audiences with his signature rope tricks while comically commenting on the politics of the day. Harry Houdini, "The Handcuff King," amazed them with his feats of escape.

This was the life to which Joe Yule, Sr., and Nell Carter aspired—the big time!

Joe was hired as a property man for Jack Reid's Record Breakers when the troupe arrived in New York. It was there that he met Nell one day when she needed a costume for one of her dance numbers; Yule could only find an evening dress that was too large for the diminutive chorine. They began to argue and she stormed off when it became clear he couldn't help her. They continued to bicker with each other and, just like in a bad movie, a relationship developed. He became more and more enamored with the feisty little dancer and he soon proposed. As it happens, Jack Reid's troupe was headed to Niagara Falls and the two were married in nearby Rochester. Reid didn't like the fact that one of his best dancers got married without his knowledge and a big argument ensued between him and the new couple. Depending on which source you believe, the pair was either fired or quit. They were not out of work for long, though, because she hooked up with Pat White and His Gaiety Girls, and he was again hired as a property man. Soon after, one of White's comedians died and Joe was asked if he would like to give comedy a try. This wasn't such a stretch because he was very jovial and kept everyone backstage in stitches with his wisecracks. This new gig, of course, was on a trial basis, but he proved to be such a natural that he was soon the featured comic or, in show business terms, the Top Banana.

* * *

It wasn't long before Nell became pregnant, although she worked in the chorus line until six weeks before she was due. Joe Yule, Jr., entered the world's stage on September 23, 1920, in a rooming house on Willoughby Avenue in Brooklyn. The couple had raised the $150 deposit for Nell to give birth in a lying-in hospital, but the terms were that you had two weeks to pay the balance or the hospital could keep the baby! This, as outlandish as it sounds, was apparently a common practice. The parents had to sign over custody to the hospital until the debt was paid. She worried that if it took a while to get the cash they might end up with the wrong baby, which was something that could definitely happen, so they opted to have the five-pound seven-ounce boy at home in Brooklyn. On the day of young Joe's birth, his father was nowhere to be found. A search was launched and the proud father was finally located: he was drunk and sitting on a pile of dirty laundry under the chute singing "Glasgow Belongs to Me." For financial reasons, Joe Senior left Brooklyn, his wife, and newborn son the following day to go back on the road with Pat White's Gaiety Girls. Nell would join him with Sonny, as the boy was called, who was just two weeks old at the time.

Rooney's earliest years were spent backstage at scores of vaudeville and burlesque houses across the United States. His crib was the top drawer of a dresser in one of the many cheap rooming houses at which the new family stayed. Every vaudeville performer dreamed of playing the Palace Theatre, at Forty-Seventh and Broadway in New York. They had to be content, at least for now, with The Gaiety Girls and cooking meals with sterno cans in their rooms while risking eviction because of the strict "no cooking" rule. They washed their clothes in a sink and hung them out the window to dry. It was a hardscrabble existence and it took strong-willed people with a romantic streak to even attempt this kind of career. Show business was not the profession most mothers and fathers wanted their children to enter.

Vaudevillians, for the most part, were in the business for the money and not the art. Just like these variety shows appealed to a mass audience and were aimed at the working class, the performers were working class as well. John Lahr, son of Bert Lahr, the great burlesque comic and, later, the Cowardly Lion in *The Wizard of Oz*, said in the PBS series *American Masters* program on vaudeville, "It was all about money. Groucho Marx and my father never got past the fifth grade. Buster Keaton had exactly one day of formal education." (Rooney's education was sporadic at best once he got into movies. It was mostly done on the MGM lot in a schoolhouse designed for the child actors under contract to the studio.)

There was a pecking order to each vaudeville show bill or lineup. Where you were placed on the bill was a good indication of your standing in the business. (To be fair, theatre managers weren't always the best judges of talent; to his dying day, Fred Astaire was indignant about having been replaced on a bill by a dog act.)

Big-time vaudeville shows usually consisted of eight acts, the first of which was silent, often featuring a trained animal. The lack of dialogue in the act allowed late-arriving theatregoers to take their seats without disturbing other audience members. The second act, known as "the burial ground," because so many acts "died" there, was often a minor singer or comic. The third act was a tab show or flash act, a condensed play or revue, complete with large sets and effects, creating a "flash." The fourth act was an established comedy team, and the fifth (just before the intermission) was a knockabout routine or a tab show, depending on what was featured in the three spot. After intermission would be a solid dance team. This was followed by the most coveted spot on the bill: next to closing. This belonged to the headliner, the star of the bill. Once that act concluded, the final act was designed to be so bad it would chase the audience out of the theatre to make room for a new crowd. It was sometimes known as "playing to the haircuts" because the performer—perhaps a second-rate juggler or magician—would be watching the backs of audience members' heads as they made their hasty way up the aisle.

The main difference between vaudeville and burlesque, aside from the quality of the acts, was the quantity. There was a performer named Birdie Reeve who was "the world's fastest typist." If there was an audience for something, anything, you could find it in vaudeville. If someone was willing to watch what you did, you could make a living doing it. There were the usual singers and comics but also acrobats, jugglers, whistlers, yodelers, strongmen performing feats of strength, iron-jaw acts, mind readers, hypnotists, and regurgitators. Yes, regurgitators! The most famous regurgitator of his day was Hadji Ali, who would drink a bottle of kerosene then a bottle of water. There was a small prop model house that had been set ablaze. He would then make the fire bigger by spewing the kerosene he swallowed, and then put the fire out with the water he had swallowed. There was even a guy who swallowed molten lead and then spit out coins.

Rooney loved growing up around vaudevillians. He rhapsodized in his 1991 biography about the sights, sounds, and smells that surrounded him in the theatres in which his parents played. The blinding spotlights, the colored mood lights, and the brightly lit marquee mesmerized him. The sounds of the instruments in the orchestra made every day have a kind of magic to it. He even recalled the rancid smell of greasepaint, the smoke pots, and the sweet makeup and powder that the chorus girls used. The costumes, the sets, the props—these were his toys. To hear him tell it, no child could have wanted for a better playground than a theatre in the early 1920s.

Legend has it that seventeen-month-old Sonny was hiding under a bootblack stand onstage during comedian Sid Gould's act when he sneezed, breaking up the audience. Gould tried to go on with his act but the tot sneezed again, so the comedian had no choice but to turn over the prop, only to find Sonny smiling up at him. In this version of the story Sonny had a toy harmonica that Gould encouraged him to play and he did it rather well and even ad-libbed a few lines, to appreciative applause. In another version he was hiding behind a prop during the act and began playing with a miniature set of drums and Gould had to stop to find out where the noise was coming from. In both versions—and there may be others—Sonny saw his angry parents in the wings and was afraid to leave the stage. In every version of the clearly apocryphal story, the audience was awed by the child's remarkable stage presence. Sonny finally left the stage and was in the process of being scolded by his parents when the theatre manager interrupted and insisted that Sonny become part of the show. He even shelled out $50 for a new little tuxedo for the lad and he would be presented as a midget smoking a candy cigar. The couple was hesitant at first, but when told that their weekly pay would increase by three bucks they quickly relented. It is hard to believe that a child just barely out of diapers could actually have any stage presence at all, but many swear to the story. Rooney stated in both of his autobiographies that he could both

The Sandow Trocadero Vaudevilles in his wonderful performance, lifting the human "dumbell" (ca. 1894).

walk and talk just a little bit after his first birthday. (In one of his monologues, Bob Hope repeated the legend of how the toddler "busted out of his bassinet at seventeen months old and stole his parents' vaudeville act and he has been guilty of grand theft ever since.")

* * *

Vaudeville was the theatre of the people, "its brassy assurance a dig in the nation's ribs, its simplicity as naïve as a circus," writes Douglas Gilbert in his book, *Vaudeville: Its Life and Times.* "The two-a-day variety show all of us knew and many of us loved was a complete characterization of a pleasantly gullible, clowning America, physically bestirring itself, sunnily unsophisticated. Its social implications, reflected in the response of its audiences, are pronounced because its entertainment was largely topical fun. The trend of its humor was the march of those times. Thus, vaudeville is an important chapter, not only of the stage, but of Americana."

Once he had made his successful debut, Sonny had to get down to the task of learning an act that could be performed every night, and Sid Gould was in charge of coming up with something. It was decided to try and get the kid to learn a popular little ditty called "Sweet Rosie O'Grady." Rooney recalled that he and Gould worked on it for about three weeks until he had it down and that even at that age he had a very good memory. Rooney also claimed that once he put on that little tuxedo he became a miniature adult—that the suit itself had transformative powers. He said he would talk like an adult all the time but wouldn't know what the hell he was saying. By all accounts, Gould and his infant colleague worked well together. They would trade old jokes onstage and the audience would always laugh whether the jokes were funny or not because everything a two-year-old says or does, especially one dressed in a tuxedo and holding a cigar, is going to get a laugh.

As rudimentary as the training was, Rooney's early days in vaudeville informed his entire career in show business, especially when it came to ad-libbing. In burlesque, and for the most part in vaudeville, too, the performers didn't have professional writers working for them; they had to come up with their own material. They had to rely on their skills as performers and picked up bits of business, jokes, and stories wherever they found them, and embellished and polished material in front of an audience. There was also a lot of thievery going on, as comics would lift material from other comedians, causing many hard feelings in the process.

One. Born in a Trunk

John Lahr said there were certain comics' names that were not allowed to be mentioned in his father's household, particularly Milton Berle (the notorious "Thief of Badgags"). But Sonny was too young to steal anything but the hearts of audience members when he performed the sentimental standard "Pal o' My Cradle Days."

Sonny continued to work with his parents on the circuit for another few years. He recalled that his mother always treated him like the star in the family. They were always on the road and had to drag their theatrical trunk from town to town. When they would check into a hotel, Joe was in charge of hauling their trunk to the room while the porter would be assigned to carry Sonny's little valise. When they traveled by train, the boy would dine on steak while his parents settled for sandwiches.

Pat White would sometimes have Sonny, dressed in his little tuxedo, stand outside the theatres with him, encouraging passersby to stop in and see the beautiful girls. According to Rooney, some local citizens got wind of the fact that there was a two-year-old dressed as a midget encouraging men to come in and see scantily clad women cavort around the stage, and that someone should put a stop to it. Sonny and his parents ended up in the office of Governor Al Smith of New York to plead their case. Rooney said that Smith was a show business fan and, after Sonny did a little song and dance for him, the Yules were given a special permit to allow the tot to keep working.

Rooney also recalled that his parents were having a hard time in their marriage. They were always arguing about Joe's drinking and philandering. Marriage and fatherhood, apparently, were not his callings. Sonny was prone to accidents and illness, like the time he fell down some stairs at a rooming house and broke his leg, or when he got diphtheria and had to spend some time in the hospital. This all cost money, something Joe had little of. Rooney recalled hearing his father muttering to Nell, "You and that goddamn kid" on many occasions. By the time Sonny was four years old, his parents broke up. Nell finally told Joe that she would no longer tolerate his behavior and they divided up what money they had. Joe left for a gig in Chicago, and Nell and Sonny headed for Kansas City to live with relatives. It would be many years before Sonny would see his father again.

Even though Sonny's career in vaudeville ended by the age of four, he was already a veteran in show business. The performance discipline that audiences and critics would marvel at over the next ninety years was already ingrained in his very being. Performing was in his blood. He was probably the best example of someone who was born on stage or, as the saying goes, "in a trunk." There was something about that intense performance training, the two-a-day (or, in small time, five-a-day) work schedule, that was the greatest preparation for a life in the performing arts.

* * *

Sonny and his mother stayed with relatives for a while, and it wasn't long before she and a friend opened their own "chicken shack" restaurant to bring in some income. Rooney later talked about the period in Kansas City as being his only taste of what most people would think of as a "normal" childhood. He had other kids to play with and his own dog, Ziggy. He enjoyed digging for worms in the backyard and going fishing with his uncle Wade. He also recalled the smell of catfish frying on Aunt Edna's big black skillet and taking the streetcar down to the Circle Theatre in Kansas City to see the latest Tom Mix movie. But after a few months of this idyllic life, Nell was back to reading *Variety* and both mother and son would become wistful at the sound of a distant train whistle.

Nell read that comedy producer Hal Roach was looking for children for his successful series of Our Gang two-reelers, which had officially begun in 1922. She convinced Myrtle, her business partner in the chicken shack, that she should join her and Sonny for a road trip to Hollywood. It was a tough four-week trip by car from Kansas City to Los Angeles. In 1924 there were few places to stay; there were no Holiday Inns or Ramada Inns and, even if there were, the ex-vaudevillians wouldn't have had the money to pay for them. The women brought along plenty of food and would take turns cooking on an open fire by the side of the road. They slept in a tent and, if it rained, they had to sleep in the car. Nobody made this kind of trip for fun; you did it as a matter of survival. The trip was also not without incident because Sonny, who, as previously stated, seemed to be accident-prone, fell off a teeter-totter and broke his arm. This required a trip to the hospital, and further expense. The trio was broke and hungry when they finally arrived in sunny California.

When Nell took Sonny to the Roach studio in Culver City, the producer's assistant was pleased enough with Sonny to offer him work at $5 a day. Nell was outraged at the offer and stormed out of the office. (In an interview late in his life, Hal Roach said that, when it came to casting his

One. Born in a Trunk

Our Gang comedies, he preferred non-actors to experienced professionals. Rooney auditioned, Roach confirmed, but was turned down. "He overacted," the producer remembered, "... he'd lost his naturalness.")

With no money for the return trip to Kansas City, Nell had to take a job as a chorus girl in a show in Oakland. Once she earned enough for train tickets to Kansas, they were soon back where they started. Fortunately, she met a theatre manager by the name of George Christman, who was putting together a group of performers to take out to Hollywood. So it was back on the trail, with eleven people in two cars, and they didn't even have a tent this time: it was sleeping bags out under the stars. Soon after arriving in Hollywood for the second time, Nell and Sonny set off on their own to find riches, and this time they were not going to be denied. She had the ambition, and Sonny had the talent.

CHAPTER TWO

Mickey (Himself) McGuire

> The movie Mickey McGuire was much like the comic strip McGuire: brash, wise beyond his years, and stubborn. So he also was much like Joe Yule, Jr.
> —Mickey Rooney, quoted in *The Great Movie Shorts* by Leonard Maltin, 1972

Rooney's mother got a steadier gig working as a resident manager at a bungalow court. The job paid no money, but it provided a roof over their heads. To generate some income she also worked for Bell Telephone as an operator. On Sundays she and Sonny would ride the trolley out to Beverly Hills to watch the new mansions being built; the swanky locale was just being developed at that time. Since she was busy with two jobs, she didn't have time to take Sonny to the studios. In order to keep his performing skills sharp, she enrolled him in Daddy Mack's Dance Studio. Rooney recalled that the first time he saw Daddy Mack he thought he looked ridiculous. Mack was very short and heavy, with a strange, tinny voice when addressing his students. Rooney said that his attitude changed toward Mack when he saw how gracefully he moved on the dance floor. Daddy Mack taught the young actor that what might appear to be ridiculous at first was ultimately in the eye of the beholder.

Sonny got his first break when he got a part in a musical revue at the Orange Grove Playhouse in Los Angeles. He had no trouble securing the role; although still only six years old and very tiny, he was already a polished show business veteran. In his audition he sang "Sweet Rosie O'Grady," the tune that made him a hit in vaudeville. The job paid a much-needed $50 per week. According to numerous biographies, the boy was the only member of the cast not suffering from opening-night nerves. In fact, he went around backstage telling all the adult performers that there was nothing to be afraid of and that they would all be great when they stepped onstage. Sonny was a natural in his role and a huge hit with the

Two. Mickey (Himself) McGuire

audience, whose sustained applause required him to perform an encore. He had already performed in front of audiences at the Roxy, the Orpheum, and the Palace, so the Orange Grove Playhouse was no big deal to him, but it did garner a positive write-up in the *Los Angeles Times*.

Even though his mother was quite busy trying to provide food and shelter for Sonny and herself, she was once again making the rounds at the movie studios. In early 1926 she received a phone call from the Fox Film Corporation and, according to Rooney, it came just in time because she had lost the job with the phone company and they were down to eating scraps. As soon as she got off the phone with the casting director from Fox, she rushed out to get Sonny, who was at the playground. She took him home and cleaned him up and then it was off to the studio.

The director of the picture for whom Sonny was to audition couldn't believe he was so young and thought that he

Young Joe Yule, Jr., vaudeville veteran at five years old, c. 1925 (Photofest).

looked like a midget, and that was exactly what he was looking for in his picture. The silent comedy short was called *Not to Be Trusted*. In the film, Sonny portrays a con man who is in cahoots with a burglar to steal some diamonds. Sonny's character is pretending to be an orphan to get some rich people to adopt him and, once in the family, he and his accomplice can steal the family jewels. Rooney remembered that members of the cast and crew treated him like an adult midget, so his performance must have been convincing. He also recalled that he was required to smoke a cigar all day and, although this nauseated him, he suppressed it because it meant five bucks a day.

Nell had the foresight to get a stack of 8x10s made of her son when he was working for Fox. These came in handy for his audition for *Orchids and Ermine*, a silent film with a synchronized musical score by Vitaphone (an early sound-on-disc system used by Warner Bros. and its sister studio First National). This 1927 comedy starred the popular Colleen Moore. Sonny was six by this time, but his mother told him to tell the producers that he was younger because they seemed more impressed the younger you were. When he told the producers he was three they were so intrigued that they took him to meet the film's director, Alfred Santell, and the gagman for the film, Mervyn LeRoy, who would go on to become a prominent producer and director. Santell and LeRoy were impressed with Sonny and he was hired, once again, to play a midget. He was taken to the costuming and makeup department and outfitted with a nifty little suit and made up with a thin mustache glued to his upper lip. He also had greasepaint applied to his face, his eyebrows darkened, and even some mascara to highlight his eyelashes.

Rooney remembered Colleen Moore as "a doll" and admitted that he would stare at her between takes. The first scene they were in required Sonny to emerge from the elevator in a big hotel then light up his cigar, walk over to a busy telephone operator (Moore) at the hotel, and begin talking to her. Although she can hear him, she can't see him while seated at her desk. When she finally stands up to look over the desk, she sees the tiny man, who begins flirting with her, causing her to smile. Everyone on the set was impressed with Sonny's performance, and Mervyn LeRoy told him that they would be working together again soon.

Rooney had appeared in just two films and was already typecast. There weren't any more midget roles available, so Nell had to find something more permanent for them. She would receive calls from studios for one role or another and they would rush over and find out that a six-year-old kid who looked even younger was not quite what they were looking for. A big break came when she received a call from a new studio in town called FBO (Film Booking Offices of America). A producer named Larry Darmour had an idea to start a franchise along the lines of Hal Roach's Our Gang comedies. Darmour collaborated with a cartoonist named Fontaine Fox who did a newspaper comic strip called "Toonerville Folks" (a.k.a. "The Toonerville Trolley That Meets All the Trains"). The strip would be the basis for a series of comedy shorts about a group of rambunctious kids. They needed a tough little character to play the lead, Mickey (Himself) McGuire, and Sonny was perfect for the part.

Two. Mickey (Himself) McGuire

Nell and Sonny gathered together all the comic strips they could find and laid them out on a table to study the character of Mickey McGuire the night before the audition. By the next day Sonny was completely prepared and had the tough little "Mickey" character down. The character was an extremely cocky kid who wouldn't listen to anybody, and that included adults as well as the other kids in the neighborhood. He was also a born troublemaker and it was his mischief-making that would establish the plot of each of these two-reel shorts. There was one problem as they approached the audition, and that was that the main character had black hair and Sonny's was blond, but that was easily corrected when Nell colored his hair with black shoe polish. "I didn't like it, but I did it anyway," Rooney later recalled.

They waited patiently all day at FBO for Sonny's audition. They both knew that Sonny was perfect for the part and was completely prepared but that didn't mean he would get it. One by one the young actors would come out of the auditions with dejected looks on their faces, followed by their equally disappointed parents. Finally, late in the afternoon, Sonny was called in and he was ready to perform for the camera. He was instructed by the director to sneak around the corner of a make-believe barn then sit down on a box, cross his legs, take out a rubber cigar from his pocket and begin to chew on it. Al Herman, who directed the test, was impressed with the youngster's innate ability to act in front of the camera and wanted him back the next day to shoot something, with Sonny in costume. Bright and early the next morning, Sonny was outfitted with the derby hat, the checkered shirt, and the torn trousers of the character from the comic strip. The producers knew they had found their Mickey McGuire.

Nell and Sonny were ecstatic when they were offered a five-year contract at $50 a week. Nell had the foresight, however, to secure the services of an agent who negotiated a salary of $250 per short. Darmour and company would make seventy-eight of the Mickey McGuire shorts between 1926 and 1932. The first eight were silent and the rest were talkies, but there was never much dialogue in these two-reelers. They consisted mainly of action, physical humor, and that old standby—a chase at the climax. What little dialogue these stories had was no problem for Sonny because he had been very verbal as an infant and spoke and sang in vaudeville. During this period, he acquired what could be called a sporadic education that included some public schools and the classrooms that the studio provided. Sonny was never that interested in books anyway. He was much too active and energetic to sit quietly for any length of time and study. He was always on the move as a kid, a pattern he would follow for the rest of his life. He was definitely a handful for the teachers he came in contact with, not just because of his boundless energy, but also because of his foul mouth. The young boy had developed quite a colorful vocabulary while working around adult vaudevillians, and when he would get angry or frustrated he would let loose with the expletives. However, the producers of the Mickey McGuire series didn't mind his behavior or language, because they felt that made him more like the character he played. This proved beneficial to his performances and the series.

It was Nell's idea to change her son's name from Joe Yule, Jr., to Mickey McGuire. Once the series started becoming popular everyone began calling him Mickey anyway, so she figured, Why not? Fontaine Fox, who created the character, didn't like the idea at all and brought suit against Darmour and FBO for instigating the name change. Rooney indicated in his first autobiography that the studio did this to try and beat Fontaine Fox out of royalties from the series. The idea was that if Joe Yule, Jr., was legally Mickey McGuire then the studio could claim their films were based on the life of a real kid and not on the comic-strip character. The lawsuit dragged on for years as the series continued. The success of the series made Mickey known to audiences and industry people alike. The steady income was a first for him and his mother and they were no longer living from job to job. Because of this, he was taken out of public school and enrolled in Ma Lawlor's professional school for children in show business. (He would meet friends like Judy Garland and Jackie Cooper at this school in the not-too-distant future.)

Mickey loved acting, and Nell was the typical stage mother, telling anyone and everyone who would listen that her son was the best child actor in Hollywood and that he would be, one day soon, a huge star. She was an eternal optimist, a trait he seemed to have inherited from her. Nell had worked so hard to escape her impoverished background. Her drive spurred him on, but nobody could have foreseen the almost supernatural energy and will to succeed that he would exhibit throughout his career. From the very beginning he knew nothing but a life onstage and he lived and breathed show business. Nell was driven too, but from the very beginning her ambition was focused on Mickey and, ultimately, his success was her personal triumph as well.

Despite their low production values, the Mickey McGuire comedies

Two. Mickey (Himself) McGuire

were very successful, often equaling the popularity of Our Gang, especially in small towns. But whereas Our Gang lasted until 1944, the McGuire series ended ten years earlier. In the related earlier legal matter, the court ordered that the Mickey McGuire name be returned to Fontaine Fox. Nell was livid at first and initially threatened to fight the ruling, but it was a hopeless exercise to fight it because they had no chance of winning. Fox created the character and therefore owned it. Nell came to accept the fact that Fox had a lock on the last name, but the courts couldn't keep her from using the first.

During a break in the series in 1932, Mickey returned to vaudeville, where he performed some of the bits from the McGuire films. When Fontaine Fox learned about this, he filed an injunction to cease and desist. They headed back to Hollywood, where Mickey had a small part in the Universal race-track drama *Fast Companions* (a.k.a. *The Information Kid*). The producers realized they needed a new last name for Mickey. Nell remembered an old vaudevillian by the name of Pat Rooney, and so now (and forevermore), Joe Yule, Jr., would be known as Mickey Rooney.

For the next few years Rooney landed some small parts in even smaller B-movies, including *The Big Cage* and a western with Tom Mix called *My Pal, the King*. He received his first mention in the *New York Times* for the Mix movie: "Little Mickey Rooney appears as Charles and does quite well." He also had a few small roles during this period in some MGM films, including *Broadway to Hollywood*, a backstage story that features a great scene of Rooney dancing his heart out with a huge smile as he bows to an appreciative audience.

His biggest break came in 1933 when Hollywood bigwig David O. Selznick saw Mickey clowning around during a table tennis tournament at the Ambassador Hotel in Los Angeles. According to Rooney, he noticed Selznick in the audience and put on a performance specifically for him. Selznick was an independent producer and would go on to make *Gone with the Wind* (1939), directed by Victor Fleming, and *Rebecca* (1940), the first American film directed by Alfred Hitchcock. Perhaps more importantly for Rooney, Selznick was also the son-in-law of Louis B. Mayer, the head of MGM studios and the most powerful man in the movie business. During the tournament at the Ambassador, Rooney put on a show that included pantomime and funny patter along with some impressions of the movie stars of the day, like Clark Gable. Selznick told his wife to make a note about this very talented young man. Selznick, as the legend goes, kept thinking about the performance all evening and couldn't sleep that night in anticipation of telling Mayer about him the following day when he went in to work. There was a new Selznick picture coming up called *Manhattan Melodrama*, directed by W.S. Van Dyke and starring Clark Gable, William Powell, and Myrna Loy. There was no part in the film for Rooney as written, but Selznick had the writers create a role for him. He ended up playing the Clark Gable character as a child. The film didn't do well initially with critics or audiences, but when John Dillinger was fatally shot outside the Biograph Theatre in Chicago on July 22, 1934, after watching *Manhattan Melodrama*, things changed. The pictures of Dillinger lying dead beneath the marquee advertising the film appeared in newspapers all over the country. As the saying goes, you can't buy publicity like that.

One month later, Rooney signed a long-term contract with MGM.

CHAPTER THREE

Shakespeare and O'Neill

> You can do it, Mickey. You can do it.
> —Nell, encouraging her thirteen-year-old son to take on Shakespeare, 1934

One of Rooney's most memorable roles was his remarkably effective performance as Puck in Max Reinhardt's production of Shakespeare's *A Midsummer Night's Dream*. Reinhardt was a theatrical legend in Europe before immigrating to the United States. He had been the director of the Salzburg Festival in Austria and the Deutsches Theatre in Berlin. Reinhardt saw the writing on the wall (probably literally) with the ascent of the Nazi Party in Germany and fled to America as so many other artists were doing at the time. He settled in New York and had done some theatre work when he received an offer from the Los Angeles Chamber of Commerce to stage a production of *A Midsummer Night's Dream* at the Hollywood Bowl.

Reinhardt, who barely spoke a word of English, jumped at the chance. It was not only an opportunity to do a big theatre piece but he also harbored an ambition to become a film director and saw this as a ticket to do just that. The *Los Angeles Times* initiated the whole idea of the Hollywood Bowl extravaganza when they shamed the Hollywood studio heads into donating $125,000 to bring "real culture" to the community. Reinhardt sent his son Gottfried ahead to try to assemble his dream cast, which included Charlie Chaplin for Bottom, Greta Garbo for Titania, Clark Gable for Demetrius, Gary Cooper for Lysander, John Barrymore for Oberon, W.C. Fields for Thisbe, Wallace Beery for the Lion, Walter Huston for Theseus, Joan Crawford for Hermia, Myrna Loy for Helena, and Fred Astaire for Puck. But, as it turns out, these stars were contractually unavailable. There were two female stars who desperately wanted to play Puck: Olivia de Havilland, then just eighteen years old, and Mary Pickford, "America's Sweetheart," who was forty-one years old in 1934. Somehow

Jean Muir, as Helena, and Rooney, as Puck, in the Warner Bros. film version of Shakespeare's *A Midsummer Night's Dream* (1935).

Rooney was called to audition for the part and he admitted decades later that he never knew why his name came up, but he and his mother never turned down an opportunity, no matter how far-fetched it might seem. He also admitted that he had never read Shakespeare before (not a surprise) or since (again, not a surprise). Rooney was baffled by the poetry and the rhythm of the language. He struggled to understand the opening lines:

> How now, spirit! whither wander you?
> ...
> The king doth keep his revels here to-night:
> Take heed the queen come not within his sight; ...

Reinhardt's assistant Felix Weissberger was handling the auditions, which were held in the Roosevelt Hotel Ballroom. Rooney waited most of the day before he got his turn to wrap his tongue around some Shakespearean prose and, when he did, he recalled that he had no idea what he

Three. Shakespeare and O'Neill

was saying. Weissberger, however, loved his enthusiasm, and the fact that he was so small and had an impish quality about him made him the perfect Puck. Weissberger was impressed enough to give him a script to take home and memorize his part so that he could get a second look, this time from Reinhardt himself.

This was going to be the tough part. Rooney was exasperated by his task and felt like it was beyond him. Nell wouldn't tolerate his defeatism and went over the text with him, line by line and word by word. This was a long way from teaching her toddler the words to "Sweet Rosie O'Grady" back in their vaudeville days. They had both come so far and stardom seemed within their grasp and they couldn't let this opportunity pass. He always had a great facility for memorizing lines so that part of the process was not a problem.

Rooney recalled in his 1991 autobiography,

> Gradually, I began to get the feel of Shakespeare's iambic pentameter, if not fully understanding the poet's words. Many of them were words I never heard before, at least not like this. I knew what "passing" meant. I knew what "wrath" meant. I knew what "fell" meant. But what the heck did "passing fell and wrath" mean?

He not only got the rhythm of Shakespearean speech but was able to grasp the meaning of the words enough to give a confident reading. The second audition sealed the deal for Rooney becoming Puck. He claimed, decades later, that the spirit of Puck magically came over him during the audition. The laugh and gurgle—and almost animal-like quality—appeared just in time for Reinhardt to witness and be captivated by it. This may seem a bit esoteric, of course, but what other explanation is there? How else could a fourteen-year-old vaudeville comic so completely inhabit one of Shakespeare's most beloved characters?

Rooney enjoyed working with Reinhardt, who gave him invaluable direction through his assistant. When Mickey uttered the following lines in rehearsal,

> Up and down, up and down,
> I will lead them up and down.
> I am fear'd in field and town.
> Goblin, lead them up and down.

Reinhardt loved his reading, shouting "Ya, ya," and called Weissberger over to give his actor the instruction to move up and down while reciting the lines. In other words, he wanted Rooney to act with his whole body.

(This was a piece of direction that he would use on stage, in films, and on television for the next eighty years!) Rooney was hired for the part and received the princely sum of $300 per week for the run of the play. The other cast members for the stage production included Walter Connolly as Bottom, Sterling Holloway as Flute, Philip Arnold as Oberon, Evelyn Venable as Helena, and Olivia de Havilland as Hermia. Erich Wolfgang Korngold adapted the Mendelssohn score, and Bronislava Nijinska and Nini Theilade staged the ballet.

The play required a thirteen-hour dress rehearsal before its opening on September 17, 1934. The Hollywood Bowl was packed and almost every movie star in town was in attendance for the gala premiere. "I felt kind of funny when I was waiting in the wings for my first cue," Mickey later told biographer Arthur Marx. "I wasn't exactly scared, but I was kind of shaky. But after I was on stage, everything was all right." According to him—and to newspaper accounts—Puck was a hit. When he recited the closing lines:

> Gentles, do not reprimand.
> If you pardon, we will mend,
> Else the Puck, a liar call.
> Give me your hands if we be friends,
> And Robin shall restore amends.

Rooney recalled that there was thunderous applause from the audience, and as he and the cast took their bows there was a sweet affirmation that some Hollywood contract players and one adolescent vaudevillian had pulled it off—with the help of the great Reinhardt. The production had a month-long engagement in Los Angeles and then was taken on tour to the San Francisco Opera House and the Blackstone Theatre in Chicago, ending up in New York City.

After the successful run of the stage production, Warner Bros. decided to do a film version, with Reinhardt co-directing it with the experienced and fellow German expatriate William Dieterle. There would be cast changes for the film because Warners wanted to utilize their own talent pool. The cast included Jimmy Cagney, Dick Powell, Joe E. Brown, Hugh Herbert, Arthur Treacher, Victor Jory, Anita Louise, and Frank McHugh. Rooney and de Havilland were the only cast members from the stage production to reprise their roles for the film. De Havilland and Mickey formed a bond during the stage and film productions. She became like a surrogate mother to him, recalling the experience with much fondness. She remembered him burying his head in her lap to take a nap and asking her to wake him five lines before his cue to go on when they were appearing at the Hollywood Bowl. (She recalled that they met again some sixty years later at a ceremony for past Oscar winners and when Mickey

Rooney as Puck. *A Midsummer Night's Dream* (1935).

laid eyes on her, he beamed and came over to whisper some Shakespearean lines in her ear.)

When Rooney was hired to play Puck in the film, the producers, knowing his history with sports-related injuries, forbade him from playing football, baseball, or any other sport during the shooting of the picture. This was going to be the most expensive production in the studio's history, and they could not afford any delays. Any work stoppage could cost the studio $10,000 per day, and that was a lot of money in the throes of the Depression. His mother kept him to his promise about not playing any sports but, knowing the energy of her child, she decided to take him up to Big Bear Lake one Sunday afternoon to play in the snow. She figured he wouldn't get hurt just running around and throwing snowballs. But he found a way. He and some friends decided to do a little tobogganing and, of course, the best seat on a toboggan ride is at the front, so that's where he was when it slammed into a tree. He was sufficiently dazed by the impact to pass out for a moment and woke to find someone's foot dangling in front of his face. The searing pain made him realize that it was *his* leg he was staring at and he had, in fact, broken it badly. Help quickly arrived and Rooney was taken to a first-aid station, where they put his leg in splints and strapped him to a small toboggan that was put in the back seat of his mom's car. She drove him to Children's Hospital in Los Angeles, where his leg was put in a cast.

During the drive from Big Bear to L.A. mother and son barely spoke because they both felt like they screwed up royally and were worried about what Warners might do about Rooney's contract. They were well aware that there could be repercussions and that the legal department had the right to void his contract and get a new actor for the part. When Jack Warner heard about the accident he did threaten to break the teen's other leg, but once he cooled down, thanks to the intervention of Reinhardt and Dieterle, he realized that they had already shot too much footage with Rooney and to start over with a new Puck would be much too costly. The directors found ingenious ways to shoot around his cast. Puck is almost always in trees or behind bushes to obscure his injury. Given that no critic ever mentioned this, the staging clearly worked.

Reinhardt and Dieterle had to go about $250,000 over budget to make the film. The movie was expected to lose money, and it did. The audiences of the period missed a golden opportunity to see a classic that would endure for generations. The film did receive mostly glowing reviews, although many Shakespearean scholars were offended at the cuts that were made in the dialogue. Rooney quoted Andre Sennwald of the *New York Times*, who said the movie was "a brave, beautiful, and interesting effort to subdue the most difficult of Shakespeare's works." He went on to praise the studio (known for its gritty gangster pictures) for a work of high ambition, adding that it was "a credit to Warner Bros. and the motion picture industry."

There were also some critics who cringed at the thought of so many lowbrow comic actors taking on the Bard's prose and, in their opinion, butchering it. In addition to Rooney's much-lauded performance as Puck, Cagney was praised for his portrayal of Bottom, although he overplays some of his scenes with manic gusto. It was also the breathtakingly beautiful de Havilland's film debut, playing an incandescent Hermia. The movie received four Academy Award nominations, including Best Picture. It won for Best Cinematography (Hal Mohr) and Best Film Editing (Ralph Dawson). Connoisseurs of the arts lauded the ambition of the filmmaking, citing cinematographer Mohr and composer Korngold for his adaptation of Mendelssohn's score. A review in the October 12, 1935, issue of *Newsweek* mentioned Rooney in a positive light:

> Reinhardt broke precedents in casting Puck, the elf responsible for mixing up the "Dream's" characters. The role had always been played by ingénues or grown men. Reinhardt wanted a boy. He chose fourteen-year-old, blond, shrill-voiced Mickey Rooney and gave him the play's longest and hardest assignment. Rooney's training as a child actor in no way fitted him for the part. Yet he interprets Shakespeare's difficult lines with incredible sensitivity. His imitations of the two lovelorn couples, lost in the forest, couldn't be surpassed.

Foster Hirsch, in his book *Acting Hollywood Style*, wrote of Rooney's performance:

> The lyric energy Rooney displays as Puck in *A Midsummer Night's Dream* became the backbone of his career. His elastic body, rather than Shakespeare's language, impels him into the play's spirit. Emerging out of a bank of leaves, he seems raw and elemental, a force of nature. As he jumps (sometimes with the help of movie magic) up hill and down, sprinkling fairy dust in the air, Rooney breaks up the lines with raucous, splitting laughter, with grunts and gasps and wheezes. With wild gesticulations and in a harsh, guttural voice, he veers from declamation to song—he seems indeed a supernatural sprite, a being from a different order.

Foster Hirsch's assertion is spot-on when discussing Rooney's acting methodology. From the beginning of his career, he was a physical and intuitive performer, traits that served him well throughout his career. It didn't matter if it was a musical, a comedy, or a drama, he got to his characters by channeling their nature through physical expression. When people think of Rooney onscreen or in a live performance it is that energy they remember most. It was not only in the rhythmic way he moved his body but also the urgency with which he spoke his lines, often in spasms of dialogue. The role of Puck became an enduring part of his legacy and a performance that still amazes audiences eighty years later.

* * *

Rooney also appeared in the screen adaptation of Eugene O'Neill's only comedy *Ah, Wilderness!* (1935). He played Tommy Miller, the youngest son of Nat Miller the local newspaper publisher, played in the film by the veteran actor Lionel Barrymore (and onstage two years earlier by none other than George M. Cohan). The play is a sentimental tale of youthful indiscretion on a Fourth of July weekend in a turn-of-the-century New England town. Wallace Beery has the role of Uncle Sid, who is the black sheep of the family because of his drinking; he also has neither a job nor a wife. The elder son, Richard (Eric Linden), is always spouting poetry without understanding it, and discussing radical politics without conviction. Richard is forbidden to court his next-door neighbor's daughter Muriel (Cecilia Parker) by the girl's father and this sets Richard off on a bender. While in this state he meets Belle (Helen Flint), who is way out of his league. The film was directed by Clarence Brown, who would direct Rooney in two of his best films, *The Human Comedy* (1943) and *National Velvet* (1944). Mickey, Brown said, "was the closest thing to a genius I ever worked with."

One critic called Rooney's performance as Tommy "amusing and interesting." However, it was Beery as the affable alcoholic Uncle Sid who stole the picture from the leads. The film did good business and the reviews were also excellent, with the *New York Times* reviewer calling it a "wise and kindly 'comedy of recollection'… and as an American comedy of manners the film explores a vein of bitter-sweet nostalgia without losing its sense of humor."

Although his part in *Wilderness* was small, this credit, combined with *A Midsummer Night's Dream* in the same year, definitely put Mickey Rooney on the map in Hollywood.

CHAPTER FOUR

Fame Comes to Andy Hardy

> "I'm seventeen; I'm no baby, Dad!"
> —The tag line for the second Hardy Family series entry, *You're Only Young Once* (1937)

When David O. Selznick brought Mickey Rooney to Metro-Goldwyn-Mayer, he and his ever-ambitious mother were hoping for great parts in great movies. What he did get were small supporting roles in *Riff Raff* (1935), starring Spencer Tracy and Jean Harlow, and *Little Lord Fauntleroy* (1936), with Freddy Bartholomew in the title role. But even though the parts were small, Rooney's performances weren't, and the top brass at MGM took note.

The biggest break of his career came in an inauspicious little package called *A Family Affair*. It was a B-movie based on a play called *Skidding* by Aurania Rouverol. The story centered on a small-town judge and his family. Lionel Barrymore was to star as Judge James Hardy, Spring Byington would play Emily Hardy, his wife, and Margaret Marquis would be Polly Benedict, the sweetheart of Judge Hardy's son, Andy. Originally, Andy was to be played by an actor named Frankie Thomas but he underwent a growth spurt in the months leading up to when shooting was to begin; the MGM studio execs also thought he looked too much like a handsome grown leading man. They decided to go instead with the short and boyish-looking Mickey Rooney.

According to Frankie Thomas, the MGM brain trust decided to add a nostalgic, romanticized family portrait to the domestic subplot of Rouverol's play, which they bought cheaply (the budget for the entire film was just $200,000, which was considered low for the "Tiffany Studio"). The movie was to have the same feeling as the recent adaptation of *Ah, Wilderness!* and, in fact, the entire cast from that film would be brought back for *A Family Affair*. According to Thomas Schatz, author of the excellent book *The Genius of the System: Hollywood Filmmaking in the Studio Era*: "Not only the casting, but the sets, props, music, even the story formula itself could be standardized, rendering what was already a low-budget enterprise that much more efficient and economical."

Schatz points out that even though the film was considered a B-picture (at only sixty-nine minutes, it was designed to be the bottom half of a double feature at Loew's theatres), MGM's superior resources gave the film an A-picture quality. The studio had little expectation that *A Family Affair* would be a success, but the public loved it, even if the critics did not. Exhibitors reported great business and wanted more of these films, and especially more of the Andy Hardy character; although he was only the fourth-billed actor in the film, he ended up stealing the picture in his portrayal of the quintessential boy next door. It was an instance of the right part being played by the right actor at the right time.

William Rogers, the sales manager for the Loew's theatre chain, was the first to suggest that MGM should consider doing a series featuring the Hardy family. When MGM started thinking about a sequel, most of the original cast from *A Family Affair* weren't available; Barrymore, in particular, wanted no part of it; he reportedly disliked working with Rooney. The sixteen-year-old was already getting a reputation as a scene-stealer, and the old pros didn't like this one bit.

The new film would be called *You're Only Young Once* and would star Lewis Stone as Judge James K. Hardy and Fay Holden as Mrs. Emily Hardy. Cecilia Parker reprised her role as Andy's older sister, Marian; as did Sara Hayden as Aunt Milly. Ann Rutherford was cast as Polly Benedict, Andy's girlfriend. Initially, Rutherford wasn't thrilled about getting the role because she was a classmate of Rooney's at the Little Red Schoolhouse on the Metro lot and he was a constant source of torment. He would follow her everywhere, pull her hair, and seemingly lived to get a reaction out of her. As much as she wished there was someone else playing Andy she couldn't turn the part down. (The two would ultimately become lifelong friends.)

You're Only Young Once was released in 1937 and included the same production crew as the first one, with George B. Seitz directing, and Carey Wilson as producer and co-writer, along with Kay Van Riper. These key production personnel and the cast would provide the core of the fourteen-film series. The story of *You're Only Young Once* is pretty simple, with the family going on a vacation to the Catalina Islands. The trip proves especially memorable, as Andy finds romance, Marian falls for a married lifeguard/lawyer, and Judge Hardy tries to catch a swordfish. A template was established for the series that included Andy's on-again, off-again romance with Polly Benedict, his involvement with other girls that causes him heartache, and the man-to-man talks with his dad that straighten everything out. Andy's sister, Marian, would also have occasional romantic problems but they were a secondary storyline and, invariably, Judge Hardy would impart his worldly wisdom to her to help resolve some crisis. Emily Hardy was the all-American mom, always in the kitchen fixing the meals and worrying about Andy and Marian, and Judge Hardy would be close by to comfort and console by assuring her that everything would work out in the end. (He must have read the scripts!) The series would also provide MGM with a platform to introduce many young starlets as Andy's girlfriends, some of whom would go on to become stars in their own right. Lana Turner, Kathryn Grayson, and Esther Williams all made their screen debuts in the series.

The series was set in a small town called Carvel, but in exactly what state is somewhat confusing. Robert Osborne said that it was Carvel, California, when introducing a showing of the films on TCM. There are references to Carvel, Ohio; Carvel, Idaho; and the Midwestern town of Carvel. This confusion is appropriate because, according to Mayer, this little idyllic enclave could be anywhere in America. The fact that these impossibly sweet people couldn't have existed anywhere then, now, or ever didn't faze Mayer in the slightest. He ran the dream factory at MGM and his goal was to produce films reflecting life as it *should* be, not the way things actually were. Warner Bros. was the studio for the gangster movies like *Little Caesar* (1930), *Public Enemy* (1931) and social dramas like *I Am a Fugitive from a Chain Gang* (1932). MGM produced musicals, sentimental dramas, and the Hardy Family series, and that's the way Mayer liked it. In fact, Rooney soon became one of the producer's favorite employees, who insisted that he call him "Papa."

Louis Burt Mayer was born Lazar Mayer in the Ukraine and grew up in Saint John, New Brunswick, Canada. He was raised in poverty and suffered physical and emotional abuse from his nearly illiterate father. His difficult childhood toughened him as he worked dirty jobs, such as junk collector and rag picker. He would do anything to make money and escape the horrific conditions of his childhood. This difficult existence gave him a steely determination that would propel him to power and riches later in life. Sometime in the early 1890s he changed his name to Louis and his birthdate to July 4, 1885, to reflect his love for and hope in America, and moved to Boston in 1904. He worked as a scrap-metal dealer until he had enough money to buy a burlesque house. He mostly presented plays at his theatre but would also show silent films. He eventually expanded by buying a small theatre chain in Haverhill, Massachusetts. As the secretary of the newly formed Metro Pictures Corporation, he decided to begin producing movies of his own. In 1916, he managed to convince Metro star Francis X. Bushman to headline his first production. The eighteen-chapter serial, *The Great Secret*, did poorly at the box office and ultimately proved damaging to Bushman's career, but it did establish Mayer as a producer. He got together with Marcus Loew of Metro Pictures and Samuel Goldwyn to form Metro-Goldwyn-Mayer Studios in 1924. He consolidated more and more power at the studio until he became its head executive, by which time he was the highest salaried employee in the country.

Mayer allowed the creative producers at MGM, like Irving Thalberg and his son-in-law David O. Selznick, free rein to produce their big-budget prestige films, but he was very hands-on as far as overseeing the Hardy Family films. He gave strict orders to the creative team to keep the films clean and uncomplicated. He liked the vanilla approach; the sentimental stories and characters would remain the same throughout the decade-long series. He demanded that the central character, Andy, always be respectful to his parents and that his relationship with girls remain in the "puppy love" stage. In short, he didn't want Andy growing up or any of the Hardy family facing any kind of challenge that couldn't be solved by the fadeout.

Mayer would transmit his thoughts on the series primarily through producer and co-writer Wilson. There was a scene in one of the early films where Andy became depressed because he saw his girlfriend Polly talking and laughing with a tall, handsome, naval lieutenant, making him feel like a little boy in comparison. At the dinner table that night he refused to eat and his mother speculated that he was ill. According to Bosley Crowther, *New York Times* critic and the author of *The Lion's Share: The Story of an Entertainment Empire*:

> Going home after the preview, Mayer took Wilson to task. "Don't you know a boy of sixteen is hungry all the time?" he charged. "You tell me you were brought up in a good American home—in the kitchen! You lied to me! You've let Andy insult

Four. Fame Comes to Andy Hardy

his mother! No boy would tell his mother he wasn't hungry! Change that line!" Mayer would then go on to tell Wilson what Andy should say to his mom, always with an eye toward how family members should interact in his idealized Carvel, America.

Not everyone at MGM was thrilled with Mayer's perfect family. When a former Broadway playwright by the name of George Oppenheimer, who was slumming out in Hollywood and taking some of the easy money to be made at the studios, was asked if he'd like to write one of the Hardy scripts he replied, "Sure, I'd love to write one, provided you let me have every member of the fucking family killed in a railroad accident in the last reel." As strange as it might seem, there were times when Rooney might have shared Oppenheimer's enthusiasm for that scenario. It is well documented that Mickey Rooney was *nothing* like Andy Hardy. Having grown up in burlesque and the fringes of the movie business, he became a very worldly teenager with all the vices of a grown man. He was a skirt chaser from an early age who frequented whorehouses, a claim he admitted to freely in his 1991 autobiography. One establishment he particularly recalled was introduced to him by Milton Berle; known as T&M Studios, it was located in a one-flight walkup off Santa Monica Boulevard. But once he became rich and famous he no longer found it necessary to pay for sex: now the girls were chasing *him*.

Rooney's behavior was of great concern to Mayer, not only because it didn't conform to his strong sense of morality, but also because it was bad for business. If Rooney's behavior became public knowledge it would tarnish the clean-cut image of Andy Hardy and, more importantly, negatively affect MGM's bottom line.

Controlling Rooney became such a problem that Mayer employed a man by the name of Les Peterson, whose purpose was to follow the juvenile lead around town and try to keep him out of trouble. This, as it turned out, was a full-time job. Rooney was not only a womanizer, he gambled excessively and drank too much (and was anything but a pleasant drunk). Peterson tried not to be too much of a drag on Rooney and would often place bets for him at Santa Anita. The purpose of this, of course, was to keep tabs on how much he was spending at the track and, at the same time, remain in the volatile actor's good graces. The idea was not to keep him from having fun, just not so much fun to create a public scandal. This was the era of the gossip columnists, and Hedda Hopper and Louella Parsons were always looking for something interesting to write about the stars. Rooney was frequently summoned to Mayer's office and lectured that he had an obligation to his fans to behave himself. However, Rooney saw Andy Hardy as just another character he was playing; he believed that at the end of a work day he should be able to live his life on his own terms.

Judy B. Woodside, in her Ph.D. dissertation "Advantages of an Arrested Development: The Onscreen Adolescence of Mickey Rooney," gives a remarkably detailed and insightful analysis of the financial incentives to keep Rooney a teenager for as long as possible. As she writes, "Mickey Rooney was a tool used by MGM to promote consumerism, to youth and to respond to a very narrow, monolithic, and conservative view of what 'Americanism' is and should be." Woodside goes on to list examples of the publicity machine of the studio that includes numerous articles in magazines and newspapers about the Hardy family values and almost treats them as if they are real people. There was a biography of Rooney that the studio put out that had virtually nothing to do with the real human being. There were even Mickey Rooney paint books and lunchboxes that further confused the relationship between the actor and the character he was playing. Basically, Woodside's thesis is that MGM perpetuated the idea of Rooney as a child because it was highly profitable for the studio. She also discusses the Hardy films in terms of their cultural significance, in the way that Mayer was using the series to promote his own conservative values and the myth of American upward mobility. The fourteen Hardy films were made from the mid-1930s to the mid-1940s, during the Depression and World War II, yet Carvel is seemingly untouched by these brutal realities. Indeed, Woodside discusses Andy's purchase of a car as a prime example of Mayer's promotion of a fanciful consumerism; relatively few people—let alone a teenager—could afford an automobile. There is almost nothing Andy wants, including a tuxedo for the big dance, that he doesn't get. Most members of the audience could only dream of the kind of life the Hardys lived, yet it didn't seem to bother them. It's hard to explain why, except that it was an escape from their own realities in much the same way as the Fred Astaire-Ginger Rogers lighter-than-air musicals. What is clear is that Mayer was pushing his ideas on what made America great because of his own rags-to-riches journey.

Every film in the series begins with a family portrait during the credits, Mom and Dad seated with Andy and his sister Marian standing on either side of them. *Love Finds Andy Hardy* (1938), generally regarded as the best of the lot, has a Norman Rockwell *Saturday Evening Post* cover

Four. Fame Comes to Andy Hardy

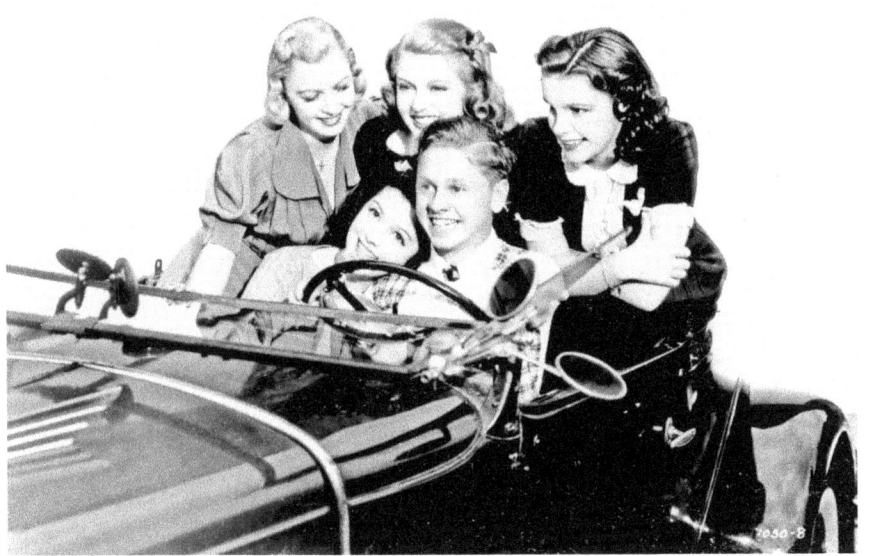

Andy Hardy (Mickey Rooney, at the wheel) is surrounded by (top row, left to right) Cecilia Parker, Lana Turner, and Judy Garland. Nuzzling up to her boyfriend is Polly Benedict, played by Ann Rutherford. *Love Finds Andy Hardy* **(1938).**

feel to it. In fact, they are like a live-action *Post* cover. There was a different writer for this particular entry in the series, William Ludwig, who would go on to have a long career that included the script for the 1955 film adaptation of the Rodgers and Hammerstein Broadway hit *Oklahoma!*

Love Finds Andy Hardy opens with a twelve-year-old boy named Jimmy (Gene Reynolds) brought before Judge Hardy because he has wrecked a neighbor's tractor. The main story concerns Andy's quest to buy a car from a used car lot. The car he wants costs $20 and all he has is $12 to put down and must pay the other $8 by Christmas Eve. Andy finds out that his main squeeze, Polly Benedict, won't be able to go to the big Christmas Eve dance because she is going away for a few weeks with her parents. Further complications in the Hardy family include a fight Marian is having with her boyfriend, and Mrs. Hardy gets a telegram from her sister saying that their mother, who lives on a farm in Canada, is quite ill and to come right away to help tend to her. Andy meets Betsy Booth (Judy Garland, making the first of three appearances in the series), who has come to visit her aunt who lives next door. "I sing, you know," Betsy shyly tells Andy. Although a bit younger than the Hardy boy, she wishes she were older and more glamorous so he would think of her as girlfriend material.

Andy's friend Beezy (George P. Breakston) is also going away for a few weeks and wants Andy to keep an eye on his girl for him until he gets back. The luscious Lana Turner plays Beezy's girlfriend, Cynthia. Andy manages to convince his friend to pay him the $8 he needs to buy the car to perform this "chore" for him. Andy takes Cynthia to the pool but she refuses to go into the water because she doesn't want to get her hair wet. She seems like a drag but she's a good and willing kisser. Betsy gets Andy a fancy radiator cap for his new car and flirts with him, but he is oblivious to her feelings because she is just a kid. When he leaves, she sings "In Between," in which she laments that she's too old for toys and too young for boys. Judy is terrific as usual, singing with sadness and feeling.

Andy gets a telegram from Polly that she can come home for the Christmas Eve dance after all but, of course, he has already made a date with Cynthia. Andy is in a pickle and has to wire Polly back that he won't be able to take her to the dance, offering no explanation. Andy receives another telegram, this one from Beezy, who informs him that he has found another girl and therefore won't be paying him the $8 he promised. What is Andy to do? It is now time to tell the used-car dealer his predicament, but the salesman threatens to sue him if Andy doesn't come up with the cash. It is now time for a man-to-man talk with Judge Hardy. Andy tells his dad about the whole sordid mess and asks if he can dip into his college savings for the money he needs. Judge Hardy doesn't want to do that because it is money for Andy's future in case something should happen to him.

Father and son are worried that they haven't heard from Mom in quite a while and have been relying on her to send telegrams because her mother has no phone. Andy tells his dad about a kid he knows who has a ham radio and might be able to communicate with one of Grandma's neighbors to get a message to Mom through the radio. The ham radio operator turns out to be Jimmy, the young tractor wrecker from the opening scene, and he is able to get in touch with another ham radio operator, this one living not far from Grandma's farm. The boy on the other end promises to get a message to Emily Hardy. The judge is so pleased he tells

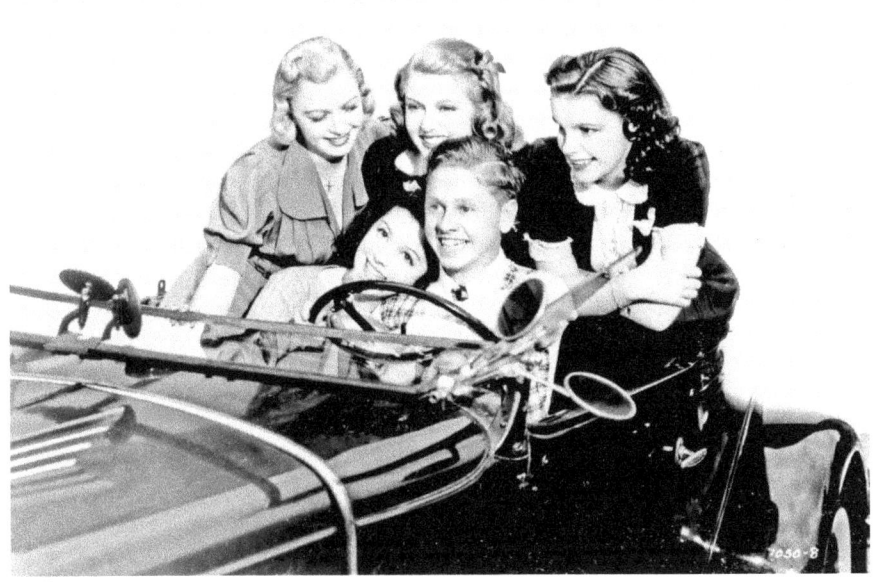

Four. Fame Comes to Andy Hardy

Jimmy that he will pay to fix the tractor for him. The judge further tells Andy that he will supply the $8 needed to pay for his car, thereby fulfilling Andy's dream of owning a car and simultaneously ensuring that Andy won't be doing hard time in the slammer for reneging on a debt. They arrive at the used-car lot in a cab, and Andy drives his dad home.

Meanwhile, Betsy does another favor for Andy when she takes Cynthia by the used-car lot and shows her a broken-down jalopy that she says is the one Andy is going to buy and must therefore be the car in which she will be going to the Christmas Eve dance. Cynthia takes one look at the heap of metal and declares the date with Andy is off. Polly has returned home and Andy goes over and tells her about his deal with Beezy. She is appalled and declares, "Oh, you are nothing but a gigolo!" She runs into her house, leaving Andy on the front step, lamenting, "I had two girls and no car and now I have a car and no girls."

At home, Marian has made up with her boyfriend and Mother arrives unexpectedly to report that Grandma has recovered her health. Betsy shows up in an evening gown so that Andy has someone to escort to the Christmas Eve dance. They drive off in Andy's new car. Polly's date at the dance knows Betsy and coaxes her into singing a few songs. One of the tunes is a bouncy number called "Meet the Beat of My Heart." Andy thinks Betsy is sensational and is a hit with everyone, including Polly's date. Andy and Polly make up.

This was a pretty typical plot for these films and probably a cut above because of Ludwig's contribution. Woodside is right that they reflected Mayer's worldview and that there was a clear attempt to keep Rooney a teenager for as long as possible. She further stated that she felt even the films that Rooney did outside the Hardy series were used for the same purpose. He was great as the toughie Whitey Marsh, who reforms with the help of Father Flanagan (Spencer Tracy) in *Boys Town* (1938). The film won an Oscar for Tracy's understated performance as the tough priest on a mission, but it is Rooney's performance that remains the more memorable. Mayer's eventual successor, Dore Schary, wrote the film about a crusading priest with the motto: "There is no such thing as a bad boy." *Boys Town* was nominated for five Oscars, including Best Picture, and won two for the writing team of Schary and Eleanore Griffin.

One of the attributes that made Rooney great was that he was able to embrace the material, however mediocre it might be, and elevate it with his total commitment to the part. Such was the case with *The Human*

Whitey Marsh (Mickey Rooney, center) cradles Pee Wee (Bob Watson), who was just struck by a car. Father Flanagan (Spencer Tracy) looks on in *Boys Town* **(1938).**

Comedy (1938). Rooney was the messenger boy Homer Macauley, who stays home to support his family in small-town Ithaca while his older brother Marcus goes off to war. The William Saroyan tearjerker, like many of Rooney's movies during his years of megawatt stardom, was criticized for being too sweet and sentimental by some critics, but his heartbreaking performance earned him an Oscar nomination.

Any film—whether it was a comedy, a drama, or a musical—was money in the bank for MGM as long as it starred that energetic perpetual adolescent Mickey Rooney. Arthur Marx pointed out that the studio kept their net profits a secret and, therefore, it was almost impossible to know what the Hardy films took in, but he stated that a conservative estimate would be about $80 million in 1930s and 1940s dollars—a truly staggering figure for the time.

Four. Fame Comes to Andy Hardy

Mrs. Sandoval (Ann Ayars) can't read, so Western Union boy Homer Macauley (Mickey Rooney) has to read the message to her: "It's about your son—it's from the War Department ..." *The Human Comedy* (1943).

The Hardy Family films made Mickey Rooney immensely popular with the American audiences of the late 1930s and early '40s. The series, along with numerous top musicals and dramas in which he headlined, made him a huge star. Rooney was different than most other adolescent actors because, although he was very successful from the beginning of his career, he didn't reach superstardom until his early twenties. This is the age when most child stars are already has-beens. Part of the reason for his ascendancy ties in with Woodside's thesis that the studio kept him in roles that a younger actor would normally play. For instance, he was twenty when he played Huckleberry Finn, who is about twelve in the Twain classic. Of course, Rooney could get away with playing younger because he was so short and had a baby face and therefore looked like a kid in his teens well into his twenties. In his musical vehicles with Garland, like *Babes in Arms* (1939) and *Babes on Broadway* (1941), despite the titles and the other "Let's Put On a Show" Busby Berkeley extravaganzas, he is age-appropriate for the parts and it is his immense talent that shines through.

According to Foster Hirsch,

> Rooney's body is musical even when he isn't performing in a musical; and when he's in song and dance shows, he's cast typically (as in *Babes in Arms*, 1939; *Strike Up the Band*, 1940; *Girl Crazy*, 1943) as someone who will explode unless he performs. (During breaks while filming, Rooney often performed for the crew.) Whenever there is a stage, Rooney's characters leap onto it to entertain. When, in *Girl Crazy*, he visits the office of the governor, where there is no stage, he nonetheless converts an anteroom into a performing arena. By chance a microphone is placed in front of him and he spins spontaneously into a vaudeville riff, parodying sports announcers. Like other unintegrated numbers in Rooney musicals, the scene is a throwaway, an entertainer's privileged way of killing time.

Rooney was a dynamo in the musicals he did with Garland. His energy was unbridled and his talent, inexhaustible. He was completely self-taught on several musical instruments, including piano and drums. He was such a good drummer, in fact, that many have said he could have made a living playing the instrument if he had not been such a great actor.

The first musical Rooney and Garland did together was *Babes in Arms* (1939) and was based on the Rodgers and Hart Broadway hit of the same name. He plays Tommy Williams, an ambitious singer and songwriter who dreams of taking a show to Broadway, but is getting nowhere fast. He meets up with Penny Morris (Garland), a singer with similar ambitions. Together they come up with an idea to stage a charity show that will raise money to send orphan kids on a trip to the country. They get some financing to produce their own show for Broadway (what ogre could stand in the way of these orphan kids?) and Tommy's success leads to ego problems as he becomes willing to ditch his friends for a great opportunity. This kind of hokey plot would be done over and over again, but the high-energy musical numbers were something wartime audiences flipped over. *Babes in Arms* became a huge success and Mickey and Judy became the new Fred and Ginger. "Mickey understood me," Garland said later in life. "He was my favorite person to work with. The genius who taught me everything I know."

"Although they are not known primarily as dancers, Mickey Rooney, Elvis Presley, and John Travolta are galvanized whenever music's in the air," Hirsch writes. "Like Cagney they are actors whose best acting has dance-like undercurrents." Rooney's versatility made him the biggest star in Hollywood and, more importantly, at his home studio MGM, which

Four. Fame Comes to Andy Hardy

Judy Garland and Mickey Rooney at their best in *Babes on Broadway* (1941). The film was directed by Vincente Minelli, whom Garland would later marry.

boasted, "More stars than there are in the heavens." What is most impressive concerning Rooney's feat is that he reached these heights during what has become known as the Golden Age of Hollywood. A quick perusal of the list of the most popular stars in 1939–1941 (cited in *Quigley's Annual List of Box Office Champions*), gives you an idea of the talent that was

Tom (Mickey Rooney), a youthful inventor, attempts to explain his latest experiment to his father, Samuel (George Bancroft), and his sister Tannie (Virginia Weidler) in *Young Tom Edison* (1940).

working in the movies at the time. Many on the list were not only stars but became legends and icons in film history.

1939	1940	1941
1. Mickey Rooney	1. Mickey Rooney	1. Mickey Rooney
2. Tyrone Power	2. Spencer Tracy	2. Clark Gable
3. Spencer Tracy	3. Clark Gable	3. Abbott and Costello
4. Clark Gable	4. Gene Autry	4. Bob Hope
5. Shirley Temple	5. Tyrone Power	5. Spencer Tracy
6. Bette Davis	6. James Cagney	6. Gene Autry
7. Alice Faye	7. Bing Crosby	7. Gary Cooper
8. Errol Flynn	8. Wallace Beery	8. Bette Davis
9. James Cagney	9. Bette Davis	9. James Cagney
10. Sonja Henie	10. Judy Garland	10. Judy Garland

Rooney's musical skills and comic energy, combined with an almost supernatural desire to please, won audiences' hearts, making him the biggest star in Hollywood. During this period of immense popularity, he also starred in many dramas. One was the highly entertaining, if fictionalized, *Young Tom Edison* (1940), in which he was the manic young genius later known as "The Wizard of Menlo Park." No less an actor than Spencer Tracy assumed the role in the follow-up, *Edison, the Man*, released later that same year.

CHAPTER FIVE

Jockeying for Parts

> I am quite sure about Mickey Rooney: he is an extremely wise and moving actor, and if I'm ever again tempted to speak disrespectfully of him, that will only be in anger over the unforgivable waste of a forceful yet subtle talent, proved capable of self-discipline and of the hardest roles that could be thrown it.
> —James Agee, 1944

The above observation from the noted critic James Agee was in reference to the actor's role in the then-new film *National Velvet*, but he was prescient about the difficulties that Rooney would soon face in his career. The sad fact is that you can trace the outline of his career in the numerous films in which he played a jockey or trainer because of the difficulty in casting him in other parts. Playing a jockey was always a good fit for Rooney, not only because of the physical requirements, but also because he knew his way around a race track. He loved going to the track and betting on the horses, something he did all of his life. It was clear that it was not just the gambling that he loved but also the unique ambience. He knew the milieu inside and out. The crowds, jockeys, flamboyant horse owners, trainers—he imbued his characters with the traits he observed as a spectator and a participant. A famously diminutive man, he no doubt related to the professional jockeys, these men of small stature who could rise to great heights with skill, determination, and luck. A gambler must believe in luck, and Rooney, above all else, was a gambler.

Through the ever-growing technology of home video, a film buff can bear witness to his transformation as a character actor over a fifty-year span just by seeing *Down the Stretch* (1936), *Thoroughbreds Don't Cry* (1937), *Stablemates* (1938), *National Velvet* (1944), "The Lady Was a Flop" (1957 episode of *Schlitz Playhouse*), "The Last Night of a Jockey" (1963 episode of *The Twilight Zone*); *The Black Stallion* (1979); and *The Adven-*

Five. Jockeying for Parts

tures of the Black Stallion television series (1990-1993). We watch in astonishment as he embodies the brash young hero-worshipper of Doc Thomas "Tom" Terry (Wallace Beery) in *Stablemates*; we see him innocently interacting with Cricket West (Judy Garland) in *Thoroughbreds Don't Cry*; and as he transitions into one of his first mature roles, as Mi, a bitter young man who learns compassion by helping to train a beautiful horse for its young owner, Velvet Brown (Elizabeth Taylor) in *National Velvet*. He is entering middle age when he plays a balding ex-jockey who walks with a limp, the result of a terrible fall he took that has made him question his purpose in life, in the uplifting teleplay "The Lady Was a Flop," and, in one of his best performances, as the banned jockey facing a very personal enemy in "The Last Night of a Jockey." He was entering late middle age as Henry Dailey in *The Black Stallion*, and reprised the role (with variations) when he took on the grind of a TV series version of that acclaimed film in his mid–seventies.

The first of these films, *Down the Stretch*, was directed by William Clemens, written by William Jacobs, and starred Patricia Ellis and Dennis Moore. Rooney plays Snapper Sinclair, a sixteen-year-old delinquent, and, as the story opens, he is about to be sentenced to a reformatory for jumping a freight car. A beautiful woman, Patricia Barrington (Ellis), steps in to ask the judge to put the young man in her care. Barrington recognizes Snapper as the son of one of the jockeys who used to work for her stables. Snapper's father had been a great jockey, but was involved in a racetrack scandal that ruined his career, prompting him to drink himself to death. The judge releases the young boy into the woman's care. She wants him to ride for Twin Orchard Farms, just as his father did. Some of the hands at the farm take an immediate dislike to Snapper because of his father's reputation.

When Barrington hires Snapper to work on her farm tending the horses, Snapper becomes taken with a horse called Faithful and wants to ride him in a race; the foreman of the stables, however, thinks the horse is a loser and wants to sell him. Willie Best plays Noah, a black stable hand Snapper befriends. There is a great scene in which Snapper, who has been bragging that he will be a great jockey if just given the chance, demonstrates how he will handle the reins and horse through pantomime. This is a direct foreshadowing of the scene in *The Black Stallion* when Henry (Rooney) shows Alec (Kelly Reno) how to ride while straddling a bale of hay.

Due to his slight stature, Mickey Rooney was frequently cast as a jockey. He undertakes that role for the first time in *Down the Stretch* (1936) (Photofest).

The next racetrack film, *Thoroughbreds Don't Cry*, released the following year, was the first non-musical film to team Rooney with Judy Garland. It would also be the first time he worked with the great character actor Elisha Cook, Jr., Rooney plays Tommy Donovan, who is recruited by an English horseman to race his prized thoroughbred in a high-stakes American race. The great screenwriter Dalton Trumbo, one of the so-called Hollywood Ten who were brought before the House Un-American Activities Committee (HUAC) during the McCarthy era in the 1950s, was an uncred-

Five. Jockeying for Parts

ited script polisher on this film. Tommy befriends the young son of the Englishman, who is played by a young actor named Ronald Sinclair. Sinclair replaced Freddie Bartholomew, who was originally slated for the role. The colorful singer and actress Sophie Tucker plays Mother Ralph, the owner of a racetrack boarding house, and Garland is her niece Cricket West. Garland also gets to sing a few songs in the movie but, regrettably, the great Tucker, who was known as the "Jazz Age Hot Mama," doesn't get to belt out a tune. *Thoroughbreds* is not really one of Rooney's better films, despite the presence of Garland and Tucker, although it is likeable. Rooney, in fact, received some very good reviews, including one in the *New York Times*, which called his performance "brilliant," and the *Washington Post* leading their review with "of all the names over the Capitol Theatre this week, Mickey Rooney's should be in the biggest and brightest letters.

Cricket West (Judy Garland) attempts to break up a fight between Timmie Donovan (Mickey Rooney, left) and Roger Calverton (Ronald Sinclair, right) in *Thoroughbreds Don't Cry* (1937). Sinclair, incidentally, was the original choice for the role of Andy Hardy.

Mickey is cashing an 'if and reverse' not to mention a long shot parlay, by reversing the usual juvenile actor's career and getting better as he gets bigger."

Evidence of Rooney's growth as an actor is demonstrated in his next racing film, *Stablemates*, in which he shares several scenes with the legendary Wallace Beery. Beery had won an Oscar six years earlier for *The Champ* (1931), for his portrayal of a washed-up alcoholic boxer who tries to straighten his life out for the sake of his young son Dink, played by Jackie Cooper. Beery was born on a farm in Missouri in 1885 and ran off to join the circus at age sixteen. He worked as an assistant elephant trainer, leaving the Big Top after being clawed by a leopard. He had a very deep voice and worked for a while in comic operas before finding work in the early film industry. At the Essanay Film Manufacturing Company in Chicago, he starred in a series of slapstick comedy two-reelers, playing in drag as a Swedish maid. He married an extra at Essanay by the name of Gloria Swanson, who would later gain immortality as Norma Desmond in *Sunset Boulevard* (1950); in the late teens, they worked for comedy producer Mack Sennett, most memorably in *Teddy at the Throttle* (1917). Beery and Swanson made this two-reel satire of old-time melodramas just before ending their brief marriage.

Beery made the transition to sound films rather easily and appeared in the MGM gangster movie *The Big House* (1930), for which he received his first Oscar Nomination for Best Actor. Rooney, of course, had respect for Beery's great talent, but it was his larger-than-life personality that made shooting *Stablemates* one of the most enjoyable experiences of his career. Rooney spends about four pages in his autobiography talking about the making of this film and the developing relationship with Beery. He liked the film and his work in it, but it was the friendship he developed with Beery that he most treasured.

The two had actually worked together a few years earlier in *Ah, Wilderness!* (1935), but Rooney was only fourteen at the time and they had very few scenes together. By the time of *Stablemates*, Rooney had already made a few of the Andy Hardy pictures and was a rising star—and also ready to go to a party with Beery at Errol Flynn's house, where they were greeted at the door by two nubile naked twins. Rooney reported in his autobiography that Clark Gable, Robert Taylor, and Spencer Tracy were also in attendance. Apparently, a good time was had by all! He also said that it took only six weeks to shoot the film, that it ended up grossing

Five. Jockeying for Parts

three times its cost, and that he never had so much fun making a movie. Sam Wood directed the film, with a script by Richard Maibaum and Leonard Praskins.

Stablemates was shot on weekends at Hollywood Park Racetrack because it would cause too much disruption to shoot during the week. Director Wood and his crew also did some filming during the $50,000 Hollywood Gold Cup race to infuse the movie with some authenticity. Rooney said that he got to ride the great racehorse Seabiscuit during one of the thoroughbred's morning workouts. He recalled with pride that he was nervous to mount the great horse but soon got over it as they sped around the track. In addition to doing great business, the film received some good reviews. Critic Nelson B. Bell, in the October 29, 1938, issue of the *Washington Post*, wrote:

> While thrilling race sequences lend the picture a high pitch of excitement, it is by no means the ordinary racetrack melodrama.... It is, rather, the deeply emotional study of a great devotion that springs up between an apprentice boy, who comes into the ownership of a potentially great racehorse, and a paddock roustabout, intent on evading the law for past transgressions and keeping himself saturated with alcohol.

The movie was intended to be another *Champ*, although the story of a young boy becoming attached to a dissolute father figure definitely worked better with the much younger Jackie Cooper. But Rooney more than holds his own with perhaps the greatest scene-stealer in the history of movies. The movie was such an audience pleaser, in fact, that *Lux Radio Theatre* broadcast an hour-long audio adaptation of it in 1941, with Rooney and Beery reprising their roles. Rooney was so taken with Beery that when his own dad died in 1950, just a year after Beery, he had him laid to rest next to his great friend.

In *The Black Stallion*, when Alec opens the old dusty door in the barn and finds trophies and memorabilia from Henry's past as a jockey, there is a picture of Rooney on horseback that was taken during the production of *National Velvet*. This 1944 film also starred twelve-year-old Elizabeth Taylor, in her first major role, as the young girl who finds a beautiful horse and wants to train him to win the grueling Grand National race. The movie came at a crucial period in Rooney's life. His marriage to Ava Gardner was already over and he was about to be inducted into the Army to do his service in World War II. In fact, the film's director, Clarence Brown, was instructed to shoot Mickey's scenes first so he could get his affairs in order before leaving to join the military. *National Velvet*, for which Rooney receives top billing, has become a classic and is one of the actor's better performances of that period. The film opens with Mi Taylor (Rooney) walking down a dirt road. The camera follows him from behind, and above, the beautiful green of the grass and blue of the sky and the ocean enrich the horizon. Mi sits by the side of the road taking in the morning air when young Velvet Brown (Taylor) stops to talk to him. They hear a commotion and look up to see a beautiful horse go galloping by. Velvet stops the horse, much to Mi's chagrin, and the owner comes along to take possession of his horse, known as The Pie. Velvet marvels at the horse and invites Mi to come to her house for breakfast. Mi, at first, declines, but when he finds out Velvet's last name he realizes that she is the daughter of the woman he has come to see. Mrs. Brown was a friend of his late father's.

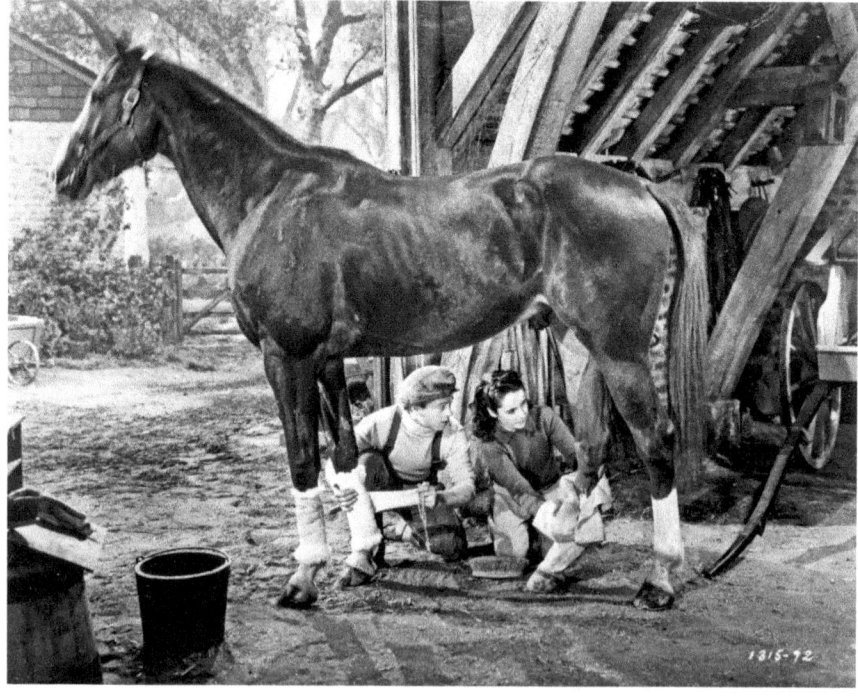

Mi Taylor (Mickey Rooney) and Velvet Brown (Elizabeth Taylor) check out their racehorse, The Pie, in *National Velvet* (1944).

Five. Jockeying for Parts

The character of Mi is a definite departure for Rooney. He is a much more subdued character than he had ever played before. There is anger and a touch of melancholy in Mi that is key to his portrayal and helps deepen the plot. Mrs. Brown convinces her husband to give Mi a job, even though neither of them completely trust him. After breakfast, Mrs. Brown puts away some of the family's money in a bag as Mi watches with a larcenous grin. But Mrs. Brown knows what she is doing. She knew Mr. Taylor and feels the son can't be too much different than his dad—at least she is placing faith in her own intuition.

Anne Revere, as Mrs. Brown, gives a lovely, Oscar-winning performance as the wise and loving wife and mother whose perceptions about people and their motivations are what guide her family. Her husband, played by veteran character actor Donald Crisp, who had won a Best Supporting Actor Oscar for *How Green Was My Valley* (1941), runs a butcher shop in town and is a good man who frets about the family wasting money on what he considers Velvet's foolish desire to buy a horse. Who is going to feed the animal? Where is the money going to come from? But it is Mrs. Brown who ultimately calls the shots in the family. In a way, the story represents a feminist paradigm: Velvet's aspirations are at the center of the story, and it is the mother who is the smartest character in the film, and it is part of her dream that her daughter will fulfill by the story's end. A key plot point is that Dan Taylor (Mi's father) was Mrs. Brown's trainer who helped her prepare to swim the English Channel. At one point, Mrs. Brown takes Velvet up to the attic to show her the medal she won for her accomplishment. Velvet wants to achieve something in her life, too.

Mi seems bitter and anxious to leave but is drawn into the Brown family, almost against his will. He wants to move on, but doesn't know where to go. He knows there is something out there in life for him; he simply hasn't figured it out yet. An opportunity seems to appear when, after Velvet wins The Pie in a raffle, she becomes determined to enter the magnificent horse in the great Grand National race. Her father and Mi both think it is sheer foolishness. Mi explains to Velvet that this isn't just a race but a grueling obstacle course for horse and rider. The horse must jump hedges with little moats behind them and it would be a miracle if the horse or the rider wasn't seriously hurt in the process. But she is determined, and Mrs. Brown backs her dream. Mi is chosen to go to London to put down the entry fee for the race. He is being entrusted with a lot of money. We see him packing all of his clothes into a duffle bag before he leaves. Mr. Brown spots him carrying the heavy bag and he basically tells Mrs. Brown that is the last they'll see of the young man *or* the entry fee.

When this writer interviewed Fred Roos (who produced *The Black Stallion*) for this book, Roos mentioned the next scene in this film. Mi has stopped at a tavern in London and is hoisting a few pints. A couple of shady characters notice his gradual intoxication and the money in his purse. They ask him where he is going, and he tells them. They encourage him to keep drinking and are looking for a way to get his money. Mickey's gift for pantomime is on great display in this scene as he gradually becomes more and more inebriated. It is one of the greatest drunk acts ever put on film.

The crooks are almost able to get Mi to split the money with them when he comes to his senses and realizes that Velvet and her family trust him and that he can't let them down. Everyone, except the ever-loyal Velvet, is surprised when Mi returns to town with the receipt for the entry fee. Mi is probably more surprised than anybody that he came back. The only thing he isn't able to do is find a jockey to ride The Pie.

There are now several scenes of Mi training The Pie and Velvet, who is riding him. These scenes, again, prefigure Rooney's work in *The Black Stallion* thirty-five years later. Velvet and *Stallion* character Alec are about the same age and they have great faith and love for their horse and affection for the trainer who is helping them achieve their ambition.

In a scene involving pathos, The Pie becomes ill and Velvet begs Mi to help him. He instructs her to get some whisky and lots of blankets. The two of them are up all night, ministering to the sick horse. In the morning, when The Pie stands up, they are elated. The entire family gathers to watch as the horse is loaded into the trailer and to wish Velvet and Mi good luck as they head for Liverpool and the Grand National Steeplechase race.

When Mi and Velvet interview the jockey they've selected to ride The Pie, it is clear that this is just a job for him and that he doesn't expect to win. Velvet dismisses him and now they have no jockey. Velvet immediately brightens and asks Mi to ride him. A pained expression comes over his face and then he tells her the reason for his bitterness. "At Manchester one fine day I saw an opening and I took it and there was a tangle, a tangle of reins and a jockey died … and that's why I'm no good to you when you need me most. I'm all soft and yellow inside."

Velvet protests and says, "There's greatness in you, Mi."

Mi replies, "There's nothing in me."

Five. Jockeying for Parts

Rooney's line readings for this scene are nothing less than magnificent. The pain and anguish that Mi has been keeping pent up inside finally come out in a flood of words and tears. In the end, Velvet—very much her champion mother's daughter—rides The Pie to victory.

* * *

After his years as a contract player at MGM, Rooney managed to land some good roles during the Golden Age of Television, once again playing jockeys. In an episode of *The Schlitz Playhouse*, Rooney played Red in "The Lady Was a Flop," based on a story by Borden Chase (an Academy Award nominee for his screenplay for Howard Hawks's 1948 John Wayne western *Red River*) and adapted for television by Martin Berkeley. Rooney, who was thirty-seven at the time of production, is beginning to show some age, with deep lines creasing his still youthful-looking face. In this half-hour episode, Rooney is a former jockey who was badly injured in a racing accident. He walks with a decided limp, the physical reminder of his spill, which has caused him to lose his nerve about racing again. He works for the owner of a stable who prizes Red's instincts about horses. Red can no longer ride and is resigned to a life that at least allows him to stay close to something he loves.

The story opens with the birth of a filly and Red smiles as he watches her struggle to her feet; he decides to name her Lady. A year or two later Red rides the young Lady around the track and has a good feeling about her racing chances, but the owner feels Lady is a washout and he wants to sell her. Red convinces the owner to give Lady a chance to prove herself in a forthcoming race. During that contest, Lady opens up a big lead but veers wildly when approaching the finish line, where Red and the owner are waiting. No one can figure out what happened and the owner wants, once again, to get rid of her. Red convinces him to give her one more chance, and the same thing happens. Now it is definite that she will be sold, and for a low price. When Red's boss finds out Red wants the horse, he lowers the price even more and lets him have Lady. Red finally realizes that the horse had veered as she approached the finish line because she had seen the man who was taking care of her, grooming and whispering words of encouragement, and had run toward him rather than the finish line.

The parallels between this poignant story and Rooney's career are unmistakable. He had been in the winner's circle many times before and, although chastened by his fall from stardom, he continued to be absorbed in his career; he needed to be in the arena as much as he needed air.

One of Rooney's all-time best performances was as Grady, the washed-up jockey in "Last Night of a Jockey" on *The Twilight Zone*.

Jockey Grady (Mickey Rooney) is enraged by his dismissal from a big race, in this scene from "The Last Night of a Jockey," a 1963 episode of *The Twilight Zone*, written by Rod Serling.

Five. Jockeying for Parts

Rooney is the sole performer in this episode. The story concerns a jockey who has been suspended from racing for horse doping and race fixing. Early in the program, Grady looks at himself in the mirror with revulsion. He screams at his reflection, calling himself a *runt* and a *shrimp*. Grady is alone in a rooming house with a bottle of booze close by. Suddenly, his subconscious produces an apparition in the mirror who talks back to him. His alter ego takes over the recriminations with glee. Grady's reflection taunts him with a list of the mistakes he has made in his life and Grady responds defensively to the heckling. At first he tries to physically remove this voice by striking himself in the head. Rooney is working very close to his own subconscious here. He is, after all, playing a performer whose best days are long behind him. It is chilling to watch this great actor literally bludgeoning himself with vicious words like *runt* and *shrimp*, knowing all too well that his lack of physical stature hindered his own career greatly.

In "Last Night of a Jockey," Grady's alter ego torments him throughout the show's first half, but then offers to grant him any wish—anything his heart desires. Grady ruminates on the possibilities and then decides that he wants to be *big*. The sight of Grady standing in the middle of the room, arms at his side, looking upward and with all his power shouting to the heavens, "I want to be big" is truly moving. The second act opens with the sound of thunder and a flash of lightning as Grady wakes up. He wipes the sleep from his eyes and immediately senses something is different. He looks and sees his feet dangle over the end of the bed. He picks up the phone and it disappears into his huge hand. He begins to giggle as he realizes this Swiftian turn to his life. He mumbles, "This is wild," as he giggles with delight. He stands up and the room shrinks around him. He is big! The first thing he does is call up an old girlfriend, who had jilted him in the past, to let her know that he is a changed man. She rebuffs him again. She thinks he's crazy when he tells her about his growth spurt: "I must be six, seven, eight feet tall. The Lakers will be scouting me soon." She doesn't buy it, and he hangs up in anger.

This being *The Twilight Zone*, the payoff comes when Grady gets a call from a racing official telling him that there was a meeting of racing officials who agreed that he should be reinstated. Grady is, of course, ecstatic at the news, but as soon as he hangs up the phone he hears his alter ego cackling madly. It slowly dawns on him that he is now too big to be a jockey. Grady's alter ego torments him further: "Your dreams were really quite small. Now if you wished to win the Kentucky Derby cleanly, that would have been something." Grady staggers around the room in angry disbelief. He begins to trash the room, like Godzilla on a rampage. He collapses in a heap on the floor, crying in anguish, "I'm too big.... I'm too big."

Chapter Six

Noir Star

> film noir / film ˈnwär /noun
> a style of cinematographic film marked by a mood of pessimism, fatalism, and menace. The term was originally applied (by a group of French critics) to American thrillers or detective films made in the period of 1941 to 1959 and to the work of directors such as John Huston, Orson Welles, Fritz Lang, and Billy Wilder.
> plural noun: films noirs
> —*Oxford English Dictionary*

Following his break with MGM, Rooney enthusiastically embarked on his new "independent" career, in partnership with Sam Stiefel. During this period, he co-produced and appeared in some fine dramatic films, in the fascinating genre known as film noir. Whereas most film buffs do not associate Rooney with this dark approach to filmmaking, it was a big part of his career in the 1950s. The movies he made during this period had extremely low budgets and, for the most part, did not do well either commercially or critically. A few of these films, like *Baby Face Nelson* and *Drive a Crooked Road*, have developed a following among critics and noir fans over the past few decades, but more obscure titles like *The Big Operator*, *Quicksand*, *The Strip*, and *The Last Mile* are also worth a second look.

Karen Burroughs Hannsberry says the era of film noir lasted from the early 1940s to late 1959. The movies involved characters who reflected, through darker stories and highly stylized black-and-white cinematography, the changing mood of America following World War II. Raymond Chandler characterized the protagonist in these films as "a knight in dirty armor." Hannsberry defined the lead male character in noir thusly:

> He can be vicious or violent, as likely to slap a dame's face as kiss her. He would be a doubtless protector of the law, nabbing hoods with a combination of instinct, fortitude, and grit. He might be vulnerable and gullible, apt to succumb to the

whims of a conniving cutie at the drop of the proverbial hat. He can be inexorably hardened by life's unforeseen knocks, brimming with cynicism, suspicion, and doubt. Or overcome with desperate disillusionment, caught up in circumstances beyond his control and urgently seeking a way out of a seemingly hopeless plight.

Films noirs are populated with characters that seem doomed from the start. They scurry down shadowy streets wet with rain and dimly lit by street lamps. The mood and tone suggests an unfair world where the little guy has no chance. The game has been fixed and all he can do is play his part. *Quicksand* (1950) fits many of the motifs and themes of the genre. Rooney plays Dan Brady, a mechanic with an eye for the ladies. He makes a date with Vera (Jeanne Cagney), a sexy girl with expensive tastes. He tries to raise the $20 he needs for the date by calling a friend who owes him that much, but the friend can't give it to him until payday. He decides to borrow the $20 from the cash register and replace it before the bookkeeper checks it out. The bookkeeper arrives earlier than expected and notices the money missing. Dan rushes out to buy a watch on credit then hocks it to replace the $20. But the store and the pawnshop compare records, and Dan is in trouble. He spirals into a life of petty crime, with Vera pushing him the whole time. She has her sights set on a mink coat and she is not going to be satisfied until she gets it.

This low-budget film provides some real tension and is well acted throughout. Rooney received some good reviews, including one from Ann Helming of the *Hollywood Citizen News*, which praises his "straightforward, mugless performance." A viewer for *Variety* notes that Rooney "portrays the hard-luck mechanic in convincingly somber tones without once having the chance for any comic capers." But the movie has a major flaw—an upbeat ending that undercuts the desperate tone of the rest of the film. The typical critical response was the following:

> *Quicksand.* Jeanne Cagney, Mickey Rooney. Melodrama. Garage employee gets in deeper and deeper as he turns to petty crime in effort to square his altered accounts. Sordid amusement pier background is distasteful; film is unethical in implication that it is hero's bad luck, not weakness and lack of moral conviction, that causes the trouble.

A failure at the box office, the movie was not one of Rooney's favorites; as he once said of *Quicksand*: "We sank in the stuff."

Rooney managed to extricate himself from his contract with Stiefel in March 1950. The actor diplomatically told the press that there were no hard feelings in the split. He indicated that they had made some bad movies and that it was time to move on, although he wished his former partner the best of luck.

Rooney's next film noir was *The Strip* (1951). He plays drummer Stanley Maxton, who has come to L.A. in the hope of opening his own nightclub. At his latest gig, he quickly falls in love with waitress and aspiring actress Jane Tafford (Sally Forrest). But Jane is mainly interested in Stanley because one of his acquaintances, Delwyn "Sonny" Johnson (James Craig), has supposed connections to the film industry. Sonny puts the make on Jane, but has no intention of helping her. He is really a gangster and, when Stanley warns her about him, Sonny's henchmen beat him badly. Jane accidentally kills Sonny during an argument, and Stanley takes the blame for it.

There really isn't much of a story in this film, but it does fit the themes of film noir and Rooney is very believable in the role. Jeff Stafford, in his article for TCM, states: "The real fascination of *The Strip* is watching Rooney play a more mature character part; that of the sad-sack loser, a role which stands in direct contrast to the actor's adrenalin-charged, hyperactive performance." Stafford goes on to say that the film's main strength is the great music throughout. We are treated to a few Louis Armstrong numbers with his musical chops and irrepressible showmanship on full display. The movie also boasts the efforts of singer Vic Damone, bandleader Jack Teagarden, and Earl "Fatha" Hines. Rooney, who was an accomplished drummer, has several solos on the instrument. *The Strip* did manage to turn a small profit, but the critics were unimpressed. Even so, as Hannsberry points out, the same critics felt the film's musical moments had merit, particularly those contributed by Rooney. Philip K. Scheuer, of the *Los Angeles Times*, writes that he "really knocks himself out on the traps ... holding his own even among such fast company."

Rooney's next picture was the excellent *Drive a Crooked Road* (1954), which reunited him with Richard Quine and his writing partner Blake Edwards. The final entry in Rooney's three-picture deal with Columbia is a stark, black-and-white crime drama. Later described by *TV Guide* as "a crisply done film noir with Rooney taken in by the universal emotional state that was at the root of many noir heroes' problems, loneliness," this was the third collaboration with Quine and Edwards and it was a mutually beneficial partnership for all three. Rooney was getting work and he, as the star, was helping the careers of two up-and-coming directors. In fact, this was the first film on which Edwards was allowed to do any directing, supervising the production's second unit.

Drive a Crooked Road, as Andrew Dickos points out, is centered around a common motif in film noir.

> The car in the film noir is a complex symbol expressing the various kinds of escape its protagonist attempts.... An interesting irony in several films noirs is that those who meet bad ends also work on cars professionally—they drive them, service them, tinker with them. Playing Don Brady, a mechanic in *Quicksand*, and Eddie Shannon, a mechanic and car racer in *Drive a Crooked Road*, Mickey Rooney finds himself in hot water because of their automotive skills and easy seduction by femmes fatales.

Rooney's performance as Eddie Shannon is unlike anything he had ever done. He plays a sad, lonely man who races cars on weekends for a few bucks but dreams of someday raising enough money to go to Europe and compete in the great races of Le Mans or the Grand Prix. His co-workers, meanwhile, rib him about never having a date and being so shy.

A beautiful woman named Barbara (Dianne Foster) drives into the garage to have her car fixed. Eddie does the work and is oblivious to her flirting. She leaves a handkerchief behind deliberately. He calls her and she asks him to bring it to her at the beach, where she is sunbathing with her friend Steve (Kevin McCarthy). Eddie feels like he may be intruding, but Steve leaves. She notices a long scar on his forehead and he tells her it came about as the result of a car accident. She coaxes him into talking about his dreams of racing. He's still reluctant to open up because we sense that he is afraid of being hurt. Barbara invites Eddie to a party at Steve's house on Malibu Beach. Eddie reluctantly attends and, at the party, he is encouraged by Steve to talk about the intricacies of car racing. Before the night is over, Steve casually mentions a plan to rob a bank and he wants Eddie to be the wheelman for the job. Eddie almost bolts out the door: he wants no part of it. Steve, with his friend Harold (Jack Kelly), asks Eddie to think it over and talk to Barbara before he makes a decision. We sense that this has all been a setup and the poor sap is being taken for a ride—literally. Barbara does her job and subtly lets Eddie know that if they are going to keep seeing each other it will take the money he gets from the bank job. Eddie is still conflicted about the bank job, but succumbs because of his desperate sense of loneliness.

There are more twists and turns to the story, including Barbara having second thoughts about her role in the whole charade. The script was written by Edwards and avoids genre clichés while providing a strong character study. Something to note is that, in Quine's hands, *Drive a*

Six. Noir Star

Crooked Road avoids cynicism. It's instead sad, romantic, and, ultimately, tragic. Rooney's marvelous work in *Drive*, like many of his portrayals, was underappreciated at the time. Philip T. Hartung, one of the more perceptive critics on Rooney's work during this period, said, "Mickey Rooney turns in another of those first-rate performances that have made him one of Hollywood's leading actors." Hartung also makes the following observation:

> The awkward age for most boys was the golden age for Mickey Rooney. But like most prodigies, one of the most talented child actors of modern times has had to pay for his precocity. At twenty-four he found himself a has-been—the public would no longer believe that he was a boy and was bored by the suggestion that he was a man. In the last five years, Mickey has made seven pictures in each of which he seemed less and less the Hardy perennial. The news of *Drive a Crooked Road* is that Rooney is still a skilled actor.... Mickey might well develop from a fine instinctive performer into a keenly conscious and accomplished character actor.

One of this writer's favorite Rooney performances is as the gun-happy sociopath in *Baby Face Nelson* (1957). The energetic movie is directed by

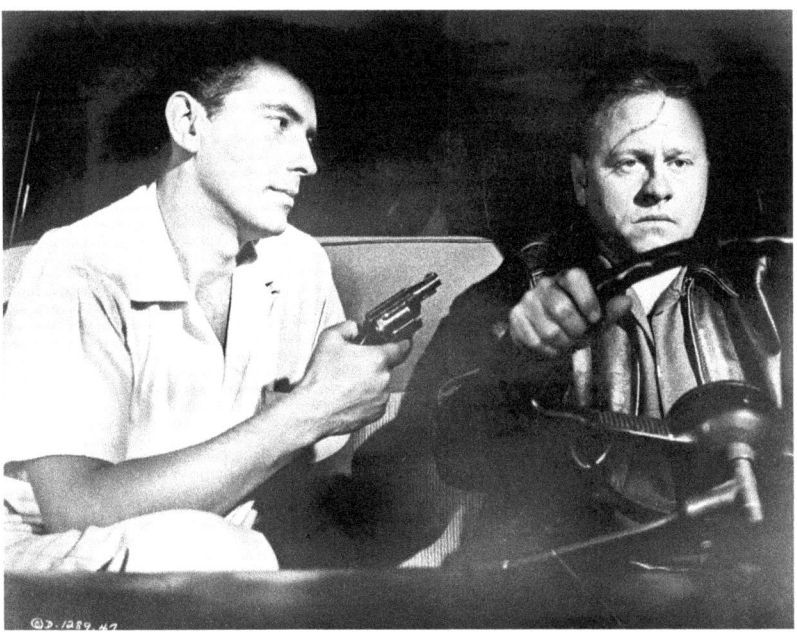

A race car driver and mechanic, Eddie Shannon (Mickey Rooney, right) is forced to drive the getaway car for two bank robbers, one of whom, Harold Baker (Jack Kelly, left), keeps a close eye on him. *Drive a Crooked Road* (1954) (Photofest).

Don Siegel, who had helmed *Riot in Cell Block 11* (1954) and would go on to direct *Dirty Harry* (1971), starring Clint Eastwood. In a chapter of his biography devoted to the making of *Baby Face Nelson*, Siegel talked about the ups and downs of working with Rooney. Siegel went to visit Rooney at his Laurel Canyon home to discuss the script and the casting. He found him in his backyard, sitting on a lounge chair guzzling beer out of the can amid some snails crawling around the back yard. Siegel began killing the snails as he tried to find a place to sit away from the predominant number of mollusks. Rooney shrieked in horror at the carnage he was causing among the snail colony and jumped up to demand that he stop killing the poor creatures. Siegel went on to say that Rooney was one of the most talented actors he ever worked with, but that he had a chip on his shoulder and, when he drank, he could become either vicious or morose. He went on to discuss the difficulties in getting a good performance out of him. "If one could hold down that wonderful energy that he would burst out with he had no peer. But if twelve cans of beer took charge—look out. To give the devil (and he was one) his due, I admired his skill and loathed his personality."

Siegel went on to discuss a perceived betrayal on Rooney's part when he heard that the actor had offered to finish directing the film because the producers were making unrealistic demands on Siegel to wrap up the shooting quickly, as they were running out of money. When Rooney heard about the demands he went to the producers, supposedly to ask for more time for Siegel, but instead offered to finish the job himself, and presumably for the remainder of Siegel's salary in addition to his acting fee. "The kind snail-saver was an evil man," the director said simply. In order to keep his job and finish the picture on budget, Siegel was forced to do fifty-five difficult setups in one day, an extraordinary achievement.

The movie opens with titles on the screen and narration dedicating the film to the members of law enforcement, which means, like most crime films, you'll be rooting for the bad guys. There is also a jazzy musical score that instantly evokes its time period. The first scene shows Lester M. Gillis (Rooney) being released from prison. He is picked up by one of mob boss Rocca's underlings. Rocca has pulled strings to get Gillis out of the pen and wants to be paid back right away. When Gillis is delivered to Rocca (Ted de Corsia), he immediately starts razzing him about his size, referring to him as "shrimp" and "little man." Gillis does not like this, and tells him so. Rocca laughs and instructs him to look out the window at a man who is talking to a group of workers. Rocca's price for springing Gillis from prison is that he must kill this union organizer for him. He refuses, which doesn't please Rocca in the least. In the next scene we see Gillis taking his first bath outside of prison; he splashes around in the tub like a kid. He then goes to a store where his girlfriend, Sue, works. (Sue is played by the luscious and talented Carolyn Jones, later to gain fame as Morticia on *The Addams Family*.) Their eyes meet and we immediately sense the passion between the two. They go to a back room where there is just one naked light bulb that he has to turn, burning his fingers so they can kiss in the dark. Reviewers failed to mention this scene, even though the sense of longing between these two characters is palpable, and they maintain that heat throughout the film.

Alan Lovell points out that Siegel's heroes are loners without families and friends who reject established society, which is certainly true of the criminal known as "Baby Face." He goes on to say, "Because of this, women have a marginal place in Siegel's films. Their absence is one way of defining the heroes. The one exception to this is the heroine of *Baby Face Nelson*. Her role in the film is not an attempt to provide Baby Face with some kind of social background—Sue is not seen as a wife but essentially as a companion adventurer." Siegel said that Rooney's only request when approached to do the role was that he find a hot young actress for his leading lady. Jones seemed to tap into what Siegel was doing with Rooney. As she plays Sue, she helps him "act taller." Sue knows how desperately Baby Face needs her. She feeds his all-consuming desire to be a big man and knows that she plays a key role in his life, and that is enough for her.

The next thing we know the cops break into Gillis's apartment, looking for something. They find a gun taped to the toilet tank and haul him back to jail. Rocca has set him up. At this point, we are siding with Gillis. He has refused to kill a union organizer; we sense his passion for Sue; and we've seen him enjoy a brief moment of freedom. The action picks up from here, with Sue helping him escape from the police at the train station where they are transferring him from the county jail to the state prison in Joliet. She gives him a gun with which he overpowers his guards and they escape in her car. They stop to get some booze by going to a pharmacy, as Prohibition is still in effect (it was actually repealed on December 5, 1933). Gillis tells the druggist what he wants and says he has his prescription. When the druggist goes to the back room Gillis pulls a gun on him and takes the liquor and his money. As he leaves, the druggist pulls a gun and shoots him. Sue takes him to see Doc Saunders (Sir Cedric Hardwicke), the hard-drinking, lecherous, Shakespeare-spouting medical man, who patches up Gillis. From there, Gillis meets up with John Dillinger (Leo Gordon) on a playground. He is much more businesslike than the trigger-happy Gillis, whom he nicknamed "Baby Face." Gillis has also taken Sue's last name: Nelson. From here it's a wild ride of stickups, car chases, and holding out at a camp from the police. On their first job, Dillinger is shot and recuperates at the camp while the others continue to rob banks. While he is recuperating, his girlfriend talks him into going to see the movie *Manhattan Melodrama*, playing at the Biograph Theatre in Chicago. (A little historical note: Rooney had a small part in that 1934 movie.) Of course, Dillinger is gunned down in front of the theatre, thanks to the "lady in red," and Baby Face Nelson is now number one on the FBI's most-wanted list.

There are wonderful moments throughout the movie. When one of the gang is killed during their first holdup, Baby Face and another gang

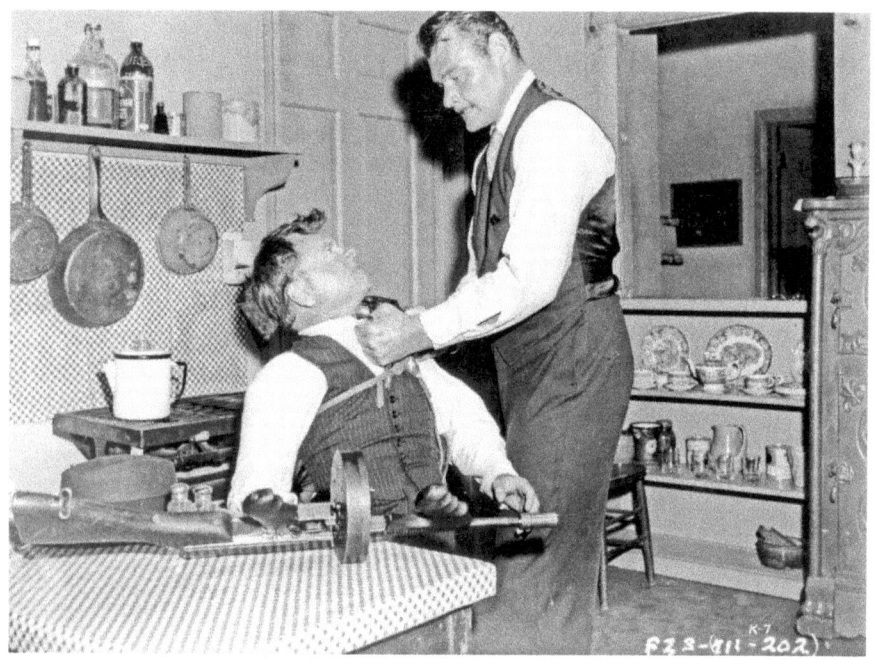

Just-released felon Lester Gillis (Mickey Rooney, left) gets roughed up by John Dillinger (Leo Gordon, right) in Don Siegel's B-movie masterpiece *Baby Face Nelson* **(1957).**

member are digging his grave. Doc Saunders wanders by and after taking a long drink of whisky, recites, "Alas, poor Yorick! I knew him well." Then Baby Face throws his shovel at him. Nelson sees Sue sunbathing and walks by with a robe to cover up her legs. Moments later the Doc comes by and sits down beside her and begins stroking her beautiful gams. She warns him to stop, but she obviously enjoys the attention. Baby Face sees this from his window and we know the good doctor's days are numbered. During one of their holdups they take the bank manager as a hostage and Nelson is amused at how short he is. "How did a little guy like you get to be a bank manager?" he asks in disbelief. He lets the bank manager live only because he is a short man like himself. After their final holdup, when Baby Face, dressed as a security guard, locks his fellow gang members in the bank vault with the employees so he and Sue can have all the money to escape the country, he spots a few boys at the camp, squirrel hunting; he raises his machine gun as Sue watches. He is about to shoot when they head in the other direction. He lowers his weapon. Sue says, "Lie to me, baby. Tell me you wouldn't have killed them."

Nelson replies unconvincingly, "I wouldn't have killed them."

The police, with the help of the diminutive bank manager's information, finally track down the doomed mobster. A final car chase, with the police in hot pursuit, ensues; they fire and hit Baby Face and Sue's car's radiator, and the car comes to a stop. Nelson stands his ground and kills several of the cops in a wild shootout, but he is badly wounded. He struggles to his feet, with Sue helping him. He is gurgling blood and coughing as they stumble into a graveyard. We hear the sirens of more patrol cars on the way. Baby Face tells Sue, "I can't make it. Don't let them kill me." He asks her to finish him off. She tearfully refuses. Then he tells her, "I *was* going to kill those kids." We hear a gunshot and Baby Face Nelson falls away from a gravestone with an inscription that says at the bottom "The End."

Baby Face Nelson has achieved a kind of cult status over the years, but it didn't do a lot for Rooney's career, receiving mixed reviews. As Hannsberry outlines in her book:

> Although one critic wrote that Rooney's portrayal of the infamous gangster "lacks ... understanding of the lust that drove Nelson to kill," other reviewers were more impressed. John L. Scott, of the *Los Angeles Times*, described the film as "a hard-hitting story in which a snarling Rooney in the title role blazes a trail of murder with his machine gun," adding that "the energetic star never goes halfway in any

characterization," and the critic for the *Hollywood Citizen-News* wrote, "Rooney delivers a most convincing performance as the gun-happy gangster, Baby Face."

The prevailing criticism at the time is best expressed by a review in *Newsweek*: "This one offers pocket-size, Puckish Mickey Rooney in the unlikeliest role of his career—that of Public Enemy No. 1, vintage 1933. It is as incongruous as Edward G. Robinson playing Pinocchio." But many critics now consider this movie a classic of the genre. David Thomson, in his *Biographical Dictionary of Film*, writes that it is one of the greatest performances in screen history and that it "achieves a fearful poetry because of Rooney's seizure of part of his own appalling destiny."

David Cairns, in his 2010 online article, "The Forgotten: Trigger Happy Punks," states in a colorful fashion:

> The cast is a delightful rogue's gallery of mean types, but astride it stands Rooney, in a remarkably buttoned-down performance of seething assholery. Initially established by the script as a man with one or two redeeming scruples, Rooney's Gillis is on an express route to damnation, and his psychopathic indifference to human life doesn't take long to come through, and once it does there's nothing that can contain it. With his head, not so much like a baby's as like a giant testicle emerging from a shirt collar, Rooney uses his pasty puffball (teeth and eyes crammed into it as with a snowman made of dough) to maleficent effect, but his body does most of the talking. With the legs of Toulouse-Lautrec and the torso of Captain Caveman, he is an unlikely action hero, but his dance training kicks in and he struts, tommy gun in hand, through Siegel's matter-of-fact compositions like Death's stunted twin.

The script by Daniel Mainwaring and Irving Shulman focuses on Gillis's developmentally arrested character. Their protagonist is emotionally and psychologically crippled. Somewhere along the line he stopped growing, in every way. He is now a time bomb of resentment in a big world in which he cannot function. Geoffrey O'Brien, in his article in *Film Comment*, states:

> Mickey Rooney gives a performance of a lifetime—mercurial, jittery, and weirdly endearing in those moments when he isn't trying to kill someone—a performance all the more powerful for being almost upstaged by [Sir] Cedric Hardwicke's lecherous, alcoholic gangland doctor and by Jones's unrelenting intensity as she makes her peace with the obscure bond that ties her to her psychopathic lover.

And Stephen Schaefer, in his 2014 online article, "Memorably Murderous Mickey Rooney," states:

> In Don Siegel's undeservedly obscure, rarely seen *Baby Face Nelson* Rooney pulled out all the stops as psychopathic gangster Lester M. "Baby Face Nelson" Gillis who, when John Dillinger was gunned down on Chicago's Depression sidewalks, became

Six. Noir Star

Public Enemy Number One. A sadistic bank robber with a real issue about his diminutive height, Rooney's Baby Face Nelson ranks as a landmark gangster in all cinema. Shot in just nine days in vivid black and white, in an unremittingly abrasive and in-your-face fast pace, *Baby Face Nelson* co-stars Carolyn Jones (who worked with Siegel previously in *Invasion of the Body Snatchers*) in one of her key performances as Sue, the only person on planet Earth who can love Nelson.

* * *

One of Rooney's key collaborators during this fruitful period was the jazz musician and arranger Van Alexander. Alexander Van Fliet Feldman was born on May 2, 1915, and died just two months past the century mark. He led bands as a high school student and studied musical composition in college. He began doing arrangements for bandleader Chick Webb in the mid–1930s. He was a frequent collaborator with Ella Fitzgerald, arranging her biggest hit, "A-Tiskit, A-Tasket," and went on to work with Bing Crosby, Doris Day, Dinah Shore, Peggy Lee, and many other singers and bands. Alexander did the music for most of Rooney's films during the 1950s and into the early '60s. He provided the music for no fewer than eight Rooney vehicles, and his driving, jazzy scores were especially important to the noir and gangster films. The urgency in the music heightens the tension and action in *Baby Face Nelson*, *The Big Operator*, and *The Last Mile*. Alexander also worked with Rooney as arranger and conductor for the many variety TV shows on which the actor appeared. He won several Emmy Awards for his television scores and was presented with the Henry Mancini Award for Lifetime Achievement from ASCAP.

Another frequent collaborator was film producer/director Albert Zugsmith. He had worked as a reporter and entrepreneur who founded the Atlantic City newspaper, *Daily World*, in 1935, also serving as its publisher and editor. He became independently wealthy and decided he wanted to get into the motion picture business. He produced mostly low-budget exploitation films with a strong story hook that featured an exposé of society's ills. *High School Confidential* (1958) was about dope pushers preying on America's youth, and *The Big Operator* (1959) concerned a corrupt labor leader, played with surprising menace by Rooney. Zugsmith is now known primarily, if at all, as a B-movie producer whose most frequent star was the voluptuous blonde Mamie Van Doren. But he was more than that. He did produce at least three certifiable classics: Douglas Sirk's *Written on the Wind* (1956), the science fiction classic *The Incredible Shrinking Man* (1957), and Welles's *Touch of Evil* (1958). Zugsmith also produced two of Rooney's worst films from this period: *Platinum High School* (1960) and the regrettable *The Private Lives of Adam and Eve* (also 1960), shot in Spectacolor, a film which has the distinction of having been condemned by the Catholic Legion of Decency. Zugsmith co-directed this mess with Rooney.

The next installment of Rooney's film noir career is the prison drama *The Last Mile* (1959), in which he plays death row inmate "Killer" John Mears. This was originally a 1930 play written by John Wexley that had Spencer Tracy play the role of Mears in the Broadway production, and Preston Foster in the 1932 film version. The setting could not be gloomier— the death house of a prison. The movie opens with the inmates in their cells saying goodbye to a fellow prisoner as he takes his final walk toward the electric chair. The movie is shot in black and white, with bare light bulbs and the bars from the cells casting vertical shadows along the gray walls. Mears hangs on the bars like an animal at the zoo. Rooney's famous energy is suppressed by the setting, but he's like a coiled spring ready to be sprung. Mears looks on with contempt at the ritual that he has seen before and he knows is waiting for him. The lights in the cellblock dim when the juice is turned on.

One inmate talks about the dreams he could have fulfilled in his life. Another talks about the women he's had. Mears paces his cell, his energy turning inward. The prisoners talk about their quests for a stay of execution. The next one to go is Richard Walters (Clifford David), a young man in the cell next to Mears. One of the guards sadistically taunts Walters about the inevitability of his death. Mears sneers at the guard, "Callaghan, your mother must bark." The guards prepare Walters by shaving one of his legs where the electrified strip will be placed. He is given his last meal, but he can't bring himself to eat it. Mears listens to the talk of the other inmates with revulsion etched on his face for the predicament they find themselves in. The prison priest, Father O'Connors (Frank Overton) comes to hear Walters's confession and to deliver last rites of the Church. Walters confesses that he did kill someone, but that it was an accident. The young man begs the priest to save him from his fate. O'Connors asks Richard if he believes in an Almighty, and he says he does. The priest stops next to Mears to ask the same question, but he will have none of it.

Walters has to dictate his last message for his mom and girlfriend to the guard who had been taunting him. The guard moves too close to Mears's cell and Mears grabs him through the bars by the neck and stran-

Six. Noir Star

gles him, then takes his keys and unlocks all the cells. Finally, Mears's pent-up energy explodes in violence. The inmates overcome the guards in the next room and seize their weapons. They put the guards in the cells and Mears calls the warden in an attempt to hold them for ransom. O'Connors, who has also been captured, begs Mears to think about what he is doing, to which he replies, "*Think?* I don't have to think. I have *faith*." He holds up his gun. The warden refuses to negotiate even after one of the guards is executed. The escape is doomed, as are all of these convicts. The guards are now in the same position as the inmates who have been waiting to die.

Rooney is excellent in *The Last Mile*. He wears a grotesque mask of hatred on his face throughout the film. The constrained energy in his body brings a dramatic tension to the film that is absent in the writing. The film lacks depth in the story other than the obvious role reversals of the inmates and the guards. But it is another strong portrayal by Rooney in a genre where his physical stature did nothing to diminish the power in his performance. It was another of his screen efforts that wasn't fully appreciated at the time of its release. The *New York Times* reviewer wondered why this old warhorse of a vehicle was being trotted out yet again: "The opening of 'The Last Mile' at the Victoria yesterday prompts an immediate question—why? Why revive a prison melodrama that has literally been done to death everywhere for the last 30 years?" Spencer Tracy had originated the role of Killer Mears on Broadway a generation before. The *Times* reviewer went on to say, "The simple fact is that John Wexley's stage antique still makes a heck of a show. And we are not quoting Killer Mears—now played by Mickey Rooney—the toughest, meanest inmate ever to create havoc along Death Row. In this United Artists release, surprisingly effective as far as it goes, the chair offers the same sizzling specter." Howard Thompson liked the cast overall, but quibbled with Rooney in the lead: "It's a man's-man set-up all right, until one of the bloodiest battles in prison fiction, when Mr. Rooney takes over for a one-man show. And herein lies the rub. Mr. Rooney is a fine, earnest, professional actor. But to watch his rather youthful countenance shifting expressions like gears as he snarls battle orders to his towering colleagues doesn't quite cut ice—for all the gore and gunfire." This is another example of a critic who watched too many of the Andy Hardy movies and just can't let go of that image and review what's currently on the screen. Rooney had already done many crime dramas by this time, including *Killer McCoy*,

Killer Mears (Mickey Rooney) talks to an unseen fellow inmate on Death Row in *The Last Mile* (1959) (Photofest).

Drive a Crooked Road, and the recent *Baby Face Nelson* and had proven his worth as a great character actor.

The final gangster film from the noir period to discuss is the Zugsmith production *The Big Operator* (1959). One critic aptly described the movie as a bargain-basement *On the Waterfront* (1954). Rooney plays corrupt union leader Little Joe Braun with great, gleeful menace. He runs the union like a brutal gangster. Zugsmith cast Steve Cochran, who usually played heavies, as an honest working stiff, and sexpot Mamie Van Doren played his dutiful wife. We see Little Joe on television in front of a congressional committee investigating organized crime in the unions, repeatedly taking the Fifth. Joe is always waving a big cigar as he barks out orders. The *Commonweal* reviewer wrote, "Perhaps some labor leaders have used Little Joe's methods, but as directed by Charles Haas the film goes so far with the rough stuff that violence seems to be used for violence sake." Bill Gibson (Cochran) is a witness to the treasurer of his union being abducted and this is of concern to Little Joe holding onto his power. Little Joe makes threats against Bill's young son if he doesn't play ball.

Commonweal concludes its review, "Except for Mamie Van Doren, who is miscast as Bill's wife, the acting is quite good, and as a slob with Little Caesar complexes Mickey Rooney is, as usual, especially effective. Nonetheless the film is so overdone that no one will take it seriously."

Requiem for a Heavyweight (1962) may seem an odd choice in a chapter devoted to noir and gangster movies, but the plot is not really about the sport of boxing but what it had become at the bottom of the profession when it mixed with the criminal element. Rod Serling wrote the original story for a live TV production of *Playhouse 90* in 1956. The teleplay was directed by Ralph Nelson and starred Jack Palance as Harlan "Mountain" McClintock, a washed-up heavyweight who has just gotten his brains beaten in by a much younger fighter. Keenan Wynn plays McClintock's unscrupulous manager Maish Rennick, and Keenan's father, Ed Wynn, is Army, Mountain's corner cut-man and, ultimately, the only friend he has. Mountain is clearly addled or punch-drunk from years of beatings even when he won, but he has developed scar tissue on his eyes and the ring doctor refuses to certify him for more fights. Some thugs are hanging around the arena looking for Maish, who owes them money for bets he has placed and who can't afford to let Mountain stop fighting. This was a live production and Keenan Wynn recalled years later that his dad, the great vaudeville comedian Ed Wynn, was having trouble memorizing his lines in rehearsals and he was afraid that this might turn out to be an embarrassing disaster on live TV. But when the lights came up on October 11, 1956, Ed performed the role perfectly and received excellent reviews for his work. The production is considered one of the classics of the Golden Age of Television and garnered Emmy Awards for Nelson and Serling, with Serling's teleplay receiving the first Peabody Award given to an individual script.

Serling refashioned his teleplay into a feature film script and, six years after the original broadcast, it became a movie with David Susskind producing and Ralph Nelson again directing, but with a whole new cast. Anthony Quinn was cast as Louis "Mountain" Rivera, the character's name changed to reflect Quinn's Hispanic heritage. Jackie Gleason was now playing Maish, with Mickey Rooney cast as his corner man and friend Army. Julie Harris rounded out the cast as Grace Miller, the social worker at the unemployment office who tries to help Mountain get work after he realizes he can no longer fight; the role was played by Kim Hunter in the TV version.

The movie opens with a tracking shot down a bar as a bunch of ex-fighters with cauliflower ears and bent noses watch a fight on TV while chugging beers. There is a cut to inside the boxing arena where we see, from Mountain's point of view, a blurred image of a young fighter who has just landed a blow to Rivera's face as he staggers to his corner. The POV continues as we see a concerned Army and a worried Maish looking at the mess their fighter has become. The referee raises the young fighter's hand in victory and he comes over to congratulate Mountain saying, "Good fight, kid." The fighter is Cassius Clay, who would soon become Muhammad Ali. Mountain leans on Maish and Army as they lead him back to the dressing room. The POV continues brilliantly in stark black-and-white cinematography through the dirty, loud, cinderblock arena to the dressing room. The POV continues until Mountain gets into the dressing room and looks in the mirror and, for the first time, we see what he sees: a battered and broken face that shows the scars of years of fights; it frightens Mountain as much as it scares the audience. Mountain lies down on the table and Maish asks him where he is. He answers, "I'm in Pittsburgh, and it's raining." The ring doctor looks into Rivera's eyes and tells Maish that Rivera's fighting days are over. Maish protests, "In nineteen-fifty-two he was the number-five-rated heavyweight." The doctor reminds him that 1952 was a long time ago and says that Rivera has scar tissue damage to his eyes and that one more punch could cause total blindness.

Maish tells Army that he'll just have to get another boy, to which Army replies, "Another boy, what about *him*?" Maish has other, more pressing concerns, like his own safety. Mountain apologizes to his manager for losing the fight and is slow to catch on to the fact that his fighting days are over. Maish tells Mountain not to worry and then heads out into the empty arena. There are a couple of thugs waiting for him and he begins to run as they chase him into the boxing ring, where they have him cornered. A heavyset character comes into view wearing a long heavy overcoat and a floppy hat. It turns out that the threatening-looking individual is actually a woman by the name of Ma Greeny, wonderfully played by Madame Spivy, who makes it clear to Maish that he not only better come up with the money he owes them, but that he bet against his own fighter. She tells him that if he doesn't come up with the money by a specific date, to "take a good look in the mirror, Maish, and then say goodbye to what you see."

Six. Noir Star

Maish has to find a way to make some money fast or his life isn't worth a plug nickel. He meets with some wrestling promoters who want to sign Mountain to a contract to play an Indian in the wrestling ring. He would be required to wear a headdress and war paint and play the bad guy in fixed matches. Army takes Mountain to an employment agency in the hopes of finding other employment. Harris is lovely as the kindly employment counselor, patient with Mountain, who is uncomfortable talking about his qualifications because he doesn't have any, other than in the ring. She feels sorry for him at first then recognizes his pride when he says that people look at him and think he is just a big ugly clown "but I was almost the heavyweight champion of the world." Just as he is about to leave she says hesitantly, trying not to offend him, that there is a job for a movie usher available. Mountain says it's honest work and

Boxer Louis "Mountain" Rivera (Anthony Quinn, center), cutman Army (Mickey Rooney, left), and manager Maish Rennick (Jackie Gleason, right) have seen better days in the searing film version of the Rod Serling teleplay *Requiem for a Heavyweight* (1962). This was Serling's favorite among all of his fine works.

agrees to go for an interview. Army takes Rivera to the theatre but they take one look at Mountain and realize that they don't have a uniform that fits him. Not to be deterred, Harris finds out about a camp counselor position where Mountain could teach young boys how to box. He is thrilled with the idea but Maish scoffs at it when he finds out because he needs his fighter to do the wrestling gig so that he can get a cut. Maish seems to agree with the idea but takes him out for a drink before the interview and, of course, gets him drunk. Army knows what Maish is up to and tracks them down at Dempsey's Bar, where the real Jack Dempsey comes over to talk to them. Army reminds Mountain about the interview and tells him to reschedule, but Rivera heads off to meet the people in his drunken condition. Army has it out with Maish, calling him "a dirty stinking fink."

The entire cast of actors is superb in this film adaptation of the TV classic. Anthony Quinn is a hulking wound of a man. He strains painfully to express himself but the countless blows to his head have caused so much brain damage that he slurs his words and has difficulty communicating even the simplest thoughts. He moves slowly but imposingly, like a large animal who knows that, despite everything, he has an innate sense of dignity.

TCM movie host Robert Osborne asked Quinn who the greatest actor he ever worked with was and he immediately said Rooney. He also talked about his work on *Requiem* and said that he would watch Rooney looking at a scene he was doing for his reaction because "he was the best actor of all of us" and knew he was on solid ground if he got a nod from him. For his part, Rooney shines as Army, Mountain's sympathetic cohort. Army says at one point, "I love this kid like he was my own brother." Army was a former boxer himself and empathizes with Rivera's plight and has the scar tissue on his own face to prove it. When Mountain is rejected at his first job interview Army says, "He's lost, Maish." Rooney even works a little comedy into this incredibly gloomy picture when he annoys Maish while playing gin rummy by constantly repeating the same phrase, "That's good to know" and then sticking a card into his rummy hand with his elbow, which really sets Maish off. It's almost a scene Gleason would have done with the great Art Carney in one of their "Honeymooners" sketches. The critic Manny Farber accused Rooney of sidelining in this scene—that is, the actor is commenting on the almost unrelenting darkness of the piece with a little comedy shtick.

Gleason is also wonderful as Maish. His approach to his character is not that of a stock villain. Maish loves Mountain in his own way, but the world around all of these men has changed radically. Everything was great when Rivera was younger and they were winning. But, as the saying goes, "Father Time is undefeated," and when Mountain got older and started losing and the arenas got seedier it all began to curdle Maish's soul. Although he cares about Mountain, his top priority became his own survival. You can see the pain on Maish's face when he does something despicable. He has become an unscrupulous man and is very unhappy about that, but he must survive and will do whatever it takes, which includes having Mountain humiliate himself in the wrestling ring.

Harris is also excellent as the social worker who sees the gentle spirit inside of Mountain and just wants to help him find a little dignity outside the ring. She befriends him and he is a man who, quite naturally, becomes attracted to her. She is lovely but rather prim and when he makes a clumsy pass at her she is repelled and then sorry that she reacted that way. All she wanted to do was help this poor lost soul and feels horrible that, in doing so, she actually may have made things worse for him.

The movie ends at the arena with the wrestling promoters and Ma Greeny closing in on Maish. The arena is loud and dirty with midget wrestlers throwing each other around the ring. Inside the dressing room, Mountain is made up to look like an Indian. He begs Maish, "I'll do anything for you. But don't make me be a clown." Maish tells him, "My life is on the line. It didn't bother you that I had every nickel saying you wouldn't go four rounds and you went seven." Both Army and Mountain now know that Maish bet against his own fighter. It is the ultimate act of betrayal. When it looks like Mountain will play along, Ma Greeny's men move toward Maish, but Rivera begins swinging at them. Once he's subdued he agrees to go along with the odious deal. Maish begs Army and Mountain to stay with him as a team, but they ignore him and head out to the ring. The last scene is Mountain dancing around the ring doing a war whoop as the crowd screams in derision. Army looks at the spectacle with tears streaming down his face.

The film received some good reviews for the direction and acting. Dorothy Kilgallen wrote a column in the *Washington Post* titled, "Film Colony Hoping Mickey Gets Oscar," but that was not to be. Surprisingly, none of the principals received Oscar consideration, but Ralph Nelson did receive a Directors Guild nod and the film was named one of the ten best of the year by the National Board of Review. Brendan Gill of the *New Yorker* gave the film and performances a rave review: "What we have here is a prizefighters-and-gangsters melodrama of exceptional humanity and finesse, which has not one, not two, not three, but four marvelous performances, by Anthony Quinn, Jackie Gleason, Julie Harris, and Mickey Rooney." The performances have grown in critical stature over the decades, and it remains one of Rooney's very best.

Although these noir and B-movies did little for Rooney's prestige, they kept him working and in the game. Critics and audiences had difficulty seeing Andy Hardy as an average Joe caught in circumstances beyond his control, or as a psychopathic criminal, but now that Rooney is gone, and critics and audiences are not as familiar with his overall career, they can look at these films and his performances and judge them on their merits alone. There was an interesting coda to this period in Rooney's career that came about a dozen years later when he co-starred with Michael Caine in a satirical look at the private-eye genre in *Pulp*.

Pulp (1972) was written and directed by British director Mike Hodges. Caine plays Mickey King, a writer of salacious pulp fiction who is hired to ghostwrite the memoirs of Preston Gilbert (Rooney), an ex-tough guy movie star who is living in seclusion with his mother and his mistress on the island of Malta. Gilbert is in hiding from some real Mafia types whose secrets he knows and that put him and King in danger. Like many of his films during their original release, *Pulp* did not receive strong reviews. Consider Gary Arnold's flip dismissal in the November 6, 1972, issue of the *Washington Post*: "Pulp comes to the screen with all the style and authority of an apple hitting the sidewalk after dropping several stories. Under the circumstances, 'Splat' would be a slightly preferable title." The critic went on to say that Rooney was miscast in his role as a gangster type. Obviously, Mr. Arnold was unfamiliar with the half-dozen or so movies in which Rooney had effectively played misfits on the wrong side of the law.

The voiceover narrator provides some laughs while reading the pulp fiction purple being satirized by Hodges in his screenplay. Despite uninformed opinions to the contrary, Rooney fits the bill perfectly as the ex-gangster movie star. He even engages in some physical shtick at the birthday party in his honor. Shooting this scene was no laughing matter for writer/director Hodges, as he explains:

> Mickey Rooney was exhausting to work with. I thought it would be like working with Caine—*Pulp* was only my second feature—but he was the antithesis, he was the wild card, he never did anything conventionally. I learned that you couldn't rehearse with Mickey, you had to shoot from the top. There's this one scene which

Six. Noir Star

is based on an old Hollywood tradition where they used to hire these guys to go in as waiters at various dinner parties, and as an awful practical joke they would pour wine over someone else's lap. As a joke I put this into *Pulp* with Mickey. So he repeats this gag with waiters and the wine and when he did it the first time it was perfect, but he never came near to repeating it again. It was all improvised, you could not rehearse with him, you just had to shoot, so that was kind of illuminating, and then you would do conventional scenes and he would be tap dancing or playing the drums on his legs.

The film never quite works because satire is so hard to pull off, but *Pulp* is an entertaining attempt to look back on a film style whose time had passed. Roger Greenspun, an insightful critic for the *New York Times*, was obviously aware of the film's source of inspiration: "You can guess where most everything comes from: the cast—Mickey Rooney, Lionel Stander, Lizabeth Scott—partly out of the nineteen-thirties and forties; the characters—imitation Bogart, Cagney, and the like—out of those pop-culture objects now made icons; the moods and tensions, out of the collective depths of film noir."

If *Pulp* is a coda to Rooney's career in film noir and gangster movies, then an appearance in an episode of *Night Gallery* performs the same function for television. The title of the piece is "Rare Objects" (1972) and, in it, Rooney once again plays a mobster who has grown tired of a life of fear. He's tired of always looking over his shoulder for some punk who wants to take his place. The story opens in an almost-empty Italian restaurant. The first shot is a fork going into a plate of pasta and the fork goes up and into the face of Augie Kolodney (Rooney), who eats with eyes darting around the room. Kolodney orders the restaurant waiter around and is angry about his surroundings and seems suspicious about the waiter and the fact that the room is almost empty. Suddenly, bullets begin to fly into the restaurant, breaking through the front window and spraying glass and debris everywhere, as Kolodney dives under his table. He has been wounded and gets up screaming at the waiter, accusing him of being part of a plot to empty the place so he could be hit.

Kolodney is injured in the assassination attempt but only winged with a bullet in the arm. He goes to a shady doctor (similar to Doc Saunders in *Baby Face Nelson*) who treats gunshot wounds, no questions asked. Kolodney tells the doctor that he has to get out of this life he is leading where everything and everyone is a threat. The doctor knows of someone who can help him out of his predicament, but it will cost him a lot of money. The gangster goes to see Dr. Glendon, played wickedly and charmingly by Raymond Massey. The doctor lives in a huge mansion filled with objets d'art, including paintings and sculptures. He is obviously an avid collector and someone who is very wealthy. Glendon and Kolodney come to a financial arrangement for his service, with Kolodney peppering him with questions about the immense amount of money he wants and how he proposes to get him out of his life of danger. The doctor just smiles and tells him that no one will ever threaten him or, indeed, find him again. He slips his latest subject a potion that adds untold years to one's life, and Kolodney begins to feel groggy. When he awakens he finds that he has joined a large colony of forgotten men and women, kept in cages, not unlike a human zoo.

"Rare Objects" is not one of Rod Serling's better efforts, but it is definitely worth seeing. The *Night Gallery* series was nowhere near as great as his trademark work on *The Twilight Zone*, but it is somehow fitting that Rooney would conclude his work in the gangster genre with someone with whom he teamed up for some of his best work over a twenty-year period. Serling and Rooney made a great writing and acting team from the live TV broadcast *The Comedian* (1957) to *The Twilight Zone* episode "Last Night of a Jockey" (1963), the film version of the TV play *Requiem for a Heavyweight* (1962) and, finally, the *Night Gallery* episode "Rare Objects" (1972). Serling was a former boxer and paratrooper during World War II, was wounded in battle, and received the Bronze Star and a Purple Heart for his bravery in battle. After the war, he went to college on the GI Bill and the disability payments he received from the military. His interests led him first to the theatre department and then to broadcasting at Antioch College in Ohio. He was one of the original angry young writers who came into TV in the mid-1950s. Serling, along with Paddy Chayevsky, Gore Vidal, and Reginald Rose, among others, turned the vast wasteland into the Golden Age of Television. Serling was not only a wonderful writer but a very shrewd businessman and he recognized that Rooney was an under-utilized talent in the movies and brought him to TV, where he was able to do some very good work.

* * *

In 1974, Michael Kernan, of the *Washington Post*, wrote of the two gangster characters Rooney had recently portrayed.

> In *Pulp* (1972) Rooney does an aging ganglord, a man with the power of death in a flick of a fingertip, a man filled with ennui in his luxurious retirement, a man

sick of himself. It is a masterful portrait. A few years ago he did a similar type for a Rod Serling TV drama. Another aging gangster, yet totally different, a unique individual. These were believable people, real, integrated, more than mere collections of observed detail.

Jake Hinkson, in his article "Fate Slaps Down Andy Hardy," writes of Rooney: "While he could dominate a screen as well as anyone in a musical or comedy, in drama he seemed to shrink." This is neither a fair nor accurate assessment. The only element that shrank when he did the noir/gangster movies was the talent around him. With some notable exceptions, he was no longer being supported by the cream of the industry that, for several years, he had enjoyed during his heyday at MGM. Gone were the days of working with directors like Victor Fleming, Clarence Brown, Rouben Mamoulian, and Busby Berkeley, writers like William Saroyan and Eugene O'Neill, and composers and lyricists like George and Ira Gershwin. In these independent B-pictures, especially without the benefit of a decent budget, a good script, and strong direction, it is unlikely that anyone in the cast is going to come off well.

It should be noted, too, that drama, by its very nature, is more realistic than musicals or comedy, and audiences (and critics) more closely scrutinize the truthfulness of the story being told on the screen. The audience who grew up with the extraordinarily talented and precocious young star of musicals was forced to deal with his ever-diminutive stature in the darker material he had to work with after coming home from his stint in World War II. What Don Siegel did with *Baby Face Nelson* was work with the actor's size as part of the character's twisted psyche. He used what would be a liability for him in other roles to the advantage of the film and created a minor classic in the process.

There is also an element of what might have been in Rooney's film career after he left the studio. Had he found a better partner than Stiefel, had the brilliant Fritz Lang, the director of *Metropolis* (1927), *M* (1931), and *Scarlet Street* (1945), been available to direct *Quicksand* (he was supposed to, with *M* star Peter Lorre in the cast) instead of the workmanlike Irving Pichel, this first venture might have turned out to be a much better film and launched Rooney on a more successful trajectory in films. But that, alas, didn't happen. In those few instances when he did work with top talent, like Siegel, Quine, and Edwards, such gems as *Baby Face Nelson* and *Drive a Crooked Road* were the result.

CHAPTER SEVEN

Ava, with the Laughing Eyes

> Ava didn't give a damn who I was, or what I was, or what I could do for her, or how much money I was making.
> —Mickey Rooney, 1965

Of all the incredible accomplishments that Mickey Rooney achieved during his life and career, including receiving two honorary Oscars, the thing he was most proud of was the fact that he married the stunning Ava Gardner. She was the love of his life and they remained close until her death in 1990. She would disparage the relationship at times for comic effect but then quickly chastise herself for doing so. In an interview with the columnist Rex Reed, Gardner was asked about her ex-husbands and Mickey's name came up; she laughed and said, "Love finds Andy Hardy." When her remark came out in print she was furious at Reed and refused to ever talk to him again. She wrote several memoirs late in life and recounted all of her relationships with men and went into great detail about her courtship by, and marriage to, Rooney. She had a bawdy sense of humor and fretted continually that her candor about her sex life might embarrass Mickey. Peter Evans, during an interview with Gardner, assured her that there was no reason to worry and that he might even be flattered by her remembrances because she repeatedly credited him for her love of sex. She also said that, of her three husbands, Rooney was by far the best dancer and that he was the most talented man she ever met. But she felt that writing of the more graphic memories of him might be at odds with his newfound faith as a born-again Christian. She needn't have worried.

Rooney was captured by her beauty from the first moment he spotted her on the set of *Babes on Broadway*. He was in full drag costume doing a comedy singing impersonation of the Latin bombshell Carmen Miranda in a scene for the movie. At the time Gardner was just a shy eighteen-

Seven. Ava, with the Laughing Eyes

year-old girl from Grabtown, North Carolina, who had been spotted by a talent scout and brought to MGM along with countless other young and beautiful girls who hoped to become glamorous movie stars. But Ava Gardner wasn't really ambitious as much as looking for something more than she could find in that small, poor North Carolina town. She was born on Christmas Eve in 1922 to a family of sharecroppers. She was the youngest of seven children brought up in a house that had no electricity or indoor plumbing. A fire destroyed the family barn and cotton gin in 1924 and the family moved to a "teacherage" (a boarding house for young lady teachers) at a local school. Jonas, her father, worked as the caretaker and her mother, Mollie, served as the cook. A shortage of funds caused the school's closure in 1935 and the family moved to Newport News, Virginia, to operate another boarding house, this one for shipyard workers. Gardner remembered her father, whom she loved dearly, and his hacking cough and chronic illnesses. He succumbed to bronchitis when she was only fifteen.

As a young woman she was painfully shy. She recalled being introduced to her new classmates when she arrived in Newport News. The moment she opened her mouth and that Southern-fried accent came out, the other students laughed. They also laughed when she told them that her father had been a farmer. She was deeply hurt by this and was reluctant to speak at all in public for some time to come. Her mother insisted that she stay in school, and she did graduate from high school. Her incredible beauty would eventually open doors for her and

The stunning Ava Gardner, c. 1950.

she would get over the shyness with a vengeance. Gardner was training to become a secretary when she decided to visit her sister Bappie (Beatrice) in New York in 1941. Bappie's husband, Larry Tarr, was a photographer and, being struck by his sister-in-law's beauty, he took her portrait and put it in the window of his studio on Fifth Avenue in New York. Al Altman, a talent scout for MGM, saw the picture and contacted her about a screen test. She headed for Hollywood with her sister as a chaperone. Because of her thick accent, Altman decided to do a silent screen test. Her stunning looks leapt off the screen. The camera loved her. Altman reportedly sent a telegram to Mayer that read, "She can't sing, she can't act, she's terrific!"

Upon meeting the up-and-coming starlet, Rooney immediately asked her for a date. The shy young country girl just laughed at the thought and undoubtedly at the sight of him with a large garish fruit-laden turban on his head, wrapped in a tight sarong, and with big ruby red lips with that indomitable Rooney smile. It was the very definition of a "meet cute."

One can only imagine what the eighteen-year-old Gardner must have looked like in person. She is breathtaking in the B-movie walk-ons she had in her early films, with her sultry dark eyes, sculpted high cheekbones, raven hair, alabaster skin, and lithe figure. Rooney fondly recalled her girlish Southern accent, which was something she and the studio wanted to get rid of quickly, but was something that he adored. He was also thoroughly captivated and put on the Rooney full-court press in wooing her. He already had a reputation in Hollywood as a wolf who was nailing every starlet he could get his hands on. (Lana Turner nicknamed him Andy Hard-on.) To Rooney, Gardner probably seemed—at least initially—to be just another of his would-be conquests, but she consistently refused his increasingly insistent requests for a date, which only made him want her more. He would call her every day and she would make up some excuse or other as to why she couldn't go out with him.

Finally, after perhaps a dozen requests, she said that she couldn't go out with him and leave her sister Bappie at home. Mickey suggested that she bring Bappie along, and the three of them had a wonderful dinner at Chasen's restaurant in Hollywood. They followed this by partying at the "in" spots, such as Ciro's and the Cocoanut Grove, where they drank and danced until closing time. This was all new to Gardner but she took to it quite readily, perhaps *too* readily. At the end of every date Rooney would drop her at her door and propose marriage. She would laugh it off as Mickey just being Mickey, but he was quite serious.

Seven. Ava, with the Laughing Eyes

A friend in North Carolina foretold that Gardner would one day go to Hollywood and marry the biggest star there. For her (and just about every other young woman in America at that time) that ideal man would be someone like the dashing Rhett Butler himself, Clark Gable. To say that Rooney was no Clark Cable was an understatement, but he *was* the biggest star in Hollywood! The first meeting between Ava and Mickey obscured the fact that he was only five-two because, in his Carmen Miranda guise, he was wearing six-inch heels. She had seen some of his films but she admitted she was rather shocked at how short he was the first time she saw him out of that costume. He was not any young woman's ideal of a leading man; in fact, Judy Garland, who admittedly adored him, once quipped that the diminutive boy with the ruddy complexion looked like a "rationed bottle of ketchup." Ava concurred, as she later told interviewer Peter Evans: "He still wasn't what I would call a handsome may-un, and his shortness surprised me, but there was definitely something appealing about him. He had thick, red-blond wavy hair, crinkly Irish green eyes, and a grin that was ... well, it definitely wasn't innocent, honey. I can tell you that." Rooney was also a big star with talent to spare, and he knew it. In public and in private, he was indefatigable. And he was rich. As a result, beautiful women were throwing themselves at him — but not this gorgeous creature from the sticks.

Rooney knew that the only way she would ever have sex with him was if they got married; he said as much to many people later in his life. Since she didn't have a car he began driving her to work every day and would drop her off at her apartment in the evening. During these drives he would regale her with studio gossip, funny stories, and impressions. When he would drop her off after work or after dinner at Romanoff's and dancing at the Mocambo he would propose marriage and she would reply, "You're crazy."

Rooney was undeterred. He would send Gardner bouquets of a hundred roses at a time, with sprays of orchids. He spent an astronomical amount of money wining and dining her, but it seemed to be fruitless. Many have speculated that she was playing hard to get and this was all a ploy to snag the biggest catch in Hollywood. But a friend of hers from that period, Ruth Waterbury, told columnist Charles Higham, "It would be completely wrong to say she used Mickey, or that she twisted him around her little finger for success. In fact, she was genuinely taken with his charm."

When she finally relented he could hardly contain his joy. Of course, there was the traditional visit to the future mother-in-law, an event that filled Gardner with apprehension. As she recalled years later: "Ma [Nell], with her legs tucked up under her, was reading the *Racing Form* with fierce intensity. At her elbow on a small table was a tumbler half full of bourbon and a bottle behind the glass as a backup." When Rooney introduced his fiancée to his mom, she said, "Well, I guess he ain't been into your pants yet." Gardner was mortified at the time, but later laughed about it and grew to like Nell's no-nonsense directness.

Their next obstacle was to receive the blessing of Papa Mayer. The boss was not pleased that his prized asset wanted to get married and potentially break the hearts of millions of young girls who coveted him for themselves. Mayer's worries seemed to be misplaced. Although Rooney had more than his share of female fans his reputation was innocent and adolescent in nature. He had none of the sexual appeal of many of the male stars of the time, including the hot young crooner Frank Sinatra. But Mayer kept those in his employ on a very short leash, and his acting skills, which he used to manipulate his stars, was legendary. If threats and intimidation didn't work, he was not beneath getting down on his knees, with tears streaming down his face, and pleading with his "children" to do what he wanted for their own good. In private, he gave Rooney the same advice he gave John Gilbert when he announced his intentions to marry Garbo: "Don't worry about marriage; just fuck her and forget her." Rooney (like Gilbert) remained steadfast. When she joined him to announce their wedding plans, Mayer pulled out all the stops. According to Rooney, Mayer was incensed that these two headstrong kids would destroy the studio's best investment. Rooney reminded his boss that the Hardy series wasn't going to last forever and that he was growing up. L.B. switched to his pleading mode. Rooney still wouldn't budge; he said he loved this woman and that they would be getting married, no matter what. Gardner recalled how proud she was of Rooney for standing up to Mayer, a man known to destroy the careers of actors he deemed disloyal.

Gardner excused herself and left the office, leaving the two determinedly stubborn men to continue their battle. Mayer's secretary, an outspoken woman, took the ingénue aside and offered the following caveat: "A leopard can't change his spots." The secretary was, of course, referring to Rooney's history with women. Her words would prove to be all too prophetic.

Seven. Ava, with the Laughing Eyes

When it became clear to Mayer that he couldn't talk the pair out of the marriage he was determined to stage-manage it for maximum benefit to MGM. He put a press agent named Les Peterson in charge of handling all the arrangements. He talked to Charles Higham in 1974; at that time,

Mickey and his mom, Nell, dance together at the height of the young superstar's career, c. 1941.

he was almost completely blind and living in a tiny apartment for retired people in Laguna Hills, California. Peterson ran his hand over a picture of Rooney and Gardner to get a "read" on them to jog his memory. He recalled that his first order of business was to keep it as quiet as possible. He found a 150-year-old, small, white Presbyterian church in the town of Ballard, near Santa Barbara. Peterson drove to the area a few days before the wedding and swore the local papers to secrecy in exchange for the first pictures that would be taken of the wedding by an MGM photographer. Peterson also arranged for a small apartment for the newlyweds in the area because returning to Rooney's home in Encino would undoubtedly bring out the press.

The wedding party consisted of Mickey's mother and her husband, Fred Pankey; Mickey's dad Joe Yule, Sr., and his new wife, Theota; Ava's sister, Bappie; Les Peterson and his wife; and an MGM photographer. The group (with the bride and groom, naturally) left Los Angeles for Ballard on the morning of January 10, 1942. Ava's mother was too ill to make the trip. The wedding service was performed by the Reverend Glen H. Lutz, who, according to Rooney, looked like a Marine. The ceremony went smoothly, except that the groom was so excited he almost dropped the ring.

The newlyweds, who would later provide the details of the wedding night in various biographies, recalled their first night together as a nerve-wracking experience. Gardner was a virgin and terrified of sex. Rooney, the consummate playboy who had loads of experience but had never been in love before, had consumed so much champagne that evening that he fell asleep, much to his bride's relief. They did, however, consummate their relationship on the second night and she has said that he was "the perfect lover."

Not long after the honeymoon, the couple went on a tour to sell war bonds. Recalling the tour with interviewer Peter Evans, Gardner said that wherever they went there were thousands of young girls screaming for Rooney and that it was every bit as frenzied as what she encountered when she later married Frank Sinatra. "But the enthusiasm, the hysteria of those kids made me understand why Mayer was so fucking desperate to keep our marriage off the front pages," she said.

The tour ended in Fort Bragg, after which they paid a visit to Ava's mother, Mollie, in Raleigh, North Carolina. Gardner recalled with great tenderness and affection how kind Rooney was to her mom, who was

Seven. Ava, with the Laughing Eyes

then very ill with cancer. Mollie had saved all the clippings from the newspaper about the courtship and marriage. She was a big fan of Rooney's, and he put on a show exclusively for her. Mollie had gotten all dressed up for the occasion and he made a big fuss over her. Ava's brother, her sisters, nephews, and nieces all showed up. Rooney sang, danced, did impressions, and was the complete movie star for her mom. Gardner told Evans, "It was probably the last truly great day of her life. I've never been able to express my gratitude for the things that touch me deeply and nothing had ever touched me as deeply as Mickey's performance for Mama that day. He treated her like a queen."

It was then off to Washington to meet FDR for his big birthday party. This was all pretty heady stuff for the son of small-time vaudevillians and a poor sharecropper's daughter. Ava's parents, like so many other Depression-era working people, loved and revered FDR. Gardner recalled that she and Rooney had watched the president give one of his fireside chats before the festivities. She recalled thinking to herself, "If only Daddy could see me now he would be so proud."

Back in Hollywood, the new Mr. and Mrs. Mickey Rooney must have made an odd couple on the proverbial red carpet. But, the truth is, they had more in common than one might expect. Although he was a huge star, he was a small man with very little education. Like many insecure people, he was very boastful and full of himself and uninformed opinions, a trait that rubbed a lot of people the wrong way. Not Gardner, though. She had her own insecurities when they met and so she understood him better than most other people. When he would get loud and boisterous in a group setting, she would simply shrug her lovely shoulders and say, "Oh, that's just Mickey."

The primary problem was that Rooney felt he could still live the life he had as a bachelor, and Gardner actually wanted a more traditional home life. She said that, initially at least, she wanted to stay home and cook for her husband, and he still wanted to party all the time. She was actually a golf widow on the honeymoon as he brought along a new set of clubs, and after plenty of sex he immediately headed for the links and she was left to play gin rummy with Peterson. The thought of spending a quiet evening at home was not Rooney's idea of a good time. He had to be always "on," to be the center of attention at parties, and conversations with Gardner drove him nuts. But they did love each other and, according to both, their sex life continued to be mutually gratifying. There were the

Newlyweds Mickey Rooney and Ava Gardner take to the links during their well-publicized honeymoon in early 1942.

inevitable moments of tension, but they had some fun, too. A friend recalled seeing them rolling around on the floor together, tickling and playing with each other at a party early in the marriage.

Rooney, displaying a penchant for foolishness that he would repeat throughout his life, actually cheated on one of the most beautiful women in the world. He thought he was still entitled to go out with the boys and

Seven. Ava, with the Laughing Eyes

leave his gorgeous wife at home. Shortly after they were married Gardner suffered an appendicitis attack and had to go to the hospital for emergency surgery. While she was in the hospital he entertained women in their home and in their bed! When she got home she discovered evidence of the betrayal and the raging Rooney battles were on.

Gardner began to display the temper that would become infamous later in her life. In 1942, Rooney was the target of her wrath, and quite justifiably. There was one evening when they were out on the town and he was ignoring her while entertaining everybody else at Ciro's. She was livid and went home early. When he got home he discovered that his fiery wife had taken a butcher knife to their furniture and cut the sofa and loveseat to shreds. Another time she locked him out of their house and he had to go stay at his mother's. During one of their separations, she moved into an apartment and one evening, he broke down the front door in a fit of sexual frustration. After the stormiest of battles came the inevitable makeup sex. But however good this aspect of their relationship was, his philandering and their incompatibility were too much for her to overcome. It came to a head one night when they were at a party and she made him jealous by dancing with the handsome MGM contract player Tom Drake. Rooney became angry at Gardner and she told him that she would dance with anyone she damn well pleased. They argued about the fact that he had not been able to get her into one of his pictures and then she shouted at him, "You know, Mick, I'm goddamned tired of living with a midget."

He recalled in his autobiography, appropriately titled *Life is Too Short*:

> This taunt hurt me more than I wanted to admit. I didn't ask to be short. I didn't want to be short. I've tried to pretend that being a short guy didn't matter. Sometimes it was an asset. It helped me get in and out of crowds, into the movies for half price until I was thirty-five, out of fights with big bruisers. I compared myself to Toulouse-Lautrec, or to Willie Shoemaker, the jockey who became a multimillionaire.... But, in truth, I didn't like it very much. I tried to make up for being short by affecting a strut, like I was a guy who knew where he was going, by adopting the voice of a much bigger man, by spending more money than I made, by tipping double or triple at bars and restaurants, by winning tennis tournaments I should have lost, by dating tall, beautiful women you'd be more likely to see on the arm of an all-American forward at UCLA. But nothing I could do, now that Ava left me, would add an inch to my height. Or to my self-esteem.

There would be a few more breakups and reconciliations, but the marriage was basically over. After this tempestuous experience with matrimony, Gardner was no longer the young, innocent girl from North Carolina. She was much more sophisticated and would become even more so. Rooney, in many ways, remained that eternally youthful, foolish, incredibly talented boy she married.

Gardner would go on to marry clarinetist and bandleader Artie Shaw, who berated her for her lack of education; she responded by reading more and taking classes to expand her knowledge. Shaw got her to go into analysis and she tried to be a good wife to him but, in the end, their marriage didn't last any longer than her first. She had a widely reported volcanic six-year marriage to Frank Sinatra (the love of her life, she later admitted, just as she was his). When they first married in 1951, Sinatra's career had temporarily stalled while her star was ascending. She appeared in such A-pictures as *Show Boat* (1951), *The Snows of Kilimanjaro* (1952), and *The Barefoot Contessa* (1954). She had torrid affairs with the likes of Howard Hughes, Ernest Hemingway, and the famed bullfighter Luis Miguel Dominguin ("It was a kind of madness, honey," she later said). Rooney just kept getting married to one woman after another. "Poor darling, he ain't got a fucking cent," she said about him late in life. "He's been raked over the coals by those goddamned wives he kept getting married to after me."

All of his wives were beautiful, but they were not Ava Gardner. Losing her was devastating to him, and the pain would only fester in the decades to follow. It was not just the loss of a woman he loved and desired but the time she represented in his life when he had everything a man could conceivably want.

On his debut studio album, *Starring Sammy Davis, Jr.*, Davis included the song "Spoken For," which Rooney wrote in 1955, some twelve years after his and Ava's divorce. The lyrics reflect the actor's undying adoration for this woman with "laughing eyes." He admits to his culpability for their breakup by saying he knows the sad ramifications of a "careless kiss." And he makes the poignant statement that, without her, paradise could never be his.

CHAPTER EIGHT

The Marrying Kind

> Marriage satisfies the need and quells the fear. I am more naturally inclined to marry than most. I seem to need a wife more.
> —Mickey Rooney, 1965

Rooney and Gardner continued to have sex on and off for a year after their marriage. When he went into the service in 1944, however, he received a call from Gardner in which she said, in a shaky voice, "I want you to stop writing—and calling." Rooney recalled that after this conversation all he could do was go back to his barracks' cot and cry himself to sleep.

While Rooney was stationed at Camp Sibert, the Loew's exhibitor in Birmingham, Alabama, asked his commanding officer if he could attend the premiere of *National Velvet*. The CO agreed and Rooney was the big star attraction at the event, enjoying that immensely. There was a party after the screening and Rooney, still mourning the loss of Gardner, started drinking. It was in a slightly drunken condition that he met the reigning Miss Alabama, Betty Jane Phillips. She was beautiful and from the South and he was carrying a torch for another Southern beauty, and Rooney—as he was to demonstrate throughout his adult life—was nothing if not foolish and impulsive. They had a few dates and he proposed. They were married the next weekend at the home of his CO.

Soon he was sent to Camp Sibert, near Gadsden, Alabama, for training in chemical warfare. However, the Army changed their minds about arming Rooney with weapons and instead decided that he would be more useful as part of the USO's Jeep Shows that entertained troops near the front lines. It's important to note that these were not like the Bob Hope USO tours that were broadcast over radio and television through several wars over several decades. The Jeep Shows were right behind the front lines and could be quite dangerous. This is not to minimize the hardships and dangers that those on the Hope tours endured, but there was a difference being this close to the actual fighting. Rooney was very proud of his service during World War II. Because of the nature of the war, troops were always on the move so he was detailed to the shows where three or four entertainers would be in each Jeep and they would travel to the soldiers to give them a little taste of home and a familiar face. And there was no more familiar face during the early 1940s than Mickey Rooney's. He took the *Queen Mary* to England, along with seven thousand other GIs, heading for the European Theatre. Rooney traveled from one battleground to another, through the cold and snowy winter of 1944, through the mud in the spring of 1945 as the Allies marched toward Berlin, constantly subject to enemy fire. He was characterized as a "real crusader" when it came to entertaining the troops. As Arthur Marx wrote: "He'd get two hours sleep, and then go out and put on three or four shows in one day, and right up front, where there was real danger of stopping a sniper's bullet."

For his bravery, Rooney was awarded the Bronze Star. He also received the Army Good Conduct Medal, the European-African-Middle Eastern Campaign Medal, and the World War II Victory Medal.

* * *

Betty Jane Rase Baker Phillips was born in Birmingham, Alabama, and was the fourth runner-up for the title of Miss America. She was just seventeen years old when she met and married Rooney. They had a very brief honeymoon before he had to ship out for the European Theatre of Operations. The impulsiveness of the whole thing was not just about his character but a part of the mood of the country in 1944. The war was obviously still raging and young people were not only caught up with patriotism (remember, this was the "good war"), but also in the romance of marrying and leaving. The soldier would then know he had a bride to come home to. In this particular case, a third party was involved: Betty Jane was pregnant with their first child by the time her husband left. Rooney was ecstatic when he found out that he was to become a father for the first time. Eighteen months later he returned home to his new family. He was obviously thrilled to see his wife and Mickey Junior but also startled to see that she had undergone a growth spurt while he was gone and was now four inches taller and obviously towered over him!

Rooney came home from the war to a far different country than the one he had left twenty-one months earlier. His first assignment was *Love*

Eight. The Marrying Kind

Rooney receives a Bronze Star for his service during the war. His ragged state may have as much to do with the end of his relationship to Gardner as it does to Army life.

Laughs at Andy Hardy, in which America's favorite teenager (now twenty-six in real life), returns home from service overseas. He is given a hero's welcome—at least in the script. Around the studio lot, according to an interview Rooney later gave to Robert Osborne in an episode of Turner

Classic Movies' *Private Screenings*, things were different. Dore Schary, who had been in charge of MGM's B-picture unit from 1942 to 1943, supposedly ran into Rooney on the lot and said, "Where've you been?" No fan of the Hardy pictures (of which the latest was the fourteenth and final MGM entry), Schary preferred what Mayer derided as "darker, message pictures." And, indeed, America had lost much of its naiveté during the war years. Andy Hardy and his idyllic family situations seemed bland to audiences who had followed the war in Europe for several long years.

In a decidedly change-of-pace role, Rooney was cast as the title character in *Killer McCoy*, with Ann Blythe as his co-star. Apparently Rooney wasn't paying close enough attention to the director, Roy Rowland, who cussed him out in front of the cast and crew for supposedly not being ready for a scene to begin because he had been talking to fellow actor Brian Donlevy. Rowland went on for so long that Rooney thought it was a joke but, when he realized it wasn't, he stormed off the set. Ever the professional, he returned and finished the picture, but he always felt that he was set up by Rowland and that the studio was behind it. He felt that MGM was sending him a message that things had changed and that he was no longer the fair-haired boy. After all, he hadn't made any money for them in a few years. *Killer McCoy* was a remake of a Robert Taylor film called *The Crowd Roars* (1938) and did rather well at the box office—but it wasn't a big enough hit to improve his stock at MGM.

He was much older than the character he played in the reworking of Eugene O'Neill's *Ah, Wilderness!* (1948). Rooney had appeared in the original film version back in 1935 as the little kid Tommy Miller; in this musical version he plays the high school senior Richard Miller, who spouts poetry and radical politics with all the conviction a seventeen-year-old can muster. He also sings to and with the lovely Gloria DeHaven, who plays his girlfriend Muriel McComber. The film is gorgeous to look at because of director Rouben Mamoulian's wonderful sense of color photography, and the music isn't bad either, but ultimately, the movie just didn't work. It was, in fact, a box-office flop, and the twenty-eight-year-old Rooney got much of the blame because he was badly miscast.

His next role was as the late lyricist Lorenz Hart, who, with Richard Rodgers, wrote many sophisticated songs for Broadway shows in the 1930s. The musical comedy-drama, released in 1948 under the title *Words and Music*, was a fictionalized biography of the legendary songwriting team, with Tom Drake portraying Richard Rodgers. The script glossed over

Eight. The Marrying Kind

Hart's severe emotional problems: he was a chronically depressed alcoholic whose homosexuality was a closely guarded secret during that less-enlightened era. The idea of Hart's drinking problem being spurred on by an unrequited love for a woman played by Betty Garrett—when the director, Norman Taurog, failed to establish any romantic spark between them—made Rooney look ridiculous. The movie made money, however, because of all the great Rodgers & Hart musical numbers. It also featured Mickey and Judy Garland in their final duet on film.

The year 1948 marked many significant changes to the once-thriving movie industry. On May 3 of that year the Supreme Court ruled that the major studios—MGM being the most major of them all—were violating anti-trust laws. Until that time, they could own theater chains, forcing the exhibitors to show only the studio's product. With this new verdict, the studios were required by law to divest themselves of their theaters. Independent producers could finally begin to compete with the major studios for actors and audiences. This marked the beginning of the end for the major Hollywood studio system.

Another major hindrance was the arrival of television, millions of which were being purchased by homeowners. Now, instead of spending an evening (and their hard-earned cash) at the neighborhood movie house, the average American could stay home and watch entertainment (fuzzy and on a tiny screen though it may have been) for free.

Rooney was obviously unhappy with the current climate at MGM, and he was determined to do something about it. Rooney had met Sam Stiefel, the owner of a number of movie theaters in Baltimore and Philadelphia, in 1943 while on a tour promoting his latest Andy Hardy picture. A slick businessman, Stiefel gained Rooney's trust when he professed to be a huge fan and wanted to manage his career. He was actually more interested in getting into the movie business and saw the star as his entrance ticket. Something that also endeared him to Rooney was the fact that his pockets were always loaded with cash and he would pony up for Rooney when he lost money at the track. He must have seemed like a good friend indeed, but Stiefel was keeping track of every penny.

Stiefel eventually convinced Rooney that he was being taken advantage of by MGM, a company that had made millions off his films while he always seemed to be broke. (It didn't occur to Rooney that his dwindling fortune might have something to do with chasing women with jewels and furs, and dropping thousands on his bookies.) Stiefel convinced the impressionable actor that Louis B. Mayer was fleecing him and that it was time for his new client to seek out greener pastures. Convinced, Rooney marched into Mayer's office in the fall of 1948, demanding that he be let out of his contract. Marx, in his book, broke down what it cost Rooney to gain his freedom from MGM.

(1) Mickey had to forgo his $5,000-a-week salary for 40 weeks and accept $2,500 for 20 weeks instead;

(2) Mickey had to give Metro a note for $500,000, "which indebtedness would be replaced by $100,000 for each picture he completed under the new picture agreement," which would call for six-month options instead of yearly options;

(3) Mickey would receive $125,000 for each picture he made under the new agreement, but $100,000 of that would go to pay off the $500,000 bond he had posted. In actual cash he would receive only $25,000 per picture;

(4) In the event Mickey defaulted under the picture contract, Metro would have the right to hold him to the old picture contract and rejoin him for rendering services of any kind to anyone else during his failure or refusal to perform services;

(5) Moreover, if Metro exercised its right to terminate the five-picture agreement by Mickey's failure or refusal to work, the unpaid balance of the $500,000 was to be paid in cash to the studio upon demand.

Of the $25,000, Rooney had to give half to Stiefel, then 10 percent to his agent, leaving him $10,000 to pay living expenses, alimony, child support, income taxes, and racetrack losses. Mayer had gotten the pound of flesh he wanted from the impudent young actor who had dared to question his authority.

Obviously, Rooney hadn't been making much money when he was working for Uncle Sam, and this added to the stress at home. His young wife was not interested in show business at all and didn't like his friends always hanging around. He took out his frustrations on her as well. She got tired of this treatment and went back home to her parents in Alabama, taking Mickey Junior with her. She was three months pregnant with their second son, Timothy, when she left. The couple lived apart for the rest of the marriage, with Betty Jane announcing that she was divorcing him with charges of "mental cruelty" in January of 1947; the divorce didn't become final until May of 1949. Eight days after their divorce she married musician

Eight. The Marrying Kind

and film composer Buddy Baker. She became a successful session singer, doing backup vocal work on recordings by Frank Sinatra, Sam Cooke, Bobby Darin, and Elvis Presley. Betty Jane and Buddy divorced in 1958 and, in 1961, she married jazz guitarist Barney Kessel.

Rooney was introduced to actress Martha Vickers in January of 1949. He was sitting alone at Ciro's, nursing a drink and brooding about his flagging career, when a friend, Nick Servano, brought Vickers over to his table and introduced her. She was a rather successful actress at the time. She was working steadily in films and had appeared with Humphrey Bogart and Lauren Bacall in *The Big Sleep* in 1946. She caused quite a stir in that film as the wild, thumb-sucking sister Carmen in Howard Hawks's noir masterpiece that was co-written by William Faulkner. She made another notable appearance in noir as the second female lead in Raoul Walsh's *The Man I Love* (1947), which starred Ida Lupino. She finally got the leading lady role in a movie with Dane Clark called *That Way with Women* (1947). Basically, she was at a better place in her career than Rooney was when they met. This appealed to him, and the fact that she was about his height was something different as well. She was also a good listener and, to someone who loved to talk as much as he did, this was indeed a very attractive quality. They began dating immediately. Vickers was not

Martha Vickers was a successful actress in films before she became the third Mrs. Rooney, on June 3, 1949 (Photofest).

only a successful actress, she had also been around the block in her personal life, having dated Jimmy Stewart and later married Paramount producer A.C. Lyles. That marriage was brief and she was in the process of divorce proceedings when she met Rooney, whose divorce to Betty Jane was close to being finalized. Mickey and Martha dated for two months, which was slow for him, and she recalled, years later, that he was actually quite subdued during their courtship. It started getting serious when she invited him to have dinner with her and her parents. She was living with them after her breakup with Lyles.

Rooney liked her parents. James MacVicker was a successful sales rep for a Japanese steel company. Rooney and James shared a love of duck hunting and deep-sea fishing. Martha's mother, Frances, was charming and a great cook. On this occasion, however, it was Martha who did most of the cooking, something that also impressed Mickey. It was a great meal and he spent most of the night talking with James about hunting and fishing. Martha pretended to be interested in the conversation because, by this time, she was determined to land Mickey. He, in turn, was so pleased with the MacVickers that he invited the whole family to come over to his place the next night for a duck dinner that he would make himself. That also went well and he soon introduced Martha to his mom, Nell, and his stepfather, Fred Pankey. The two couples even went to Santa Anita to watch the races together.

Once he had started a serious relationship with Martha, he became determined to extricate himself from what he soon realized was a disastrous business partnership with Stiefel. Rooney talked to Johnny Hyde, his former agent at William Morris, who wanted him back. The Morris Agency attempted, unsuccessfully, to get Rooney out of the deal with Stiefel to do two films for United Artists: *The Big Wheel* (1949), a romantic drama with a race track setting, and *Quicksand* (1950), another noir.

Martha got a quickie divorce from Lyles in Las Vegas, and Mickey accompanied her there. He immediately began gambling and losing, which she should have taken as an omen, but at the time she was unaware of his dire financial situation. They were married on June 3, 1949, just six hours after he picked up his divorce papers. He told a reporter after the wedding, "I've got me a wonderful girl this time. If this one doesn't last, there's something wrong with me."

Martha, who also went by Mart, seemed to be a very sharp young woman who was doing quite well in her own career. One has to wonder

Eight. The Marrying Kind

what possessed her to marry Rooney, who, at the age of twenty-eight, was already a two-time loser in the marriage sweepstakes, and as anyone in Hollywood could plainly see, in a career-downward spiral. According to friends, she felt that, with her encouragement and love, he would make a comeback. Like so many in the business, she knew how talented he was and remembered the heady days when he was king of the box office. He was also very persuasive; it had something to do with that incredible energy and sincerity that seduced audiences and could also do the same with the opposite sex. A friend from the studio days and a creative partner in years to come, Richard Quine, commented on that energy: "Mickey was frenetic. It was impossible for anyone to keep up with him. He used to wear me out. In fact, I use to slip a phenobarbital into his drink every so often, just so I could get some rest."

Before long, marriage stalled Mart's budding career. She quickly became pregnant and gave birth to their son, Teddy, nine months after the wedding. As usual with the actor there were money troubles and he was about to face one of the lowest points in his career. He was invited to be a presenter at the Academy Awards, and then, as he recalled in his autobiography:

> Mart and I were sitting at the kitchen table. We'd gotten dressed early and were having a bite to eat before we made the drive into town. Then the phone rang. It was Johnny Green, the show's musical conductor, who had drawn straws down at the Academy and lost. He had to tell me the bad news: The Academy had second thoughts about my presence. "You've been married too many times to be a presenter."

He described this as one of the worst moments in his life; he felt emasculated, utterly humiliated at the rejection. So soiled was he by the whole experience, in fact, that he attributed the death of his marriage to Mart to the industry slight. Neither was working at the time, and the two began to drink and snipe at each other. At one point, Rooney said he was considering quitting the business and she agreed, saying, "Maybe you should become a milkman." He resumed his philandering ways, scrambling to shore up an ego in tatters. Mart became more depressed because she was left alone with the baby while her husband was out carrying on all around town. When he was home and she was drinking, she would ride him about his failing career. She would correctly point out that he was blaming everyone but himself for his predicament. Six months into their marriage, even before Teddy arrived, they both knew their union was a failure.

During this difficult period, Rooney's father, Joe Yule, Sr., died of a heart attack on March 3, 1950. It must have seemed to Mickey that he was in a bottomless pit. Luckily, he found work in two low-budget films in rapid succession: *He's a Cockeyed Wonder* (1950) for Columbia, and *Fireball* (1950) for Twentieth Century–Fox. Neither film did much for his career long term, but it brought some much-needed money into the Rooney household and kept the breadwinner out of the house for days at a time, no doubt a relief to both husband and wife. He had also landed a job on a syndicated radio program, *The Hardy Family*, reprising his role as Andy Hardy, who was still having his man-to-man talks with his father, the wise judge (again played by Lewis Stone). This may have seemed like a major step back in Rooney's career, but the radio-listening public obviously had fond memories of the original movie series. His previous venture into radio, *Shorty Bell, Cub Reporter*, folded within three months. *The Hardy Family*, on the other hand, managed to remain on the air (both in the U.S. and abroad) for several episodes. Rooney spent so much time away from home, in fact, that it was the family maid who drove Mart to the hospital to give birth to her son, Teddy, on April 13, 1950. Rooney showed up later in the day and the joy of seeing the baby made him push his wife to try and save the marriage, but that kind of thing only happens in the movies.

Love, money, fame, and marriage—none of it seemed to last for him. During the divorce proceedings, Rooney pretty much let Mart spell out her case against him. She alleged that he was abusive to her and that he drank too much. As compensation she was awarded "$2,000 a month alimony for the rest of the year; $1,875 a month for the following year; $1,750 a month until July of 1955; at that point it would drop to $950 a month for six months." The scale would drop down to a minimum of $300 a month and she was awarded full custody of Teddy, for whom she would receive $150 per month in child support. Needless to say, Rooney desperately needed to keep working and pretty much accepted any offer that came along.

After their marriage ended, Martha found that roles in films were hard to come by because, then as now, there was always someone ready to take your place if you were not available. Although the marriage was brief, the courtship, childbearing, and divorce had taken about two and a half years out of her career and that in Hollywood can cool off a hot actress. She married Chilean polo player/actor Manuel Rojas in 1954. They had two children, Tina and Tessa. She didn't get another film until the low-budget crime drama *The Big Bluff* (1955), but that movie did nothing

Eight. The Marrying Kind

to regenerate her career. She did make a somewhat successful transition to TV, appearing in many episodic dramas, including *Perry Mason*, *The Millionaire*, and *The Rebel*. Her final film was a western, *Four Fast Guns* (1960). She was only forty-six when she died of esophageal cancer in 1971.

* * *

At this point most men would just give up on the whole idea of matrimonial bliss, but not Mickey Rooney. He must have felt loneliness as an almost existential threat to his very being. The best scenario for him might have been to just stay married to one woman even if it was in name only and see other women on the side, which he was always doing anyway, just to avoid the emotional and financial costs of another divorce. He seemed incapable of doing that, however, and maybe it wasn't his call to make because, ultimately, his wives would get fed up with his roving eye and his carelessness with money. Ava, Betty Jane, and now Martha had made an effort to be a wife to him and the latter two even bore his children but, although he could play husbands and fathers on the screen, he seemed incapable of pulling off those roles in real life.

Despite his abysmal track record in marriage, perhaps the reason women were still drawn to him, regardless of his financial situation at any given time, was his extraordinary talent. Who knows? Maybe he could strike it big again. Just as Rooney bet on the horses at the track, many women were betting on him—even if the odds were against them. He was also the life of the party and was always putting on a show for the attractive women he met. When he had a beautiful woman on his arm it was validation that he was still a player in Hollywood on the personal level, even if his professional life was skirting minor-league territory.

Despite his outward sense of bravado, it was clear that the divorce from Martha Vickers had taken its toll on him. Richard Quine, who directed Rooney in *Sound Off* (1952), recalled that his old friend was in a state of depression during the entire production. Apparently, on the first day of shooting he called in sick. Quine tried to talk him into coming to work, reminding him that he was okay when they were out together the night before. No amount of coaxing worked, however, and Quine was worried about him so he got in his car and raced toward the actor's house, only to pass Rooney in his car heading toward the set. No amount of personal pain, it seemed, could keep the ex-vaudevillian from hitting his marks.

Sound Off, the first of a three-picture deal with Rooney and Columbia Pictures, is the story of an obnoxious nightclub comedian at Ciro's who is drafted into the U.S. Army during the Korean War. Typical of a militaristic wartime comedy, the protagonist undergoes a personality change, brought about by strict discipline, becoming an exemplary soldier along the way. Shot in a process called SuperCinema Color, the film is a comedy featuring several musical numbers. Rooney, who would be paid $75,000 for each of the three films, worked in collaboration with director Quine, producer Jonie Taps, and writers Blake Edwards and Dick Crockett. The same team was responsible for the follow-up, *All Ashore* (1954), another service comedy, this one in Technicolor and in the tradition of MGM's '40s musicals *Anchors Aweigh* and *On the Town*. In *All Ashore*, three happy-go-lucky sailors (Rooney, singer Dick Haymes, and dancer Ray McDonald) are on shore leave in Santa Catalina, California, where the majority of the film was shot. He still had one more film to complete his Columbia contract, and it would prove to be a welcome change of pace. (That 1954 film, *Drive a Crooked Road*, is explored in depth in Chapter Six.)

* * *

In the fall of 1952, Rooney was at the Woodland Hills driving range working on his golf swing when he spotted a tall, beautiful redhead nearby, practicing her technique as well. The young lady, Elaine Mahnken Devry, had a cute Maltese terrier named Pepy, whom he found adorable. He loved animals all his life and always had a menagerie of pets. He was also partial to redheads. Needless to say, they began dating and were out together every night for a month. Rooney's approach hadn't changed. He asked her to marry him every night they were together. "Mickey had quite a way about him," Elaine had to admit. Within a month's time, on November 15, 1952, the two were married in a Las Vegas wedding chapel called Wee Kirk o' the Heather. He told a reporter, "This one's for keeps." She was very beautiful and had started modeling when she was only fifteen.

Born in Compton, California, Elaine attended Compton Community College, where she became their "Beauty Queen." She met her first husband, Dan Ducich, at the school. He was a big athlete in high school and later became a Utah State University basketball star. They got married in the fall of 1948 after moving to Butte, Montana, where her husband had opened an aluminum siding business. In April 1949, Ducich was convicted

Eight. The Marrying Kind

of armed robbery in Los Angeles and was sentenced to only five years' probation because several leading citizens in Montana vouched for his character. The couple divorced in late summer of 1952 and she moved back to Los Angeles to live with her mother, who was an animator with Walt Disney Studios.

Elaine said that she remembered Rooney's movies from the late '30s and early '40s, when he was Andy Hardy and was doing all those musicals with Judy Garland. She was just a kid at the time but recalled that her whole family loved him, partly because he greatly resembled her kid brother. She said she felt like she already knew him even before they met, but quickly realized he was nothing like Andy Hardy. She also said that she was in awe of his musical talent because, while they were dating, he would sit down at the piano and compose tender love songs for her on the spot. She felt that he had a beautiful soul. For the first two years of the marriage they lived in Rooney's Woodland Hills home. It was a small house, but, according to the fourth Mrs. Rooney, a comfortable one. He had a valet and a housekeeper and wouldn't let his new bride do anything around the house. She did, however, examine his financial records and was appalled by her husband's reckless spending. She immediately set about to put his financial affairs in order. This was to prove a daunting task.

Elaine strongly disapproved of gambling and therefore refused to go to the races with Mickey. Her ex-husband also had a gambling addiction but this still did not deter Rooney from continuing this expensive and self-destructive habit. One of the early rifts in their marriage occurred when her ex-husband got in trouble with some shady people in Las Vegas and he desperately needed some quick cash to get him out of deep trouble. Dan Ducich contacted his ex and appealed to her to ask her husband for some money to bail him out of his current jam. Rooney refused, and Ducich was later found with a bullet in his head. Rooney was not only remorseless, he was incensed that she'd continued to stay in touch with her nefarious ex-husband. Asking Mickey to intercede on his behalf was the first nail in the coffin of their relationship. But money—or, more accurately, the lack of it—would be the ultimate undoing of the marriage.

Rooney liked Elaine's father, Fred Mahnken, from their very first meeting; indeed, it seems as though he was more compatible with the parents of his wives than with the wives themselves. Fred also loved the racetrack and gambling, and had great admiration for Mickey. At a time when the actor needed an ego boost, Fred was there to remind him of his many accomplishments in the field of entertainment. They spent a lot of time together at the track and just hanging out around town. It was at this time that Rooney decided that he and his new wife needed a bigger house; he found what he was looking for in Studio City. He even insisted that Fred move in with him, but the older man initially balked at the idea because he didn't want to mooch off his new son-in-law. Rooney got around this by hiring Fred as a handyman. Rooney would later claim that Fred took advantage of their relationship and didn't do any work around the house. Elaine was especially incensed by this when she talked to Arthur Marx some thirty years later. She said that Fred wanted to do the handyman chores, but Mickey wouldn't let him. It seemed he wanted a companion to go to the races with more than he wanted the yard work done.

Elaine had been poor, and the thought of being poor again terrified her. She was determined to get Rooney's many creditors paid off and make him financially solvent for the first time in ages. It didn't start off well: he used the last $12,000 he had for the down payment on the house, leaving no money in the budget for furnishings. Rooney had to scramble to get some money quickly because he and Elaine were scheduled to be on Edward R. Murrow's TV show *Person-to-Person* in a week and "we couldn't very well be sitting on orange crates when Mr. Murrow showed up." He said that when they moved in they only had two mattresses, one for him and Elaine and one for Fred. Again, Elaine told Marx that Mickey's recollection of these events was "utter nonsense." She also declared that she didn't have a clue that he was broke because he would brag to her when they were dating of all the property he owned, leading her to believe that he was loaded. Rooney claimed that he bought the house in Studio City knowing he couldn't afford it, but that Elaine insisted they needed a bigger house. Again, she flatly denied this, saying that she was perfectly happy in Woodland Hills. She was convinced that Rooney needed to keep up the trappings of a superstar, with a valet, a large wardrobe, a maid and cook. He couldn't afford any of these luxuries but he had established a certain lifestyle when he was a big star and wasn't going to change anything just because his circumstances had changed.

Things began to look up for Rooney thanks to his new manager, Maurice Duke.

Born on October 27, 1910, in New York City, Duke was a colorful former vaudeville harmonica player with the Cappy Barra Harmonica

Eight. The Marrying Kind

Ensemble. Once the demand for his specialty dried up, he became a manager and, later, a film producer. He was a loud, brash, cigar-smoking Damon Runyon–type character that many in Hollywood found irresistible. He walked with a cane and had a brace on one of his legs, the result of childhood polio. Rooney credited this character with getting his career off the ground again. According to Rooney, one day in late 1952 Duke knocked on his door. He came in and promised Rooney that he would be able to get him some work and resurrect his career. They had already been friends for a few years and Duke had witnessed Rooney's decline with great sadness. He had been a big fan of his talent and felt that one of Hollywood's great natural resources was being underutilized. Rooney agreed: "My heart has been broken so many times, it has cauliflower valves," he said, only half-jokingly. Duke's career as a producer, it should be mentioned, was less than stellar. In 1952, he produced what may be the worst picture ever made, *Bela Lugosi Meets a Brooklyn Gorilla* (a.k.a. *The Boys from Brooklyn*). Co-starring with the down-on-his-luck former Dracula was the comedy team of Duke Mitchell and Sammy Petrillo, the very poor man's Dean Martin and Jerry Lewis.

Duke's appearance on the scene was fortuitous because Rooney had just fired his agent, Nick Servano. Servano recalled to Marx some thirty years later, "I wouldn't agree with him about what he wanted to do with his career. For example, he wanted to direct and I thought he was a lousy director because he had no discipline." Servano went on to explain Rooney's problems with marriage and women:

> He only married for the sex part of it. He never went home. I could tell the minute he was bored with a wife. He'd say to me, "What are you doing tonight, Nickeroo? I thought we'd have dinner." You see, he was always on the make. A beautiful woman would drive him up a wall. But lots of times he couldn't lay the girl of his dreams unless he married her first. The man had deep insecurities because of his size. He was the Huckleberry Finn of America. Every kid wanted to be like him, but no dame wanted to be married to him. Because he wasn't handsome. To them, he was just a crazy little kid. But a lot of dames used him as a stepping stone to movie careers. That's why he had to get married so many times.

There was a little luck involved in Rooney's resurgence as well. Duke had secured for him a nice gig in Las Vegas performing at the Flamingo hotel just a few weeks after it opened. On the plane back from Vegas, Rooney and Duke met the Pulitzer Prize-winning writer James Michener. Michener and Rooney began to talk and the actor impressed him greatly.

In fact, Michener liked him so well that he promised to write a nice part for him in the screenplay he was doing based on his book *The Bridges at Toko-Ri*. Rooney did the picture and, although he wasn't paid a lot of money, the 1954 film was a major Hollywood production that starred William Holden and Grace Kelly. The movie was a success and Rooney received some very good reviews; there was even talk of a possible Oscar nomination for Best Supporting Actor. He caused quite a stir during the shooting. His was a small but pivotal part as rescue helicopter pilot Mike Forney. Because it was a supporting role there was a lot of down time during the shooting. The location was an aircraft carrier, and the director, George Seaton, went looking for Rooney for one of his scenes and couldn't find him. There was a frantic search and genuine fear that he may have fallen overboard. Then late in the day one of the carrier's planes landed and a smiling Rooney emerged. He had gotten bored and bribed one of the pilots to fly him to Tokyo to one of their better racetracks and a day of admiring and betting on the ponies.

Duke was instrumental in helping secure some of Rooney's best work during the mid-to-late '50s. The actor did a low-budget war movie called *The Bold and the Brave* (1956), for which he received an Oscar nomination for Best Supporting Actor. He also appeared in the title role of Don Siegel's *Baby Face Nelson* in 1957. This is one of his truly great performances and, although it received mixed reviews when it was released, it has grown in stature over the decades. Rooney received the Caesar, the French equivalent of the Oscar, for his performance.

Duke also secured for Rooney a headlining stage gig with his partner Joey Forman at the Riviera in Las Vegas. Mickey's salary was a tidy $17,500 a week, but he ended up blowing it all when he lost fifty grand at the crap tables in one night. He became so depressed after losing the money that he told the audience at the following performance that he was retiring from show business. It was headline news in the papers, but everyone knew it would be short-lived. The mild-mannered comedian Wally Cox was performing at the Dunes Hotel and his dry humor was not going over well with the rambunctious Vegas crowds. Duke called and asked if Rooney might un-retire for $17,500 per week, and he was on the next plane back to Vegas.

It was not long after the Vegas episode that Duke reached his boiling point with Rooney and his craziness. The agent told him in no uncertain terms that he could no longer work with him. As he explained

Eight. The Marrying Kind

it, "There was no particular incident. I just got fed up with him because he does stupid things. He won't listen to you, and he thinks everybody steals from him and blames all his problems on them. No one ever stole from Mickey. Mickey steals from himself. Mickey's his own worst enemy."

They parted company, but not before Duke produced one of Rooney's most forgettable films, *The Atomic Kid* (1954). Elaine had expressed some ambition to act in movies, and Rooney got her a small part in this science fiction comedy, based on an original story by Blake Edwards. She is billed (in small type) on the theatrical poster as Elaine Davis (Mrs. Mickey Rooney). The film might best be described as an atomic bomb.

And things were no better at home.

Elaine was unnerved by her husband's ever-present friends hanging around the house at all hours of the day and night, a common complaint from all of his wives. The lack of privacy spurred her to ask him to buy a boat so that they could get away and enjoy the outdoors. He liked to golf and go to the races but other than that he was perfectly content to stay at home and pal around with his cronies. According to Rooney, he was first pressured to buy the house, then a boat, and then a cottage in Lake Arrowhead—all for Elaine. She insisted that she needed to get away from the traveling circus that life with him had become. Even though she was young and beautiful—and, according to Marx, was still a knockout when he interviewed her decades later—it wasn't enough for Rooney. She reportedly slapped him across the face when she caught him trying to give his phone number to a serving girl at a party in their home. She began to spend more and more time at the cottage in Lake Arrowhead, which allowed him to run wild in Hollywood. In addition to chasing women, he was chasing acting jobs, and apparently catching both.

One of Mickey's films of that period had an oddly familiar ring to it: *Andy Hardy Comes Home*. It was 1958, twelve years since the last Hardy Family movie had been released (and eight years since the syndicated radio program concluded), yet Rooney still believed that there would be enough interest in the characters to generate a new series. To put it mildly, he overestimated the public's sense of nostalgia. Rooney himself contacted some of the original cast members, including Fay Holden, who was willing to reprise her role as Andy's mother, Emily. (By this time Lewis Stone, one of the most beloved actors from the earlier films, had died. The seventy-three-year-old Stone, whose career dated back to the silent era, suffered a heart attack in 1953 while chasing some juvenile delinquents who were throwing rocks in his carefully tended garden.) Cecilia Parker and Sara Hayden were back in their characters of Marian and Aunt Milly, respectively. Missing in action, however, was Ann Rutherford as Polly. This was a disappointment to Rooney, who had hoped his former onscreen girlfriend would play his wife in the update. Rutherford told interviewer Walter Wagner for his book *You Must Remember This* that she turned down the offer because, as she informed Rooney, *no one* actually marries their high school sweetheart. Rooney, ever the optimist, cast a little-known actress, Patricia Breslin, in the role of Andy's wife, Jane, added some kids to the family, and went on with the film. Instead of a traditional "The End" title, it read "To Be Continued ...," obviously leaving the door open for a new series of Hardy films. None were forthcoming.

* * *

When Elaine announced to her husband that she had someone new in her life, Mickey didn't bat an eye. He claimed he still wanted her to come back, even though by then he was essentially living with his latest girlfriend, actress Carolyn Mitchell.

Born Barbara Ann Thomason in Phoenix, Arizona, on January 25, 1937, she developed into a beautiful girl and made the inevitable trek to Hollywood to seek stardom. She landed a role (billed by her professional name) in a low-budget feature, *The Cry Baby Killer* (1958), directed by the King of the B's Roger Corman and starring a then-unknown actor named Jack Nicholson in the title role. Corman, who took pride in making low-budget movies that never lost money, admitted that on this particular effort the box-office returns were a disappointment; he added, however, that the production costs were later recouped off the television rights.

Carolyn, a.k.a. Barbara Ann, won a host of beauty contest titles, including Miss Muscle Beach, Miss Surf Festival, and Miss Southwest Los Angeles. She was introduced to Mickey Rooney by Bill Gardner, a car salesman she knew from her time working as a dance instructor at Arthur Murray's. The affair between the two began quickly; they shared an uncommonly strong desire for sex—and histrionics. There were headlines when Barbara Ann, supposedly distraught about her on-again, off-again relationship with Rooney, took an overdose of sleeping pills. Many suspected the whole sordid episode was a publicity stunt.

It wasn't.

Eight. The Marrying Kind

"My partners weren't what we call in horse racing parlance 'routers,'" Rooney told *People* magazine in 1993. "They were sprinters." They went out of the gate, but who was reportedly threatening suicide if he didn't get a divorce and marry her? By this time (1959), she was also pregnant with their first child and—understandably, especially given the moral climate of the time—even more desperate to give her baby a legal paternity. She and Rooney went to Mexico, where he got the obligatory quickie divorce, this time from Elaine; he and Barbara Ann were married there as well. Four months later, Kelly Ann Rooney was born. They ultimately had four children together, Kelly Ann, Kerry Yule, Kimmy Sue, and Michael Kyle, in rapid succession.

There was trouble throughout the marriage, which should come as no surprise given the circumstances at the beginning. She later claimed, "Our home was in a constant uproar. I never knew when he was coming home." She said that he embarrassed and humiliated her with vile and abusive language, and sometimes left guests in the middle of the evening to go to bed. Rooney's finances, too, were in a shambles again due to the latest downturn in his career and the toll taken on his bank account by gambling debts and alimony payments. Although Elaine had told Rooney about her boyfriend, when she began to threaten to sue him for divorce, he sent some private investigators to her house to take pictures of the two *in flagrante delicto*. Rooney acted shocked when the pictures were revealed during the conference with the lawyers. It looked like he would get off relatively easily, but guilt overcame him and he fell to his knees and wrapped his arms around her legs and once again begged her to take him back. She refused and knew that she had him by the balls, financially speaking. Rooney tried to plead poverty to the judge during the divorce hearing, stating that of the $12 million he had made in his career, about $10 million went to taxes.

By the time it was all added up, Elaine got a total of $381,750. She got the house, the cabin at Arrowhead, the motorboat, the Chrysler, the horses, assorted jewelry, $40,000 in cash, and $1,750 a month for the next several years—and, of course, she got to keep her young, tall, good-looking boyfriend. Rooney would later quip that she got the goldmine and he got the shaft. He would ultimately only pay alimony for a year and a half. He agreed to the settlement because he had already obtained a quickie Mexican divorce from her five months before their California divorce became final. He did that in order to marry Barbara Ann, but the legality of the

Mexican divorce and marriage was dubious from the start. (Elaine knew about the whole sordid affair when she was getting her divorce, although she didn't want to make things any worse for Rooney legally.) The legality of the divorce and marriage was in dispute even before his fourth marriage officially ended, so Rooney and Barbara Ann were married again in Los Angeles in early 1960 to make everything official.

Elaine, it should be said, was not blameless in this whole mess. She told *Parade Magazine*, in January 1967, when Rooney was at possibly the lowest point in his life,

> Mickey's always in hot water, and I'm not going to downgrade him with a recitation of what marriage to him was really like. But I'll tell you this: After being married to him for eight years, I'm marriage-shy. I've had half a dozen proposals in the past few years, but I turn chicken, especially when the proposals come from actors. I'm sure some actors make good husbands, but after Mickey, I'm afraid to take the chance. As for my divorce settlement, Mickey let his imagination run riot on that. I got a $75,000 house in Studio City, with a $45,000 mortgage. The reason I have to work now, doing bits here, feature parts there, is that I still have to pay that mortgage off. I don't live in that house. I rent it to meet the payments. Mickey's business manager used to give each of us an allowance. I put mine into a piece of mountain property. He put his into horses. The Chrysler I got was eight years old. All the jewelry consisted of my wedding ring, my engagement ring, and a watch. The $21,000 a year for ten years—that's a joke, too. I got it for one year. Then it was cut back to $500 a month. It's been more than a year now since I've gotten a single payment. I don't know who ghosted Mickey's autobiography, but whoever did tried to make me look like a heavy. But I entered my marriage to Mickey in all honesty. I told him I didn't love him, that I was still in love with my first husband. He said he didn't care. I was lonely at the time. I was young and foolish. I thought I could learn to love him. I gave the marriage everything I had. I tried everything Mickey suggested. After years and years, I had enough. Living with Mickey Rooney is no bed of roses.

Rooney's financial troubles continued into his new marriage. The divorce settlement with Elaine was just the tip of the iceberg. He outlined his unique approach to finances in the above-mentioned ghostwritten autobiography.

> I'll tell you about money. It's like this. Stanley Kramer wanted me to play a role in his comedy *It's a Mad, Mad, Mad, Mad World* (1963). He wanted four months of my time and offered $100,000. Here's what happened to that $100,000 during those four months. Salary $100,000 minus 10 percent agent's commission leaves $90,000 minus 10 percent manager's commission leaves $80,000, minus $25,000 in U.S. and California back taxes leaves $55,000, minus $30,000 in U.S. and California current taxes leaves $25,000, minus $6,000 for lawyer, accountant, and secretary leaves $19,000, minus $3,500 for Sig Frolich [Mickey's lifelong friend] for helping me per-

Eight. The Marrying Kind

form leaves $15,500, minus $2,400 for Mrs. Rooney No. 4 (Elaine) leaves $13,100, minus $600 for Mrs. Rooney No. 3 (Martha) leaves $12,500, minus $1,800 in child support for Mrs. Rooney No. 2 (Betty Jane) leaves $10,700, and business expenses at $500 per month leaves $8,700. That's it, I work four months for $100,000 and get to keep $8,700. Rooney's law of economics.

He would file for bankruptcy in 1962, with liabilities totaling $346,513.12 and assets of just $1,500. Rooney would make cursory admissions over the years that his money troubles were his own fault, but these statements seemed to lack conviction. Managers, agents, and, yes, even ex-wives, were right: Rather than looking in the mirror, Rooney tended to blame everyone else for his problems.

Chapter Nine

Murder, He Wrote

> My poor Barbara ... what is going to happen to my babies?
> —Mickey Rooney, 1966

"When I met Rooney in a small office near Sunset Boulevard in Hollywood, he was primed," said Roger Kahn, a famous sports writer of the time. Kahn had been offered the job of ghostwriting Mickey Rooney's autobiography, and the famous actor was outlining his story the way he felt it should be told. "This book is the story of a loud little guy who doesn't want to be loud," he said in a tempo that reminded the writer of a Gatling gun. "It's the story of somebody who thinks well—twice a month. It's about a man who loves women so much he's married five of them and every time for love." Rooney continued this rapid-fire performance for twenty minutes.

Kahn met with Rooney's lawyer, Dermont Long, to discuss the terms of the book deal. During the meeting, Long gave the writer the following advice: "Don't fuck Barbara Ann."

The beauty in question had traded in her dreams of stardom for the role of Mommy and was attempting to make ends meet on a tight budget. Rooney continued to get work, however, and their finances became more stable. One role he was offered came from Roger Corman. The independent director, who had hired Barbara Ann for *The Cry Baby Killer* about six years earlier, now wanted Mickey for the supporting role of demolitions expert Terrance Hanlon in a World War II action-drama called *The Secret Invasion*. Mr. Corman told this author what it was like to work with the supposedly difficult Rooney: "I never experienced any problems. Mickey was really a pleasure to work with. He was very focused and needed little rehearsal. He would get it on the first take. Even when he had to fire a big machine gun in *The Secret Invasion*, he got it on the first take."

While making the film in Dubrovnik, Yugoslavia, Rooney befriended

Nine. Murder, He Wrote

Mickey Rooney and his fifth wife, Barbara Ann Thomason (a.k.a. Carolyn Mitchell), whose life was cut tragically short. This picture was taken in 1962.

a young actor named Milos Milosevic, whom he later invited to stay at his Los Angeles residence. Milosevic began to get a few bit parts in Hollywood, including one in the popular Cold War comedy, *The Russians Are Coming! The Russians Are Coming!* (1966). At this time Rooney had to travel to the Philippines to do another action film called *Ambush Bay* (1966). He asked his new friend Milosevic to keep an eye on Barbara Ann while he was on location. Milosevic did more than keep an eye on her: they became intimate. When Rooney returned stateside and learned about the affair, he immediately moved out of the house and began divorce proceedings. Barbara Ann became frightened when he demanded custody of the children, claiming that she was an unfit mother; he also got a court order to have Milosevic removed from the house. Rooney was also admitted to the hospital at this time because he had contracted a rare blood disease while shooting in the Philippines.

Marge Lane, Barbara Ann's best friend, said that Thomason was so afraid of losing the kids that she told Milosevic to leave. He did as he was told but was enraged that she was essentially throwing him out of the house. Thomason began to think about returning to Rooney and giving the marriage another chance, which, of course, only made Milosevic angrier. He wanted her to tell Rooney that she would not be returning to him and planted a microphone on her so that he could hear her tell him that *she* would be the one filing for divorce. Milosevic and a private detective would be in an adjoining room at the hospital to listen in on the conversation. However, when she went to Rooney's bedside, they began talking, and her attitude softened toward him. Forgetting that she was wearing the wire, she swore that she would never see Milosevic again. Rooney recalled that they talked for about an hour and, when she left the room, he could hear a commotion in the hall. Milosevic, apparently, was none too pleased at what he had just heard.

Milosevic and Thomason left the hospital and met Lane and a few other friends for dinner. They left right afterward and the couple went into the house, alone. In retrospect, their friends should have been more apprehensive of leaving the volatile couple unchaperoned. Everyone knew Milosevic had a fiery temper, but none of them could have expected what happened next.

One of Barbara Ann's friends was staying at the Rooneys' guest house and thought it odd that Milosevic's car was still in the driveway the following afternoon. When Wilma Catania knocked on Thomason's bedroom door, there was no answer, and the door was locked; Catania and the maid had to break the door open with a hammer and screwdriver. They found the pair lying next to each other in the bathroom, with Thomason having suffered a fatal gunshot under her chin, and Milosevic having shot himself in the temple. The gun Milosevic used to kill Thomason and then himself was the very same weapon that Rooney bought for her protection.

The murder-suicide was huge news in the papers and there was an infamous photograph of Rooney's lawyer shepherding the children, with bewildered looks on their young faces, away from the house to stay with their maternal grandparents. Apparently the children never heard the gunshots and so they were spared walking in on the grisly scene. Rooney was still in St. Johns Hospital and was due to be discharged in a few days. His doctor asked one of Mickey's old friends, Sig Frolich, to break the news to him, but he couldn't bear to do so. Dr. Buckley then called Mickey's son Timmy, his press agent Red Doff, and his longtime friend Red Barry to come to the hospital to help break the news and lend emotional support. The doctor set up something of a little drama as a way of alerting Rooney to the tragedy. With Rooney's son and friend there in the

Nine. Murder, He Wrote

hospital room, the doctor received a prearranged phone call and answered it with a shocked expression, saying, "What? They are *both* dead?" and then confronted Rooney with the news. Weakened by the effects of the blood disease, Rooney became disconsolate and completely lost his bearings. He kept muttering about "my poor Barbara" and asking, "What is going to happen to my babies?" He tried to get out of his bed and go to his wife and the kids, but his doctor insisted he stay where he was. Now being treated for severe shock, his hospital stay had to be extended.

Rooney recalled in his second autobiography that he felt like he died when he got the news. He was in a daze leading up to the funeral; not being able to eat and already in a weakened condition, his weight dropped below 100 pounds. Milosevic's mother wanted her son's body shipped back to Belgrade and, in some kind of denial, she was telling reporters that Rooney had been plotting to have her son killed, and that the murder-suicide was actually a double murder. She even tried to bring federal charges against Rooney in late 1967. She claimed through her representative, Julijana Stamenkovic, that her son's arm was broken before the fatal shooting, proving that there was some kind of struggle before he was shot. Her theory was that Rooney had put a hit out on her son. The feds felt that the charges were baseless and stuck with the LAPD's ruling on the case.

Michael Rooney, one of Mickey's children with Barbara Ann, talked to Emma Brockes of *The Guardian* about the murder of his mother and the years that followed. He was only three years old at the time and admitted that he didn't remember anything about the actual killings; all he recalls about the event is that he and the other children were rounded up and told they were going to see *Mary Poppins*. He also said that he was glad that he went to live with his maternal grandparents because they provided a stable home environment in which the children went to school, did their homework, and had chores to do to earn their allowance. What little contact he had with his father always focused on show business matters; as he came to realize, this was the only subject in which Mickey was conversant.

As Michael Rooney pointed out, the children were sent to the actor's in-laws, and there they would remain. Kahn recalled that Rooney originally wanted to dedicate his first autobiography to Thomason, but they had a fight and he instead dedicated it to his mother. Kahn concluded his chapter on Rooney with this observation: "He and almost everyone close to him was out of control. If you venture too far from the norms of society, I thought, as these people were doing, if you live simply on whim and impulse, you place yourself in nothing less than mortal peril."

Feeling sorry for her best friend's ex-husband, Marge Lane helped Rooney attempt to take care of the four kids. She was a regular at the house for a long time; the kids referred to her as "Aunt Margie." Mickey was still reeling from the tragic events and desperately needed the help. He soon had to leave the country to shoot a film in Italy, and Lane couldn't stay with the kids all the time because she had a job as a real estate agent. Rooney asked his friend Bill Gardner to move into his house and watch them while he was gone. This was a job well beyond his friend's capabilities and eventually Gardner called Mickey's former in-laws for help. The Thomasons jumped at the chance to keep the children away from Rooney. At first he was livid that the grandparents had taken the kids, but when he saw how happy they were and realized that he would probably have to leave again for work, they came to a co-guardianship arrangement that would allow him to see them whenever he wanted. Rooney would have the kids stay with him for long stretches of time while he was home and he came to depend on the help of Aunt Margie more and more over the next six months.

Lane was rather matronly and not exactly Rooney's type and that was primarily what appealed to him at this point in his life. He needed her help and soon the idea of marriage, although not in the sexual tradition of his previous unions, seemed like the logical thing to do. She would provide some stability and perhaps he could get full custody of the kids with a wife who could take care of them when he was away on location. She was also very religious and a woman about his age. In an interview with Marx, Lane said that Rooney's management team felt that a marriage to a respectable, middle-aged, Christian woman would help his badly damaged image. They were married on September 10, 1966, in Las Vegas. It was on their honeymoon night that she first became aware of his dependence on narcotics. He took sleeping pills as soon as they got to their room and was out like a light until the following day. Shortly after the wedding she accompanied him on a tour of Australia, where he was doing a comedy/musical act with singer and dancer Bobby Van. Rooney was still a big name in Australia and had to deal with autograph hounds, something he abhorred. His method of avoiding the fans was to stay in his room the whole day and not come out until it was time to work. This bored his latest wife to tears.

Nine. Murder, He Wrote

Because of his new marriage there was a lot of positive publicity in the newspapers and magazines about how he had finally matured. These reports were premature, however. Once they got back from Australia, Rooney began seeing other women. Marge knew about this behavior from Barbara Ann and wasn't really shocked by it. "But she hadn't told me about the sexual things she had to put up with. Not just that he only satisfied himself, but the, well, you know, 'imaginative' things he wanted to do. I truly believe he has an aversion to women—quite a complex about proving his manliness."

When she told Rooney that she didn't want to have sex with him, it sealed the deal as far as the marriage was concerned. Even though she told him she was willing to stay married and take care of the kids and didn't care if he had a girlfriend or not, he still wanted more. Between dealing with her demanding husband and taking care of the kids, her immune system gave way and she contracted the flu. Rather than remain in the house and spread it to everyone else, she decided to stay with a girlfriend for a few days. It was during this period that she got a call from his manager, Red Doff, that Rooney was filing for a divorce and that she wasn't to come back to the house. He admitted in his autobiography that he didn't remember much about the 100 days he was married to Margie Lane. He was still in shock over what happened to Barbara Ann and had only married Lane to have someone to take care of the children. Late in his life when talking to an interviewer about his marriages he mentioned Margaret and said, "At least I *think* that was her name." It took a full year after the separation for the lawyers to work out a deal that required Rooney to pay only $350 a month for a year, and court costs, which meant he got off relatively unscathed. She originally wanted half of his estate. He was flabbergasted at the demand and told the judge he couldn't understand this in light of the fact that they had been married only a few months; the judge agreed.

* * *

During this difficult period in Rooney's personal life, an opportunity arose to appear in one of the finest films of his career, a film that, unfortunately, is too often overlooked. *The Comic* (1969), written by Aaron Ruben and Carl Reiner, is the realistic story of a silent film comedian named Billy Bright. Although brilliantly talented, Bright is an egotist whose star fades with the arrival of talkies. He is a philandering husband,

Martin "Cockeye" Van Buren (Mickey Rooney, left) and Billy Bright (Dick Van Dyke) are two elderly former silent film comedians who pass the time playing a game in which they try to recall the order of the stars on Hollywood and Vine. When they come to Bright's star, they are disgusted to see a wad of gum stuck to it. "That," Bright says bitterly, "is where your civil disobedience starts." *The Comic* (1969).

Nine. Murder, He Wrote

an absent father to his only son, and an alcoholic. The role of Bright was conceived by Reiner as a character for Dick Van Dyke, a man who, according to his late friend Stan Laurel, was one of the few modern-day comedians who knew how to use his body to get laughs. Billy Bright may have a bit of Stan in his character, but he is also an amalgam of other great silent stars, particularly Harry Langdon, Charley Chase, Buster Keaton— even Mickey Rooney. "As a matter of fact," Reiner said, "when we researched the movie to do it, we found that all the great ones had the same history: much married, fooled around, drank a lot—Keaton, all of those guys. As a matter of fact, going to Mexico and marrying somebody and waking up and saying, 'Who are you?' after getting married the night before actually happened to Keaton."

Bright is fortunate to have one true friend throughout his adult life: Martin "Cockeye" Van Buren, Bright's onscreen second banana. Like his name implies, Van Buren is cross-eyed, not unlike another great silent clown, Ben Turpin. Rooney was cast by Reiner to play Cockeye. "I was in awe of this man," Reiner told this author in a lengthy interview about the film. "I considered him maybe the most talented human being ever in motion pictures. He could do *anything*."

Anything, that is, except cross his eyes.

> On the first day on the set I told him, "You know Mickey, I know it's a strain to cross your eyes so you'll keep your eyes down unless we're in a close-up or a two-shot, you know, and then you open your eyes and you'll have them crossed." ... And he said, "You know, I can't cross my eyes." Of course I laughed. The man who could do everything in the world but he can't cross his eyes? I said, "I could teach you in a minute unless you are kidding me." He said, "No. No, I never could." I said, "Well, listen. Anne Bancroft and I talked the other day about doing eye crossing. We can cross our eyes, hold one eye to the edge, and make them look funny." I said, "All you've got to do is put your finger on the bridge of your nose and look at the tip of your finger." He couldn't do it. I could not believe it.... So because the character was so important to the look of the picture, we sent him to an eye doctor and had a prosthesis made. He said, "You know, I can't put anything in my eye. It's so red and swollen; I can only keep it in for a few seconds." We had to have a doctor on the set every day he was there. We'd say, "Roll 'em" and "Action" and put in the eye because we didn't want a second wasted with the eye in. It was hysterical.

In spite of this one hurdle, Rooney was a total pro to work with, Reiner insisted, if a bit hyper. Did the other actors feel as positively about him as the writer/director? "Oh yes, they loved him, everybody loved him because he was a pain in the ass," Reiner laughingly recalled. "He wouldn't let us get any work done; he would rather play. I mean, after he did his work, after he was finished, he'd come to the set on his off days and have fun with people."

Rooney gives a highly nuanced performance as Cockeye, bringing depth, humor, and empathy to his role as Bright's loyal friend. Even after both men have reached old age, they spend their days together sitting in the park, while Bright, for what must be the millionth time, laments not having bought more property in the '20s, which would have made him a wealthy man. Bright still believes he can make a show business comeback, but Cockeye seems to accept that times have changed. In an era of burgeoning political correctness, he is told by one casting director that his crossed eyes "are in bad taste." Cockeye retorts, "When the world stopped laughing at these," pointing at his eyes, "they started *killing* each other!"

In one particularly sardonic moment, Bright suffers a heart attack during a ludicrous wedding ceremony to a much younger gold-digger. Cockeye visits him at the hospital, even bringing his friend's antique Billy Bright tin toy to "give you something to play with." Another visitor is Bright's adult son, Billy Junior, a gay designer known as Lucinda (also played by Van Dyke), dressed immaculately in white. Having not seen the boy since he was a child, the elderly man enquires about the approaching guest, "Who the hell is that, Cockeye?"

"I don't know," he replies, "but I bet he smells good."

Billy Junior speaks with both his estranged father and "Mr. Cockeye" respectfully, although it is clear he remembers meeting neither one. After delivering a box of thin mints, he takes his leave. "Nice boy," Cockeye says. "Someday he's gonna make you a grandfather, Billy."

"Don't hold your breath," Bright says knowingly.

With his health failing, the old man is wracked with a bad cough. Cockeye, though, smiles encouragingly, adding, "You got good color, Billy!" Reiner laughed at the memory of Rooney's reading of that repeated line: "He did it such a way he made me laugh each time."

Loyal to the end, Cockeye grants his dying friend's last request. At the sparsely attended funeral, during an insincere-sounding eulogy by the unctuous president of the Academy of Motion Picture Arts and Sciences, Edwin G. Englehardt (the straight-faced Ed Peck), the eulogist is the recipient of a pie in the face, thrown with deadly accuracy by Cockeye himself.

It is a fitting tribute.

Chapter Ten

Sugar Babies

> 2nd COMIC sings a few bars of an aria.
> 1st COMIC: Just a minute. What are you singing?
> 2nd COMIC: Paganini.
> 1st COMIC: Whattya mean, Paganini? Let me see that.
> 2nd COMIC: See, it says right here, Paganini. (shows 1st COMIC the book)
> 1st COMIC: Paganini. You idiot. That says *page nine*.
> STRAIGHT: Well, we've got to sing something. Have you any suggestions?
> 2nd COMIC: "I Want a Girl."
> 1st COMIC: Let's sing first.
> (audience laughs raucously)
> —Burlesque routine from *Sugar Babies* (1979)

Rooney believed his career reached its nadir when he did the narration on a documentary about soft-core porn movies called *Hollywood Blue* (1970). He was so embarrassed by the work, in fact, that he fled Hollywood and settled in Florida. There he met wife number seven, Carolyn Hockett, who worked in customer relations at the *Miami Herald*. She was a pretty blonde who somewhat resembled Barbara Ann and she was not interested in show business, which was a relief to Rooney. She was a divorcée and had a young son named Jimmy. Before they got married, Rooney asked Hockett if she would be interested in being a part of a larger family because he was still thinking of trying to wrest his kids with Thomason away from their maternal grandparents. He took Hockett and Jimmy to meet his kids and claimed they all got along well. After she agreed to bring the kids into the fold, Rooney proposed and they flew to Las Vegas; you know the rest. He again tried to get work in Hollywood, but with no luck. The idea of trying to get his kids back was put on hold and Mickey, Carolyn, and Jimmy headed back to Ft. Lauderdale, Florida.

But work was again scarce and Rooney actually found employment by attending cocktail parties, pretending to be a friend of the host and mingling for an hour or so; for this he was paid $500. Word of his predicament reached his old friend Eddie Bracken, with whom he had worked in a film called *A Slight Case of Larceny* (1953), nearly twenty years earlier. Bracken was part-owner of the Coconut Grove Theatre in Miami and he had what he thought would be the perfect vehicle for Rooney: *Three Goats and a Blanket*, a play in three acts by Woody King and Robert J. Hillard. The theme of the show is alimony, a kind of comic treatment of an age-old custom of giving one's ex-wife "three goats and a blanket." Rooney played an out-of-work TV producer who is paying $500 a week in alimony while taking in $28. The show, with which Rooney toured the dinner theater circuit through much of the decade, was, he readily confessed, his meal ticket during this time period. On a more artistic note, he made a brief return to one of his most prestigious early projects, *A Midsummer Night's Dream*, this time essaying the role of Bottom. He played this on the straw hat circuit in summer stock theatres in 1973.

Around this time, Mickey and Carolyn went back to L.A. so that they could petition the court to grant him custody of his children with Thomason. Her parents had retained high-powered attorney Marvin Mitchelson to make their case. Mitchelson claimed, on behalf of the Thomasons, that Rooney was an unfit parent. Carolyn spent two days on the stand trying to convince the court that they were now capable of providing a good home for Kelly Ann, Kerry Yule, Kyle, and Kimmy Sue, as well as Carolyn's son Jimmy and their daughter, Jonelle, who was born in 1970. In the end, the judge sided with the Thomasons and they were awarded permanent custody, but Mickey and Carolyn were given generous visitation rights. Even Rooney agreed that the Thomasons did a great job in raising his children.

After he lost the custody battle, he went back to Florida and, though he continued to work in dinner theater, it didn't begin to pay all the bills that he piled up. This, of course, continued the pattern of marital strife because whenever the money was tight, he blamed his wife. Now it was Carolyn's turn. He thought she was too free-spending with his money. One of the main complaints of all of his ex-wives was that whenever things got complicated in the relationship Rooney would just take off, sometimes for weeks on end. He seemed to be consumed with coming up with ways to make money that would allow him to live like the king he was when he was in his early twenties. Mickey was undoubtedly one of the most tal-

Ten. Sugar Babies

ented actors of all time, but he was no businessman. Consider just some of the hare-brained schemes he came up over the years: He tried to sell Ralston-Purina, the makers of pet food, on a plan to manufacture soda pop for dogs and cats. (He was careful to point out that these cola drinks should not contain sugar as that would be unhealthy for animals.) He tried to push a product called Mickey Rooney Macaroni and a product called Rip Offs, disposable underwear for adults who don't want to do laundry on trips. He opened several restaurants, among them Mickey Rooney's Star-B-Q that featured menu items like Claudette Cole Slaw and Dandy Hardy Sandwiches. There was also a Mickey Rooney Café in Ft. Lee, New Jersey, and countless other business ventures and product ideas that went nowhere. It is safe to say that these schemes were a further drain on his finances. Carolyn finally had enough of the monetary instability and filed for divorce. He, as usual, pleaded with her not to leave him, to no avail.

Marriage number seven was officially over.

* * *

In 1971, his agent, Milton Deutsch, died suddenly. That led him to Ruth Webb, whom he credited—right before God—with getting his career going again during his Oscar acceptance speech in 1983. Webb was a bit of a show business legend herself; she began her career as an actress and appeared in many Broadway productions, including the Leonard Bernstein–Adolph Green–Betty Comden musical *On the Town*. She later became a well-known agent who specialized in resurrecting the careers of older actors who had fallen on hard times. Some of the stars she represented were Dorothy Lamour, Kathryn Grayson, Donald O'Connor, and Gig Young. Rooney was right up her alley: a great star from the past who everyone realized had immense talent but who could not find steady work. She was also his first female agent and so this was a new experience as well. Webb was a colorful character who liked to conduct business from her home—her bedroom, to be precise. She usually made and took calls for her clients in a reclining position. Rooney called her one day and, in essence, said, "I've tried everything else, if you're willing to take a shot on me I'm willing to do what you say."

Webb immediately began to work like a tiger on his behalf. She got him more stage work and, according to Rooney, when he became quite ill during an engagement in Houston and was confined to a hospital bed for ten days, she stayed in his room, sleeping in a twin bed, and helped nurse him back to health. She later invited him to come stay in her Hollywood Hills home. Since he had no place else to go, he took her up on her generous offer. Rooney described his new environment:

> Ruth already had a houseful of people and assorted other critters: Jamie, her live-in lover; her son, Mike; her ninety-six-year-old mother (who was a painter), an actor named Dean Dittman, two live raccoons (who lived in a wire cage just outside the library window), an alley cat named K, a mutt named Tippie, and a big scarlet macaw named Sidney.

He went on to say how much he enjoyed his stay there because she threw a lot of parties and her other clients would come, old friends like Martha Raye and Ann Miller, and he would get to talk to them about their careers and what Webb was doing to help them. She not only got him more work and let him stay at her house rent-free, she also introduced him to a Christian Science healer, whom he credited with helping him bring God into his life. Whether the Deity or Webb's tireless efforts were responsible for the surge of work that was coming his way, he was grateful to both.

She booked him on *Hollywood Squares* and he appeared on several episodes of the *Merv Griffin Show*. She wanted the audience and the industry to know that he was still around. Letting Rooney loose on a talk show seemed like a questionable career move at best. He was, after all, a product of the studio system, an era when the publicity department worked overtime to produce ghosted articles and invent quotes attributed to the stars. Without this assistance, many screen gods and goddesses would have been revealed as the ordinary, under-educated people they really were. Had Clark Gable, Gary Cooper, or Marilyn Monroe, to cite just a few examples, lived long enough to be on the talk show circuit, who knows how they would be perceived by today's film buffs. Mickey Rooney came across as a blowhard and, although he talked non-stop, he rarely said a goddamn thing.

The most famous (or, more accurately, *infamous*) Rooney talk show appearance was on December 1, 1959, when he had a disastrous encounter with Jack Paar, then the host of *The Tonight Show*. This occurred during one of Paar's infrequent trips with his show out to the West Coast (most of the year *Tonight* was telecast from New York). Paar felt that the actor came to the show drunk, which Rooney vehemently disputed at the time. Paar later told Arthur Marx:

Ten. Sugar Babies

I never met Mickey Rooney before he was on my show that night. He was a legend to me, of course. I knew about him and liked his work very much. As a matter of fact, often on *The Tonight Show*, we'd sit around talking about who was maybe the best motion picture actor who ever lived. And [the answer] would usually be Mickey Rooney or James Mason. Later, when Mason was on, he was told that and asked who he thought was the best actor ever, and he replied, "Mickey Rooney."

According to Paar, Rooney found out that the show was to be broadcast in Los Angeles, and called *The Tonight Show* to inquire about being a guest on the program. Paar didn't know why he wanted to be on the show because he didn't really have anything to plug, but he was happy to accommodate him. Paar said that he usually tried to have lunch with a guest of this stature before their first appearance on the program if he had not met them before, but Rooney demurred, citing a previous engagement. He was at an anniversary celebration with his wife and, although the show was live at 8:30 p.m., he knew that he wouldn't be on until about 9:00, so he arrived a little late. Paar recalled that he didn't even get a chance to go backstage to shake Rooney's hand during the commercial break because the actor's handler said he didn't want to see him. Still, Paar didn't read any hostility into this because he thought Rooney didn't want to spoil the spontaneity of their meeting. Rooney later admitted that he *did* have a few drinks at the celebration but insisted he wasn't drunk and that Thomason never would have let him go on the show if he was.

Paar said that Rooney was belligerent to him from the moment he came on the show and that he kept mentioning a tire business that he was a partner in with some pro football player. He kept mentioning the location on Sepulveda Boulevard. Paar felt it was all very boring and so did the audience. Rooney apparently kept needling Paar about how he thought a local talk show host named Tom Duggan was a better interviewer than he was. Attempting to change the subject, Paar asked Rooney, "What kind of a woman was Ava Gardner?" Rooney took this as an affront and replied, "She was more woman than *you* will ever know." At that point, Paar asked him if he liked the show and he said he didn't, and then Paar said, "Perhaps you'd like to leave?" The headlines in the paper next day were "Rooney Walks, Staggers off 'The Tonight Show.'" After he left, Paar said, "It's a shame. He was a great talent."

Rooney would later apologize to Paar for his behavior, but never forgave him for the comment he made to the audience after he departed. During Rooney's guest appearance on *The Late Show with David Let-*

terman in the early '90s, the host attempted to interview the veteran star about his career, but it soon became apparent that he was there to merely promote his latest autobiography. Letterman became rankled by his guest's hawkish approach. The following evening, he opened his show with an apology for the previous night's program. For his part, Rooney began to intentionally mispronounce Letterman's name as Waterman.

Of course, not all of Rooney's talk show appearances were disasters. In the early '70s, when MGM was tearing down its backlot (making way for the inevitable condominiums) and selling the contents of the prop department, Johnny Carson surprised Mickey on *The Tonight Show* by raising the curtain to reveal Andy Hardy's original roadster, still in perfect shape a quarter of a century after the series officially concluded. Rooney was delighted. He ran over to the automobile, jumped in, and immediately started it up.

* * *

Thanks to Ruth Webb's dogged persistence, Rooney began to get better work in films in the mid-to-late '70s. He was cast in *The Domino Principle* (1977), a big Hollywood picture directed by Stanley Kramer and starring Gene Hackman and Candice Bergen. He also had a role in a very successful Disney film starring Helen Reddy called *Pete's Dragon* (1978).

It was while he was staying with Webb that he met his eighth and final wife, Jan Chamberlin. A gifted singer, she had been working with Mickey Rooney, Jr., who introduced her to his father. She recalled in a TV interview her first meeting with him at the Ruth Webb party. She said that Mickey Junior had to coax her into going to the party, but was glad she went when she met Rooney. He started playing the piano and she began to sing "I Won't Last a Day Without You," the Carpenters' hit, written by Roger Nichols with lyrics by Paul Williams. Jan said she felt like Garland in one of the Mickey-Judy musicals.

Mickey and Jan immediately hit it off and as soon as he left Webb's sanctuary, he moved in with Jan and her two sons, Chris and Mark. About a year after they moved in together, Rooney asked her to go with him on a business trip to Hong Kong, but she was hesitant to go public with their relationship. She must have felt there would be no turning back once the press got hold of it. She said that she got to know the *real* Mickey and not the one she thought she knew from his many interviews.

Rooney characterized their relationship as one long fight. He said

Ten. Sugar Babies

they argued about everything and that the reason the relationship continued to last was because the fight was not over yet. Although the couple met in 1974 they didn't get married until August of 1978. The wedding took place at the Conejo Valley Church of Religious Science. Frolich, who had been a friend of Rooney's since they appeared together in *Boys Town* in 1938, was best man; Chris Aber, Jan's son from a previous marriage, gave the bride away.

They were interviewed in *People* magazine less than a year after the wedding. The article focused on the difficulty of being married to someone with such a disastrous marital record. Rooney admitted that he wasn't the most mature individual when he said, "There's a child in me that's being a man and there's a man in me that is being a child.... I'm hard to live with." The last part of that would certainly qualify as one of the great understatements of all time. Jan told Laura Stevenson, "He treats me extremely hard and I rebel. Being married to Mickey is like a game of chess. I'm not sure who will win. It'll probably be a stalemate."

* * *

When he was first approached about doing a burlesque show he felt it was a "bullshit idea: burlesque is dead." The project began in the mind of a college professor by the name of Ralph Allen who loved reading about and listening to old burlesque routines and the artists who performed them. Allen's academic background included an undergraduate degree from Amherst and graduate work at Yale. When he was an assistant professor he translated some plays by a 16th-century dramatist, then later, when he landed a teaching job at the University of Tennessee, he became very interested in the history of burlesque. Allen was a full-fledged scholar but he also had a funny bone and would incorporate comedic bits into his academic presentations. Broadway producer Harry Rigby heard about a paper the professor was to deliver about burlesque at a theatre history conference at Lincoln Center and his curiosity was piqued. Allen was a hit, and Rigby, who had been thinking of doing a burlesque show, stopped the professor after the presentation to tell him how much he enjoyed his talk. Over drinks, Rigby was delighted to find out that Allen had collected almost three thousand burlesque sketches and routines. There would, in other words, be no shortage of material. Rigby and Allen agreed to a deal that would give the professor 2 percent of the profits from the show in exchange for his work and access to the material. According to Rooney's autobiography, it was Allen who told Rigby that the key to the show would be the top banana, and that was Joe Yule, Jr., the son of another top banana.

Rigby next contacted one of the best producers on Broadway, Terry Allen Kramer, who also had connections for the financing. Kramer thought it was a good idea and might be fun. Rooney, though, had to be convinced. He had a bad experience in an earlier attempt at a pre-Broadway show called *W.C.*, a musical biography of W.C. Fields, based on a memoir by Fields's on-again, off-again mistress Carlotta Monti.

Rooney had been touring the straw hat circuit in *George M!* (this show, a musical based on the life and songs of George M. Cohan, opened at the Palace Theatre on Broadway in 1968, with Joel Grey in the title role). Rooney's interpretation of Cohan was so successful that he won the Straw Hat Award for Best Actor during the 1970 season. Producers interested in doing a play on Fields felt that Rooney would be a good choice to play the late, great comedian, who was then enjoying a cultural renaissance. David Black went backstage after *George M!* and pitched the idea of a Fields musical to him, and he loved it. Black then commissioned Arnold Weinstein to write the book and lyrics, and Larry Rosenthal, a motion picture composer, to do the music. Black didn't like what they came up with and didn't feel the material was good enough to show Rooney. He then turned to Milton Sperling to do the book, and Al Carmine for the music. Black felt the new version was a great improvement. Rooney liked it as well and was officially on board. Black then hired Bernadette Peters, a talented singer/actress with more than a decade of stage experience, to play the part of Monti. Ted Wannamaker was brought in to stage the production. The play opened in Baltimore to some pretty good reviews and then played in several summer stock theatres along the East Coast.

There were some problems with the script that Rooney would try to fix by ad-libbing. Sperling told Marx, "Before the tour was over, we had to fire the original director and bring in another one. Which, of course, was unnecessary; Mickey was doing most of the directing himself, as he always does." Marx points out that Rooney was not the problem, when he quotes Black: "He was absolutely brilliant as W.C. Without him, we would have had nothing on the stage. The problem was the book. It didn't seem to be going anywhere, and most of the songs weren't very good either." The writers never could figure out what they wanted to stress in Fields's character. Was he a jerk? a drunk? a lech? or all of these and more? Meanwhile, Rooney was begging, "Give me something funny to do. Fields was a funny man."

Ten. Sugar Babies

Black closed the show in August 1971. The official reason was that the financial backers wouldn't be able to come up with the money based on Rooney's name value at the box office. But as Black later told Marx, "Mickey was unhappy with the script and refused to play it on Broadway."

Now with the burlesque show proposal, Rooney was naturally wary of getting burned again. He was also worried that if the play *did* make it to New York it might hurt his new marriage because he would be away a lot. Chamberlin, however, was so enthusiastic about the project that she told him she would come and stay with him when they took the play on the road and—if they made it to the Great White Way—they would set up house for the run of the show. She was instrumental in convincing him that the time was right for a burlesque comedy musical. Rooney began to realize the potential of the show and the idea of being the top banana— the *star*—was also quite appealing.

Finally, Rooney was involved enough to read the script the writers had put together; its working title was "The New Majestic Follies and Lyceum Gardens Review." Rooney didn't like that title at all. He continued with his dinner theatre work while Rigby, Allen, and Kramer were trying to tweak the production. At one of Mickey's dinner theatre gigs, Allen showed up backstage to talk to him. The professor told him that they were thinking of former MGM tap dancer Ann Miller for his co-star, and that really intrigued him. In Rigby's pitch to Rooney he told him that there would be lots of singing and dancing, and the choice of Miller gave him a much better feeling for the whole enterprise. Rigby then announced the show's new title: "Sugar Babies." Sugar Babies were the candies sold during the burlesque shows, but also what the stage door Johnnies called the chorus girls. The double meaning appealed to Rooney.

Although very much interested, he still worried about whether a burlesque show would work in 1979. He was especially concerned about the comedy bits. Rigby would perform some of the gags for Rooney, who seemed to like most of them. The actor also realized that the project would be lucky to break even during tryouts on the road and they could close in a week if they even got to Broadway. Rigby finally got him to sign on the dotted line once he promised him five grand a week for the extent of the run, no matter what happened. Once Rigby had Rooney signed up, he next approached Ann Miller, who was delighted by the idea. Rigby remembered that Miller had dated composer Jimmy McHugh. He had passed away but, with Miller's help, it was discovered that McHugh had

The glamorous Ann Miller and a bewigged and be-gartered Mickey Rooney take to the stage in the Broadway hit *Sugar Babies* (1979).

about seventy songs stored away that had never been published. Rigby negotiated with the McHugh estate and secured the music, then hired Arthur Malvin to write the lyrics. Rigby also landed Ernest Flatt to do the choreography. Both Malvin and Flatt had worked on *The Carol Burnett Show*.

Kramer was crucial to getting the show off the ground because she had the financial connections. It was going to cost $1.6 million (more than four times that amount in 2016 dollars) to mount *Sugar Babies*, which was a little more expensive than other musicals of the time. The costumes, sets, and labor it was going to take to essentially mount a period piece variety show made it a rather costly endeavor. But Kramer had connections in her own family, as her husband, Irving, was on the board of Columbia Pictures. He was able to get Columbia to invest $500,000, and she was able to raise another $300,000 before putting up the final $500,000 herself. Once the money had been raised, Rooney was now sure that the play

Ten. Sugar Babies

would at least open and he and his wife moved into a motel suite in New Jersey, right across the river from Manhattan.

Once Rooney was in and they began rehearsals, he started complaining about the script. His main problem with the material was that it may have read funny on the page, but it didn't play. According to producers and actors, the first few weeks were utter chaos. Because of Rooney's unhappiness with the way things were going there were many firings, including the first three straight men who had been hired. Many of the other comics in the rehearsals were thoroughly pissed at these demands and vowed never to work with him again. For his part, Rooney complained that the jokes weren't funny and stated over and over that the show didn't stand a chance. These were not the words that anybody whose work was based on whether the show succeeded or not wanted to hear. He failed to see that everyone involved with this play had a lot at stake and was trying to be positive and they were all doing their best. Rudy Tronto, who directed the sketches for *Sugar Babies*, told Marx that Rooney was right about the fact that most of the sketches weren't very funny. He pointed out that although Allen knew a lot about the history of burlesque, he was not a comedy writer and had no idea what would work on stage in 1979. Rooney was adamant that the sketches needed "buttons," or punch lines, or they weren't going to work. Later on, as the show began its tryouts on the road, two TV gagmen, Ralph Goodman and Paul Pompian, were called in to punch up the sketches.

Norman Abbott was the first director of *Sugar Babies* and, along with Rigby, had the original idea of doing a burlesque show on Broadway. He neglected to nail down a contract before showing up in New York for rehearsals. Abbott's background was in TV, directing sitcoms and variety shows, and Rooney thought he didn't have the feel for burlesque comedy material. Rigby reluctantly fired his friend at the star's urging and hired Tronto, who had worked with Rooney as an actor in *W.C.* and had directed a play a few years earlier called *The Best of Burlesque*.

When Tronto arrived in New York on his first day, he encountered some frantic actors. Miller rushed up to him to complain about the dances Flatt was making her do and Tronto reminded her that he was just there to direct the sketches. Then Rooney came running over and grabbed him and said, "Rudy, we've got to get rid of all this shit. This stuff is terrible. My father did it fifty years ago." While they were still in rehearsal Rooney was anxious to get the sketches "on their feet" but they couldn't because they still did not have a straight man to work with him. He finally approved of Peter Leeds as his straight man as they had worked together before, and Tronto did put the material on its feet to see what would play. He and Rooney would also write some new material while pruning and adding to the old, and the sketches began to come together.

There were other problems as they prepared to take the play on the road for the all-important preview audiences. If audiences and critics didn't like it in Chicago and Detroit, it probably wouldn't even get to Broadway. One of the main problems in the early days was that the choreographer, Flatt, wanted to do a musical number featuring Rooney on roller skates and singing "I Just Want to Be a Song-and-Dance Man." He was not too steady on the skates and wanted no part of it, but Flatt insisted it was a great idea. The experiment lasted through a few of the previews, and some lucky people got to see a man approaching sixty, wheeling around the stage singing at the top of his lungs. The early preview audiences were great and the show was getting some good reviews when, during one of the shows, Rooney lost his balance and landed on his keister. The producers might have been willing to risk injury to their star if the play was not doing well, but this was beginning to look like a hit and they could no longer take any chances, so Rooney on wheels came to an abrupt halt. The show continued its pre-Broadway run to mostly full houses and good reviews—so much so that by the time they got to New York the producers already had over $1 million in advance sales.

The show opened at the Mark Hellinger Theatre on October 9, 1979. Despite the advance sales and the strong audience response, everyone was nervous on opening night—except Rooney. Like he did as a youngster before going onstage in *A Midsummer Night's Dream*, he went around offering encouragement to the cast, telling them there was nothing to worry about and that they were all going to be great. There was no reason to worry because once they hit Broadway, the sketches, and the musical numbers with Rooney and Miller—choreographed by Flatt with the music by the aforementioned McHugh and lyrics by Dorothy Fields and Al Dubin—were running on all cylinders. The show was an immediate hit with audiences and, to everyone's surprise, the tough New York critics. Walter Kerr said that *Sugar Babies* was "essentially a Rooney occasion (it seems to me extremely unlikely that anyone would have shaken the mothballs out of sixty-year-old burlesque routines and done them full throttle and all flags flying, without him), and indefatigable Rooney is exactly as

Ten. Sugar Babies

Mickey Rooney is reunited with his ex-wife (and eternal flame) Ava Gardner backstage at the Mark Hellinger Theatre, New York, during the 1979-1982 run of *Sugar Babies*. Ann Miller (right) seems as excited as the former lovers (Photofest).

energetic and exactly as talented as he was when, at the age of three or four, he rammed a cigar into his mouth, raked a derby over his brow, and made a star of himself. Which is very, very energetic and even more talented."

Clive Barnes, at the *New York Post*, remarked that "the show is solidly on the shoulders of Broadway's most promising newcomer of the year (yes, oddly enough, it is a first), Mr. Rooney. Rooney delivers with manic grace ... he is the glorious epitome of the clown. With his lopsided grin, his geriatrically boyish air, his warmth and total naturalness, Rooney is something to experience.... Rooney is the icing on the *Sugar Babies*, a Top Banana if we ever had one."

Rooney, who had been reminding everybody for decades that he had once been the number-one box-office star in the world in his youth, had once again reached the heights as a balding, paunchy man in his late middle age, proving that miracles do, in fact, happen. This was the beginning of a three-year run on Broadway in front of sellout houses, and he was the center of attention again. So popular was Rooney that Kramer recalled that it was almost impossible to sell tickets to the show when Rooney took a vacation. On the night that Rooney took his final bow at the Mark Hellinger Theatre in 1982, he was a rich man once again in terms of his finances, his career, and his personal life. His marriage was also going well, and he was headed out on the road with *Sugar Babies* for another five years.

For Jan and Mickey, it was a great way to start their marriage. It was the focal point of his incredible career comeback, and Rooney, who had been broke for what seemed like a lifetime, was very much in the money again. He started out making $10,000 per week because, true to form, he wanted the quick cash rather than a percentage deal. He changed his mind later in the run when he saw the grosses—and was probably reading the trade headlines that said whenever he took time off from the play the producers couldn't *give* tickets away—and he signed for 10 percent of the gross receipts. He was soon taking in over $30,000 per week; eventually, it would top $65,000 per week.

He continued to hang around Webb's office when things were going well, but she was afraid that he would leave for a bigger agency. A young man by the name of Mark Russell Bell worked as her assistant during the 1980s. He recalled that the actor had filed a legal appeal of the Screen Actors Guild agreement in the mid-'60s that actors were not to be paid residuals for film and TV productions made before 1960. More than 100 of his colleagues supported him in this legal action. The suit was actually sent to the Supreme Court, but they refused to hear the case. This occurred just a week after he received his honorary Oscar in 1983. Bell reported that Rooney took out ads in *Daily Variety* and *The Hollywood Reporter* that read, "Even Though We Lost, Thank You for Your Support."

Rooney did eventually have a positive experience with SAG when they brought him in for a conversation about his career in front of an

Ten. Sugar Babies

audience of his fellow actors on May 11, 2004. Todd Amorde, an actor and executive with SAG, was the host and interviewer for the event. Rooney did go on about how Walt Disney named his famous mouse after him and how he discovered half the stars in Hollywood, but there was a very real moment when Amorde broached the subject of the lawsuit and said, on behalf of all actors, "I want you to know that you *did* help and everyone in here now enjoys residuals on virtually every job that they work on. The problem was it didn't reach back to help the people behind, but you helped create a legacy that will give to actors for years to come. So we thank you for fighting the good fight."

Rooney was living with Chamberlin and her two sons at that time, and his son Tim was very much involved in his life as well. Bell also notes that he observed the actor attempting to become a better person and even becoming more introspective. He said that Rooney was originally offered the role of Archie Bunker in 1970, but turned it down because of the kind of racist character that Norman Lear described to him when he made his pitch. Bell also shed some light on the homophobic vibe Rooney would sometimes give off, attributing that to his interpretation of religion. He also points out that Rooney was a good friend with Harry Rigby, the producer of *Sugar Babies*, who was in a same-sex relationship.

As he approached his twilight years, Mickey Rooney seemed to have it all: a thriving career and, finally, a seemingly lasting happy marriage.

CHAPTER ELEVEN

The Black Stallion

> The beginning of production was kind of tough. A lot of people standing around waiting for direction and it would be tense and he was, like, the old pro.
> —Tim Farley, observing Rooney on-set

Mickey Rooney has an astonishing 340 film credits listed on IMDb, and one that was released in 1979 may just be his best, which is a debatable point. Beyond debate is the fact that it is the film for which most contemporary moviegoers are likely to remember him. *The Black Stallion*, based on the classic 1941 children's book by Walter Farley, was adapted for the big screen by Melissa Matheson, Jeanne Rosenberg, and William D. Witliff. An eleven-year-old boy, Alec Ramsey, is shipwrecked on a deserted island off the coast of North Africa with a wild Arabian horse, whom he befriends. After being rescued and returned home to America, it is decided to enter the horse in a race against two champions.

The film, which officially began production in 1977, was produced by Fred Roos, Tom Sternberg, and Francis Ford Coppola (whose father, Carmine, composed the score). It stars Kelly Reno as Alec, Teri Garr as his mother, Hoyt Axton as his father, Mickey Rooney as Henry Dailey (a retired race horse jockey), and the Arabian horse Cass Ole. The director was Carol Ballard. (This author managed to secure interviews with Walter Farley's son Tim, producer Roos, juvenile lead Reno, and director Ballard. All of their quotes herein are exclusive to this book.)

Tim Farley, son of Walter Farley (1915-1989), the author upon whose book the film was based, was deeply moved that his father's story was being immortalized on film. "I was grateful right from the beginning because of my dad. I was there for pre-production, which was selecting the horse. I was attending USC in Santa Barbara. I was a freshman. Me, my dad, and Carroll went looking at stallions for a day. We went to look for the stallions at some incredible farms in northern California. My dad

Eleven. The Black Stallion

had a horse that he was trying to show to Carroll. We ended up getting a couple of horses, one from California and one from Texas."

Early in the film, we see Alec making contact with the magnificent Arabian black, and, slowly, the horse learns to accept him. In tracking shots that are stunningly vivid, the boy rides the horse along the shore. Audiences and critics of the time were mesmerized. One critic who was especially impressed was Roger Ebert. As he stated in his review:

> The first half of *The Black Stallion* is so gloriously breathtaking that the second half, the half with all the conventional excitement, seems merely routine. We've seen the second half before—the story of the kid, the horse, the veteran trainer, and the big race. But the first hour of this movie belongs among the great filmgoing experiences. It is described as an epic, and earns the description.

Ebert, of course, is correct in describing the first half of the film as an epic, but the second half is far from routine. This is due, in great measure, to Rooney's brilliant performance as Henry Dailey, the retired jockey who coaches Alec on the art of racing. Fred Roos believed from the start that Rooney would be perfect in the role, although he admits sometimes he wasn't sure if Mickey was simply stretching the truth or merely kidding. "I think he ... sometimes he would tell jokes, you would never know. Sometimes he would say that he would go over in the morning and work thoroughbreds on the track as an exercise jockey. I don't know if he really did because that can be dangerous." Despite Mickey's tendency to exaggerate his abilities, as an actor, Roos believes, he could do no wrong. "I was always an admirer but *The Black Stallion* was *it*. We just got along fabulously on that movie. He was so much fun to be around."

Carol Ballard had never directed a feature film before *The Black Stallion*, and he was apprehensive about working with Rooney. He had heard that Rooney was difficult, an egomaniac, and wouldn't take direction. Francis Ford Coppola's Zoetrope Studios produced the film and when Ballard voiced his concerns about Mickey, Coppola told him not to worry: "He's an old pro. It'll work out."

Because the actor had been accused of playing fast and loose with the text in the past, one wonders just how much of his dialogue in the film was ad-libbed. According to Ballard, "All of it." This didn't bother either the director or the producers as they were not too partial to the script they were working with; given that it was faithful to a children's book from the 1940s, it had a somewhat corny feel. Mickey's fresh

Rooney (right) and producer Francis Ford Coppola (left) on the set of *The Black Stallion* (1979) (courtesy Tim Farley).

approach was actually welcomed. Ballard also stated that the film was shot out of sequence, with the second half completed before the first.

The film's second half is redolent of Frank Capra's depictions of 1940s small-town America, and Carmine Coppola's exquisite score follows the majesty of the first half with a playful, jaunty vibe that perfectly captures that era.

There is a great deal of attention to the visual splendors in the second half of the film as well. The Black, temporarily housed in the Ramseys' backyard, is frightened by a junkman wearing similar headgear to that of the man who beat him on the ship. He runs through a field alongside factories spewing smoke in silence. He gallops through the town, his hooves *clip-clopping* on the pavement. In the background one can see the classic cars and colorful period costumes of the townsfolk who gasp at the wild stallion as he goes flying by. Alec, panicked by his horse's escape, runs through the town looking for him, later sitting forlornly on warehouse steps on a foggy morning with the sound of ships in the distance. Through the fog we hear hoofbeats on the pavement and a white horse wearing a funny hat emerges pulling a wagon carrying an old black man with a white beard, wearing a beret and smoking a pipe, who stops to talk to Alec. Snoe (the wonderful Clarence Muse) asks Napoleon (his horse) if he has seen a black

Eleven. The Black Stallion

stallion. Snoe gives Alec directions in a lyrical tone and then we see Alec running through a golden wheat field toward a large red barn on a beautiful summer morning.

There is a shaft of sunlight coming through the roof of the barn as Alec falls through the hay chute, landing in the stall where the Black is waiting. The sound of hesitant footsteps is heard as someone makes his way down the stairs. Through the shaft of light, the individual appears to have a white beard, like Snoe, but as he gets closer, we realize the "beard" is actually shaving cream. The man, a former jockey trainer, is Henry Dailey, making his entrance in an odd, side-to-side manner (Ballard told Rooney to come in like a crab).

Rooney was back working with top talent, and he didn't disappoint. According to Ballard, they were waiting for rainy weather to pass and Rooney suggested he teach the kid how to ride. So he pulls together a couple of bales of hay and puts Alec on one of them and teaches him how to hold the reins and go with the rhythm of the horse and tells him to kind of "throw it away" and not to "pump him" and "he'll be making that rhythm." Ballard also mentioned the scene where he is describing the "ice man" George Wolf as being ad-libbed. Henry turns his cap around and again begins to demonstrate how George Wolf would sit chilly on a horse and wait to make his move, and when he saw an opening he'd scoot in front and everyone would say, "Here comes the ice man."

Many critics hailed *The Black Stallion* as an instant classic, with *Variety* calling it "a perfect gem." David Thomson gave special attention to Rooney's contribution to the film: "Carroll Ballard's *The Black Stallion* is a film that never fails with audiences. One reason why is that after the lyrical stuff on the island with the horse and the boy, the story moves on to horse racing where Mick is the trainer who teaches the boy to be a jockey on The Black for the big race. It is one of the finest tributes to education in American cinema."

David Denby said of the director, "Ballard has made a grave, meditative, but highly sensuous film; watching it is like entering into a first adventure with all the pleasures and terrors intact." Roger Fristoe, in his article on the film for TCM, wrote, "One viewer said that in watching the film he felt he 'was discovering the emotional sources of mystery and enchantment'—and, indeed, *The Black Stallion* has a transporting power that can engage a receptive imagination in the way that only the best movies can. With its exceptional cinematography by Caleb Deschanel and the splendidly played interactions between horse and boy, this is one of the most beautiful films of all time and a moving celebration of the bonds that can be shared by animals and humans."

Indeed, the movie can cast a spell over an audience, even though its tropes are familiar to the experienced film buff. Judith Martin listed all the clichés of horse-racing movies and then said, "Each of these scenes is in *The Black Stallion*, but in a restrained manner that seeks to jerk no tears. The emotion, and it's considerable, is produced, instead, entirely by the beauty of the film." Martin, like many critics, took note of the paucity of dialogue in the film. Ballard and his cinematographer Deschanel were concentrating on telling this well-worn story in a new way. They were part of the film school generation. Ballard had attended UCLA, where one of his classmates was Francis Ford Coppola, and Deschanel was a USC graduate. They were part of the "new Hollywood" and working with a show business veteran was a new experience for both parties. As mentioned earlier, Coppola had no trepidation about working with Rooney. He had hired him when he was still thinking of directing the film himself,

Mickey Rooney (center) seems a bit out of sorts as he goes over the script for *The Black Stallion* with director Carroll Ballard (1979). The unidentified individual on the left looks like he'd rather be anywhere else (courtesy of Tim Farley).

Eleven. The Black Stallion

but all the production problems with *Apocalypse Now* negated that idea and he turned to his old film school buddy to direct it. Coppola was the oldest of the film school generation and actually came in at the end of the studio era, with his first big production being *Finian's Rainbow* (1968), starring Fred Astaire. In another intriguing link with the past, Rooney's father, Joe Yule, Sr., appeared in the title role on Broadway a generation before.

Many of the scenes rely on Rooney's economy of expression. When he is playing cards at a table near the barn and Alec asks him about his racing career, Henry says very little but the scene is memorable when he shudders, as though caught by a sudden chill. When Henry is lying in his bunk on the train as they head for the big match race, we see the look of apprehension on his face as he contemplates a possible change in his fortune. The look of worry and the way he holds the leash in his hands as The Black is taken away from him for the big race reveal that he has lost all control—and this is all said without uttering a word. This ability to express emotions without words was important to the filmmakers because it allowed them to tell the story visually and therefore keep it cinematic

Henry Dailey (Mickey Rooney, back) and Alec Ramsey (Kelly Reno, front) are an effective team as trainer and jockey, respectively, in *The Black Stallion* (1979) (courtesy of Tim Farley).

without sacrificing the story. Rooney helped Ballard convey the familiar story in quick brushstrokes, thereby maintaining the filmic rhythm established in the first part of the film.

Critic Janet Maslin offered the following praise: "Mr. Rooney lends humor and humanity to the proceedings, and he fits surprisingly well into Mr. Ballard's careful scheme."

The Black Stallion was a long, difficult project. It was in production for two years before its release in 1979. Ballard said that he shot everything he could and that the first cut of the film was eight hours long. Guy Flatley did a profile of Rooney in 1977 about the film in production. The actor said of Kelly Reno, who plays Alec, "He's your original boy on the cover of the *American Weekly*, right out of a Norman Rockwell painting. I think he's more American than I was. By the time I was Kelly's age, I had been working nine years in vaudeville."

Reno, now a middle-aged man with a wife and three kids, has very fond memories of making the movie. Prior to appearing in *The Black Stallion*, Reno had no acting experience. He credits his finding out about the role through a

> friend of our family in Pueblo, Colorado. She lived in town and we lived out in the country on a cattle ranch. There was an ad in the *Denver Post* that a company was going to be making a new feature film and they were looking for a young boy for a lead role in this film. Basically the ad didn't say you needed to act but just that you had to know how to ride horses. She called my dad and mom and told them she thought I would be perfect for this movie. So my mom looked into it and asked me about it. At the time it was like, "Sure. It would be a day out of school."

Reno remembers having to audition not just once, but several times. Obviously, the producers were impressed with the boy—after all, he got the job. Asked if the amazing action shots of his riding The Black were the result of trick photography, he answered emphatically, "No, no! Absolutely not!! I had to learn. So once I got the job all the riding I did on the cattle ranch was bareback. I mean, you just *do* it ... it's not much different than riding with a saddle. It kind of is because you know you've got your stirrups and you can balance yourself and you can kind of keep yourself in the saddle, whereas when you haven't got a saddle you've got to rely on balance and wit." Reno admits, however, that he was doubled in the actual racing scenes, as he explains: "At eleven years old there was no way that I was going to be able to ride and control that thoroughbred. They had a double in the long shots when he has opened up.... Then they

Eleven. The Black Stallion

would cut to close shots of me on Cass Ole. I mean, he was a show horse and I can handle a show horse."

He has especially fond memories of working with Hoyt Axton, who played his father, and the legendary Rooney. "Mickey was Mickey," he says with a smile. "He was just down to earth." Knowing the boy lacked on-camera experience, Rooney shared some invaluable advice. "Mickey would tell me to look off to the shoulder, look off to this side, and look off to that side," Reno recalled. "'Don't look directly in it, look over the top. You can't look into that camera! The only time they do stuff like that is when you are doing comedy and somebody in the movie is talking to the audience. But usually if you're at the movies you don't want the actor staring at you.' Mickey did help me a lot there."

Tim Farley recalls that Mickey, who suffered from arthritis, would become tired at times, and it showed in his attitude toward Ballard. When the director asked for a retake on some scenes,

> Mickey might say, "We've already got the shot." Carroll is, like, "No, I want another shot." This went on for a few more takes and then, I remember, I used to go to the dailies. I wanted to be a part of every element of the film. You could see he did this like one of Mr. Rooney's, I mean, he was a pro. He knew when they had the take; he used to wear one of those copper bracelets for arthritis, or whatever. So what he did was he would move the bracelet from one wrist to another. He knew that if you had a close-up on him it wouldn't cut in the editing. The continuity would be lost.

Laughingly, Farley explained that he did that on purpose. Mickey, it seems, could still be playful on set. "He was strong and, every once in a while, he would break into a song and dance. He would do that because it would get really edgy on the set."

One interesting element to Farley was the company to which Rooney would gravitate between shots. "He hung around with the jockeys a lot, which I thought was really funny," he recalled. "They were all about his size. He always enjoyed hanging out with those guys because they talked the same language. I mean, Mickey was kind of a tough-talking guy and so were the jockeys. The jockeys always had girlfriends, they like the sports cars, and they like the fast and flashy life. That's why he liked the jockeys, too; he was hoping for some tips for betting. He spent his whole life betting on the goddamn horses. He lost a fortune on gambling."

Kelly Reno admits that the shoot could indeed become tedious—and lengthy. "We did footage in Toronto; we did footage in California. All of the city scenes and all of the scenes of the house and the barn and finding my horse, that was all done in Toronto. Most of the beach scenes were done in Italy, in Sardinia. The helicopter scenes, they were done in Oregon." Overall, it took two full years to shoot the picture. "It was a long time," Reno laughs. "They got lucky that I didn't have a growth spurt!"

Success in Hollywood breeds spinoffs and imitators. There was the inevitable sequel *The Black Stallion Returns* (1983), in which Rooney did not appear. The first of the imitators was *Lightning—The White Stallion* (1986), which was directed by William A. Leavey, with a screenplay by Peter Welbeck, co-starring Susan George and newcomer Isabel Garcia Lorca. In this rather forgettable film, Rooney plays a millionaire gambler and horse breeder who agrees to help find a prized white stallion that has been stolen and then, once the horse has been retrieved, he agrees to teach a young teenage girl who is losing her sight to ride the horse. The young actress (Lorca) is quite beautiful, but the script and direction are subpar.

Two years later Rooney appeared in a television movie called *Bluegrass* (1988), which is a romantic drama about the Kentucky horse farms and racing culture but primarily a starring vehicle for actress Cheryl Ladd, who had become a TV star in the series *Charlie's Angels*. It is a well-made TV movie, thanks largely to the fine direction of Simon Wincer, who would go on to great acclaim for his efforts in bringing Larry McMurtry's masterpiece *Lonesome Dove* (1989) to the small screen. There are some other good actors in the cast, including Diane Ladd and Anthony Andrews. The movie seems a rather accurate depiction of the thoroughbred industry in Kentucky, but it is mostly concerned with the love life of Cheryl Ladd's character, as you might expect. Rooney is good as an eccentric character named John Paul Jones, who is a successful businessman and an expert on thoroughbreds, but, as in most of the vehicles after *The Black Stallion*, producers were merely trading in on his name and association with horse-racing films; they were not roles that required him to stretch as an actor.

Rooney also appeared in a Canadian TV production, *The Adventures of the Black Stallion*, that ran from 1990 to 1992, in which he reprised his role as Henry Dailey. In the series, Henry and Alec (now played by Richard Ian Cox) work toward winning races with The Black, but the half-hour episodes are more about the relationship between Henry, Alec, and his family and their home, Hopeful Farm. The show is uneven, with thin storylines as the series progresses. Alec is now fifteen years old and has dif-

Eleven. The Black Stallion

ferent problems than the eleven-year-old Alec from the book and film. Richard Ian Cox is excellent as Alec, and Rooney, who seems much older than he did in the film, kind of reinvents the character for the series as a mischievous old-timer who must be watched and can be quite cranky with people other than Alec. This author spoke with Sam Waterman, who produced the series, and he raved about Rooney's contribution to the series and said that he made everyone on the production look better because of his complete professionalism and generosity.

But it was *The Black Stallion* that was the culmination of all of these performances with a racetrack setting and is a crucial role in Rooney's historic career. The movie plays constantly on cable TV, attesting to its continued popularity with contemporary audiences. It has also gained in stature with film critics over the decades since its release. A Blu-ray version was finally released in late 2014 because fans of the film had been clamoring for it for years. This was followed in 2015 with a Criterion Collection deluxe edition that includes interviews with director Ballard and cinematographer Deschanel. In both interviews the filmmakers lavish high praise on Rooney's performance and say that his contribution was crucial to the success of the film. Deschanel echoes Ballard when he states, "Mickey Rooney is really a great actor." The Criterion edition also boasts five of Ballard's documentaries and for those who are fans of *Stallion* and other Ballard features such as *Never Cry Wolf* (1983), *Fly Away Home* (1996), and *Duma* (2005), the inclusion of the director's nonfiction films is a real treat. One of the best is called *Rodeo* (1969) and covers the 1968 National Rodeo Finals in Oklahoma City. The film focuses on rodeo champion Larry Mahan and captures the color, action, and sound of a vibrant piece of Americana. The cinematography is once again by Ballard's college friend Deschanel, who captures the feel of competition, the men, the horses, and the bucking broncos from every angle. The images are expertly edited together to give the audience the feeling of watching an action feature film.

As gorgeous as *The Black Stallion* is visually, it would not work without the sizeable contribution of Rooney's performance. No matter how much Ballard struggled with shooting the story, they were going to have to get back to the material in the Walter Farley book, regardless of how corny the filmmakers felt it was. This author agrees with Thomson when he says that Rooney's performance drives the second half of the film. Despite all the bad movies Rooney did in his career, this masterpiece continues to connect with audiences today.

Part of the reason Rooney was crucial to Ballard and the success of his first feature was because he had done so many of these movies before and knew the life of the racetrack inside out. He had not only done about eight different film and TV horse racing projects over the decades but was also an inveterate gambler and bet on the ponies for most of his life. In fact, the last public picture taken of Rooney was when he ran into Mel Brooks at an outing with his stepson Mark and his wife at the Santa Anita racetrack just a few days before he died. But it was in the work in all these horse racing films from *Down the Stretch* to *The Black Stallion* that we can see Rooney not only age but grow as an actor, from a callow youth to a man who has known great sorrow, triumph, and defeat and—in between— a man who must wrestle with his own inner demons and insecurities. The industry he loved may have put him in a box with their limited vision in casting, but within those constraints he managed to create some great and memorable work that will stand the test of time.

CHAPTER TWELVE

Small Screen, Big Star

> When I was twenty years old I was the number-one box-office star in the world. When I was forty nobody wanted me. I couldn't get a job.
> —Mickey Rooney, 1983

As Rooney indicated in his 1983 honorary Oscar speech, there were long stretches in his career where he couldn't find any film work at all. His lament to the Academy of Motion Picture Arts and Sciences audience included references to the stage production *Sugar Babies*, which he said resurrected his career, and to the television film *Bill* (1981), for which he won an Emmy—the only American competitive acting award he would ever receive. He was pointedly referring to the fact that it was his work in other show business mediums that brought him to the Oscars, not films. It was a moving speech and Rooney made a point of accepting the award as a part of his current career renaissance as much as, if not more than, his early film career. He was right, of course, because although his film career went through long dry spells, that didn't mean he ever stopped working. Aside from his forays into radio, nightclubs, and live theatre, he made innumerable appearances on television. Some were good, some were great, and some were downright embarrassing.

His first official effort at a sitcom was *The Mickey Rooney Show* (a.k.a. *Hey, Mulligan*), which made its debut on August 28, 1954. The half-hour show, produced by Mickey Rooney Enterprises, was the brainchild of Rooney's three-time partners Blake Edwards and Richard Quine. Mickey, thirty-four at the time, played an Irish American twenty-three-year-old studio page (and aspiring actor) at the (fictional) International Broadcasting Network (IBN). He lived at home with his parents, former burlesque star Nell Mulligan (an obvious nod to his mother), played by Claire Carlton. Nell met her future husband, Joe (Regis Toomey), a vice cop, during a raid on a burlesque theatre. Pat Harding played Mickey's girlfriend, Carla Balenda, who is a secretary at the studio. Joey Forman plays Freddy Devlin, Mickey's friend and fellow page. (Rooney and Forman proved to be an excellent comedy team. It's easy to see why they became a headlining act in Las Vegas in years to come.)

In one of the early episodes of the series called "The Moon or Bust," Mickey and Freddy are building a rocket in Mickey's parents' garage. Why they are doing this is never made completely clear, but it provides a great premise for some wacky comedy. Mickey tells his mom that he is planning a trip to the moon and, of course, she thinks it is her son's imagination running wild again, or perhaps this is just another one of his acting exercises. The budding astronauts take their rocket out to a park and Mickey christens the space vehicle with a bottle of champagne that breaks the rocket's cone off. (Mickey in a spacesuit is a great sight gag without his doing a thing.) His parents and Mickey's science teacher from high school play along by showing up for the launch. A farmer and his wife see Mickey and Freddy land in a nearby field and when the battered and smoking astronauts emerge from the wreckage, they are convinced they have landed on the moon. The farmer, on the other hand, thinks he is witnessing the landing of a UFO, and he and his wife cower in fear.

Freddy, recovering from the blast and looking around, becomes a little skeptical about the place at which they have arrived being the moon. Mickey, though, is convinced and plants the American flag in the middle of a cow pasture. When a cow wanders by, Mickey thinks it is a moon man disguised as a cow. The would-be space travelers and the frightened farmers approach one another warily. Mickey and, to a lesser extent, Freddy think they are approaching moon people and Mickey speaks space gibberish, which is translated at the bottom of the screen.

Mickey: Where are we?
Farmer: Glendale.
Mickey: (*to Freddy*) I swear I've seen this guy at Sam's Market.

When it becomes clear that they have not landed on the moon he turns to Freddy again and says, "I can't believe I just claimed Glendale for planet Earth!"

The series had many strong episodes and the writers provided Rooney and Forman with some great opportunities at verbal and physical comedy that they took maximum advantage of, but the series was doomed because the critics had a real problem with Rooney playing a much

Twelve. Small Screen, Big Star

younger character again. In many of the reviews critics even thought that he was still playing a teenager, although in one episode it is mentioned that he is a mature twenty-three. While the critical response was mixed at best, the real problem was the stiff competition it was facing. NBC put the show up against the powerhouse *The Jackie Gleason Show*, which dominated that time slot on Sunday evenings. Rooney recalled that Gleason would taunt him on nights when his own show was pre-empted with calls at three in the morning, saying "Hey, Spider, I want you to know that one loyal American watched your show tonight." Then Gleason would cackle and hang up before he could respond. Rooney and Gleason would become good friends and would co-star a few years later in the film version of *Requiem for a Heavyweight* (1962). Gleason once remarked, "If Mickey were six feet tall he would be Sir Laurence Olivier." Gleason may have had high regard for his fellow performer but Rooney did not endear himself with his business partner Maurice Duke or the sponsors of the show. Duke claimed that once things started going south in the ratings and the writing was on the wall for the future of the show, Mickey lost interest in the whole enterprise and began not showing up for work. He also attended a party at the Pillsbury Family estate and got into a spat with the president of the company and stormed off. Despite the silly idea of him playing a needlessly younger character, it was a very funny show and can now be viewed on DVD.

Rooney would have similar luck with his second series, simply called *Mickey*, which was co-created by Arthur Marx—the son of Groucho—who would go on to write a very good biography on Rooney more than twenty years later. The ABC series, which ran during the 1964 season, looked like a winner both in terms of its non-competitive time slot and its premise. Rooney plays a Midwest family man who inherits a waterfront property in Newport Beach, California, and pulls up roots and moves his family out west. Marx recalled in his biography of Rooney that he could be difficult to work with at times, but that he was also a comedy genius who brought all his gifts to the series. Marx remembered an episode that co-starred the very patrician-looking actress Dina Merrill, who is playing a rich heiress trying to seduce Rooney on her yacht. (Merrill was, in real life, an heiress, being the only child of Marjorie Merriweather Post, of Post Cereals.) There is a sequence where she has stolen his clothes and he grabs a short fur coat out of her closet to hide his nakedness. He escapes in a dinghy, wearing only the fur coat. Marx said that, on paper, there wasn't much to the scene, but by the time Rooney finished adding comedy bits, including a confrontation with a police officer, the scene played much better than written. Marx also mentioned that Rooney could give direction as well. In the seduction scene with Merrill she had been fitted with a padded pushup bra and she says, "Mickey, it's such a beautiful, clear moonlit night. You can even see the Big Dipper." He responds, "Where?" She is to turn and point, thereby thrusting her bosom in his face. Merrill didn't understand that the "Big Dipper" line was a double entendre, and the director was too embarrassed to explain it to the regal actress, so Rooney took over. He put his arm around her shoulder and said, "Look, Dina. The idea of the scene is very simple. When you say 'Big Dipper,' you're supposed to shove your clydes in my face!" At which point he buried his nose in her bosom. "By George, I've got it!" she exclaimed with an amused giggle.

Merrill was amazed at her co-star's ability to memorize lines. He told her, "It's easy. I never do a scene the way the writers write it. I just glance down the page and get the gist of it, and make up my own words. I just use the script as a blueprint." The problem with that is that the other actors are relying on the lines in the script for their cues. There would be bigger problems as the series progressed, including getting Rooney to show up for the read-throughs. He always had an excuse for not showing up, usually delivered to the producers by his manager, Bullets Durgan. No matter the reason given for Rooney's absence, the truth was he was always at Santa Anita, betting on the horses. On the rare occasions he *did* show up for a reading of the script, he would just sit in a corner with a copy of the racing form and a transistor radio, listening to the race results. But with all the problems his obsession with the horses created on the set, the biggest obstacle to the success of the series turned out to be the stiff competition again. ABC decided to put *Mickey* up against the acclaimed CBS sitcom *The Dick Van Dyke Show*, and *Mickey* faded quickly out of the gate.

The third and final series was again for NBC, and ran from January to June of 1982. Rooney took this series as a day job; at night he was performing in the sold-out run of *Sugar Babies* on Broadway. The series was called *One of the Boys* and featured some fabulous young actors, including Dana Carvey, Meg Ryan, and Nathan Lane. Rooney plays sixty-six-year-old Oliver Nugent, who decides he wants to go back to college and moves in with his grandson Adam Shields (Carvey) and his roommate, Johnathon Burns (Lane). Tom Shales, in the *Washington Post*, wrote of the premiere episode:

Twelve. Small Screen, Big Star

> Commences now another in the nine lives of Mickey Rooney, who is in phase three of his amazing, daunting career.... He is at his pushily lovable best.... Perhaps Rooney is not universally irresistible; it's just that there is no longer any point in trying to resist him. He's safely in the legend class, and his clowning and camaraderie with Scatman Crothers is extremely appealing. This is a Super Bowl of ham, and a fairly routine comic vehicle is elevated into a rarified plaything, just right for bouncing on the national lap. Experience does count, after all.

Rooney seemed to enjoy doing the sitcom, despite the slim premise. Before a taping would begin, he would take questions from the studio audience. Nathan Lane recalled that someone asked Mickey to do Puck's closing speech from *A Midsummer Night's Dream*. He obliged, delivering a letter-perfect rendition, bringing the audience to its feet at the conclusion. Despite the affection the public obviously had for the veteran actor, the show barely lasted a season.

Rooney may have been more temperamentally suited to be a guest on a sitcom, not the star. One of his most memorable guest spots was on an episode of *The Lucy Show* in early 1966, called "Lucy Meets Mickey Rooney." In the series, Lucy Carmichael (Ball) was the semi-competent secretary to banker Theodore J. Mooney (Gale Gordon). The plot of this particular episode involves Rooney coming into the bank to apply for a loan for an acting school he wants to start. His pitch to Mr. Mooney is that everybody wants to be an actor. Lucy comes in from lunch and spots Rooney and is, as usual, star-struck. Mr. Mooney is receptive to the idea of loaning him the money because he knows he is a hard worker. Rooney's reply to the compliment: "When you've been married as many times as I have you *have* to be a hard worker!"

Both Lucy and Mr. Mooney end up taking Mickey's class and he has them do acting exercises that have them imitating the movements of animals, with Lucy doing a duck walk and Mr. Mooney hopping like a kangaroo, and then all of them walking and crowing like chickens. The highlight of the show is when Mickey and Lucy do a silent movie pantomime, with Lucy dressed as Chaplin's Tramp character, and Mickey as The Kid (played in the 1921 silent classic by Jackie Coogan). Ball is adequate as the great Charlie, but Rooney, a genuine veteran of the silent era, takes his performance to another level. He perfectly captures the movement of both his body and his mouth as he speaks the dialogue silently with his lips moving a mile a minute, and the shrugs and movement of his feet as if he were being photographed at a different speed. (Silent comedies were indeed shot at a slower speed—known as "undercranking"—so the action would appear much faster when projected.) It is an astonishing pantomimic achievement. Maybe that's why, when Ball was asked by Robert Osborne in an interview for TCM who the most talented person in Hollywood was, she said, without hesitation, "Mickey Rooney."

Rooney was also a regular on variety shows during the early days of television. The first big TV hit (in 1948) was *The Texaco Star Theatre* featuring Milton Berle, who was someone right out of vaudeville and burlesque. Television, in its infancy, needed trained performers so they could simply turn on the cameras and broadcast. You didn't need to be very inventive with the camera and it was almost impossible anyway because they were heavy and not very mobile, and technicians had to use a ton of lights just to get an image on the screen. Vaudeville performers were used to coming out, doing their act, and making an exit, and that's what television needed.

In addition to Berle's show, Rooney made countless other appearances on other variety shows, including *The Ed Sullivan Show* (originally known as *Toast of the Town*), *The Hollywood Palace*, and a show he co-hosted with Sammy Davis, Jr., called *NBC Follies*, in 1973. For the debut episode of *The Judy Garland Show* in 1963, Rooney's former MGM partner insisted that he be her first guest. In fact, Rooney would appear on three of the series' twenty-four episodes.

Rooney worked up a comedy skit with Joey Forman that was a takeoff on the hit TV show *Candid Camera*. The show featured a hidden camera that would catch people off guard doing and saying silly things. The setup was that Forman tells the audience that he is from the show and that he is pretending to be a hardware store clerk and will be interviewing people passing by. He tells us that a moose head on a far wall actually contains a camera, and that the fishing rod in front of him is a microphone. Rooney walks by and is very uncooperative. He turns his back to the camera and Forman turns him back around to face it. It's Rooney's reactions to Forman trying to keep him from turning away from the moose and speaking into the fishing rod that are priceless. At one point Rooney goes to pick his nose and Forman pulls his hand down. It's all Rooney's physical shtick in reaction to the setup that makes it a classic routine—one he would do on many shows and in his live act with Forman, and later with Bobby Van.

Rooney also appeared on the September 17, 1967, episode of *The Smothers Brothers Comedy Hour*, not long after the tragic death of his fifth wife. His fellow guests were Bette Davis and the British rock group The Who. Keith Moon, the group's drummer, bribed a stagehand to put some explosives in his drum kit to create a memorable effect. The stagehand cooperated too well, putting *ten times* the amount Moon had expected.

Mickey Rooney gives a taut performance in "Eddie," an Emmy-nominated episode of *Alcoa Theatre* (1958).

When the detonation occurred, Moon was thrown off his drum riser and cymbal shrapnel cut his arm, guitarist Pete Townsend's hair was singed and his ears were ringing, and a camera and studio monitor were destroyed. As for Miss Davis—lead singer Roger Daltrey recalls that the legendary actress was "knocked right on her arse and was thoroughly pissed." Rooney, completely unscathed, apparently immensely enjoyed the ruckus.

But perhaps the most enduring of Rooney's television appearances were on episodic dramas and specials. He worked on most of the major series from the 1950s to the late '90s, everything from *Combat!* to *Wagon Train* to *ER*. One of his greatest dramatic portrayals was a one-man tour de force as "Eddie," an *Alcoa Theatre* presentation in 1958. In this taut drama, a small-time gambler owes $1,000 to a gangster who is on his way to collect his money—or else. The half-hour show consists of Eddie on the phone desperately trying to raise the money to save his life. As the appointed hour approaches, Eddie becomes more and more frantic. The action takes place in one stifling room on a hot summer day, which lends to the claustrophobic feeling of the piece. Jack Smight received an Emmy for his atmospheric direction, as did William Froug for producing, and the writers Alfred Brenner and Ken Hughes. Rooney was nominated, but didn't win. Froug, in his Archives of American Television interview, recalled going to the men's room after the Emmy ceremony and seeing Rooney washing his hands and looking in the mirror and saying, "Fuck 'em. Fuck 'em all." He was understandably disappointed—it was, after all, a one-man show in front of the camera, and everyone *behind* the cameras was picking up awards and he was going home empty-handed—again.

Rooney also appeared in a few episodes of the long-running TV western *Wagon Train*, starring Ward Bond. One episode, "The Greenhorn Story" (1959), was directed by Bretaigne Windust and written by Jean Holloway. Rooney plays Sam Evans, a big-city editor who wants to start his own newspaper out west. Of course, being a greenhorn, he has no idea what a trip across the country in a covered wagon entails. The wagon master, Major Seth Adams (Bond), has a strict list of the things that can be taken on the months-long trek, mostly dictated by the need for the items with an eye toward the overall weight that a member of the wagon train can carry. Evans wants to bring a printing press along, and the major almost goes through the roof.

Rooney is excellent as a man out of his element who ultimately finds a way to adapt to his new, rustic surroundings. One of the better scenes involves a kind of trial run as the wagon master must instruct members of the train to travel in an orderly fashion. Each man is assigned a position in the train, but Evans gets confused and runs into another wagon, causing mass confusion. Later in the program, he earns his spurs when he stops a runaway wagon.

"The Greenhorn Story" was so popular with viewers that the producers of the show brought Rooney back to reprise his role as Sam Evans in "Wagons Ho!" (1960), directed by Hershel Daughty and again written by Jean Holloway. The wagon master and the other members of the crew read the book that Evans wrote about his experiences on his trip cross-country; shown, in flashback, are some of the misadventures of a tinhorn trying to adapt to the ways of the West. The story also tells of Evans meeting his wife-to-be on the train, their marriage, and the birth of their son while on the trail. The scenes of Rooney as a shy bridegroom and an expectant father are perhaps the highlight of the two episodes.

Rooney's greatest triumph during the Golden Age of Television was a *Playhouse 90* drama called *The Comedian*, written by Rod Serling and Ernest Lehman, and directed by John Frankenheimer (who called Rooney "the best actor I've ever worked with"). The pristine kinescope, which was originally broadcast live on February 14, 1957, is now available on DVD through the Criterion Collection. An added bonus to the DVD is a group of interviews with Frankenheimer, Rooney, and co-stars Kim Hunter and Mel Tormé.

The Comedian is a scathing look at the behind-the-scenes turmoil of putting on a weekly live comedy/variety series. Rooney plays Sammy Hogarth, the star of the show, who browbeats everyone around him into submission. His favorite target is his weakling brother Lester (Tormé), whom he keeps around as a gofer and to be the butt of jokes in his weekly monologue. Lester has grown tired of the abuse—or rather his wife, Julie (Hunter), has—and she has threatened to leave him if he doesn't stand up for himself. Al Preston (Edmund O'Brien) is Sammy's dried-up head writer who, in desperation, uses the work of a dead colleague to infuse life into his latest script. Lester finds out about the plagiarism and threatens to take this information to a columnist unless the jokes at his expense are dropped from the monologue. The acting is superb from the entire cast, but it is Rooney who steals the show. His Sammy Hogarth is a despicable human being, but a recognizable one.

Sammy is always looking into the mirror in his dressing room. He has a mammoth ego and worries about getting older. There is a sense that Sammy looks on the weekly broadcast as similar to preparing for a championship fight. There is even a scene where he is stripped to the waist and shadow boxing. Rooney doesn't speak his lines; he bellows them. He must invade the space of his subordinates in order to be recognized as someone of stature. Everything about Sammy is excessive. His laughter is a wide-open-mouthed guffaw, an angry one. When he eats, he stuffs spaghetti down his kisser like a condemned man having his last meal. He devours everything and everyone around him.

Director Frankenheimer reminisced about working with the talented, if unpredictable, Mickey Rooney: "the problem during two and a half weeks of rehearsal was to keep Mickey Rooney from changing the performance he came in with. He would change it every day. We would have a different performance. It was absolutely incredible to see. And he would start improvising the script and I wouldn't know what he was saying." Tormé mentioned in his interview that while everyone in the cast began rehearsals with simple line readings, Rooney "gave a full-blown performance every time we rehearsed the material."

His energy and improvising caused some concern for the director. "I recall one day going up to Mickey and saying, 'These lines are not in the script.'" Frankenheimer then did an impression of Rooney saying, "Listen Johnny Boy, the only guy you do line for line is ol' Billy Shakespeare." Frankenheimer responded, "'Well, Mickey, I'm just a stupid SOB because I got written at the end of this line in the script, 'close-up Mickey Rooney.' *See it*? Unless you say this line, there ain't gonna be no closeup of Mickey Rooney.' He was letter-perfect from then on, absolutely letter-perfect."

Rooney had always been known for the incredible amount of energy he put into his performances, but in this live telecast he is on overdrive. Frankenheimer pointed out that there was a practical reason for the accelerated pace. The show was running two minutes long and Rooney was trying to help the director out. Frankenheimer shakes his head in wonderment, saying that Rooney had picked up three minutes in the first act and now they were one minute short; Frankenheimer relayed this information to Rooney, who obligingly slowed it down, and they finished right on time.

There is a point in the program when Lester, who has been thwarted in his plan, wanders onto the live broadcast of the show-within-the-show to confront Sammy on camera. Sammy ad-libs as long as he can before

Twelve. Small Screen, Big Star

he picks Lester up and throws him over his shoulder, then runs off stage carrying him until he can throw him down and begin to pummel him. All of this is done on live TV, with no breaks, no doubles, no stuntmen. "It was working without a net," Rooney remembered. "Once the show started, you were live all the way. What went wrong went wrong." Frankenheimer worked with six cameras, and he had his shots so carefully planned that you never would have thought it was all happening in real time.

Rooney makes the monster that is Sammy human with little gestures and looks. Sammy gives Lester an anniversary present and is noticeably ill at ease doing so. He is awkward doing something nice for his brother, and we see in Rooney's face a kind of sadness that this little gesture is so painful for him. When O'Brien tells him off by speaking the truth that Sammy's hunger is for something he will never have—love—we see the pain and hurt on Rooney's face even as he is screaming at O'Brien. In the final scene, after the show is over and the set has been stripped to an empty sound stage, Sammy spots Lester and his wife comforting each other. Sammy looks on in silence and envy for a moment before yelling for Lester to come to his dressing room. Lester slowly and reluctantly moves away from his wife as she reaches out for him, but it's no use. Sammy's hold on his brother is too strong. Sammy wins again, but he will never be happy.

In the interviews, we learn that Rooney got feedback on his performance the very night it aired. "After I had gotten home and gotten several calls from friends and then I received a telegram ... a telegram I still have today and it is framed, and the telegram was from Santa Barbara, California, and it just simply said, 'Thank you for the acting lesson—Paul Muni.'" Muni was an acting god to performers of Rooney's generation.

The same year Rooney did *Mr. Broadway* (1957), a musical TV special directed by Sidney Lumet, in which Mickey portrays George M. Cohan, the role for which James Cagney won his Oscar in 1942.

A few years later Rooney guest-starred on the hit ABC show *The Naked City* (1961). This hidden gem of a program is called "Ooftus Goofus"; it was directed by Arthur Hiller, who would later gain fame as the director of *Love Story* (1970). Howard Rodman and Jo Pagano wrote the teleplay, and the series starred Paul Burke and Horace McMahon as the lead detectives in a New York City precinct. Lawrence Dobkin does the narration that sets up the story. George Bick (Rooney) is a lonely and frustrated forty-year-old man who, in many ways, has never grown up. He plays pranks on local people and businesses as a way to protest his

Two talented men at the peak of their powers: Mickey Rooney (left) and James Cagney (right), c. 1941.

invisibility. The story opens with George walking down the street in the early morning hours, stopping to pet a cat. The narrator intones,

"Young George Bick worked at twelve in his father's grocery store. He took it for granted that he would grow up, but he didn't." It is suggested that, by growing up, it is meant that he would grow taller. The narrator

Twelve. Small Screen, Big Star

goes on to list George's failures before observing: "A man who has not been heard has not been born."

George still works at the grocery store and is angry at the world for his lack of advancement. He plays pranks, like changing all the price tags on the products in the store to much lower ones, causing a stampede of customers looking for a deal, as George stands by and giggles. The NYC detectives show up to quell the commotion and deduce that it is a child's prank. Once they restore order, they figure that's the end of it. George follows up his pranks with letters to the newspapers, using the pen name Ooftus Goofus to air his grievances. Next George stink-bombs a movie theatre because he is angry that they are showing a movie featuring a handsome star on whom his wife has a crush. His letter to the editor laments that he could never compete with a movie star.

The wonderful Maureen Stapleton plays George's wife. George feels that she drinks too much, so he breaks into the neighborhood bar and puts weak tea into their whiskey bottles. He then writes a letter complaining about bartenders serving women who should be home with their husbands. We get a glimpse of George's life when he comes home to an empty apartment and gets busy doing the cleaning. As he is writing his latest missive to the newspaper, he stares into a mirror. His image talks to him and encourages him to write the letter and suggests words to reflect the bitterness he feels for his lot in life. George tells his alter ego, "I'm so lonely."

A short time later we meet Abby arriving in a cab with a load of packages. She meets George, who has been waiting for her, and is asleep on the front steps of their apartment building. She has been out on a shopping spree and talks nonstop, but not to her husband, who is trying to get a word, any word, in edgewise. He mutters complaints about her spending too much and never being home. He gets a bottle of beer and wants to sit down and talk and just share a beer together, but she is too tired and falls into bed fully dressed and falls asleep, leaving George alone again. Abby works in a beauty shop and it's all she talks about. In an act of revenge, George sabotages the hair dryers at the salon, and a woman is badly injured. George's pranks have gone from mischievous to dangerous, and the detectives now have a crime to solve.

Rooney's performance as George is truly astonishing because it is so far from who he is off screen. He conveys loneliness—and even shyness— with utter conviction. There is a scene in the back room of the grocery store, for example, where the workers are having lunch. George sits, alone, away from the group. He is reading a magazine and is telling his co-workers what's in the article, but no one is listening. The man's sense of isolation is heartrending.

The story climaxes when George emerges from a cab wearing a suit of armor and carrying what looks like a bomb into a boxing arena. Spectators step aside as he goes through the arena and enters the ring. He grabs the microphone and sets the bomb down. He pulls up the plunger on the bomb and tells the crowd that he will detonate the explosive if his wife isn't summoned to the arena so he can talk to her. The police detectives arrive and ask for his wife's name and address so that they can go get her. The cops also attempt to reason with George to stop this craziness before anyone gets hurt. The shrewish Abby arrives and immediately assails George for his foolishness. Although he pleads with her to just listen to what he has to say for a few minutes, she refuses and tells him she doesn't care what happens to him and rushes out of the arena. George begins to weep and, completely defeated, pushes down on the bomb's plunger. Nothing happens. The bomb is a fake. The detectives rush over to him and begin patting his sweaty brow, as though we were a boxer and they were his corner men.

A little-remembered Rooney television movie (upstaged, no doubt, by *Bill*, which aired the same year), is *Leave 'Em Laughing* (1981). This was a Charles Fries Production, directed by Jackie Cooper, one of Rooney's contemporaries from the studio era. The script is by Cynthia Mandlelberg and Peggy Chantler Dick, and is based on the real-life story of Jack Thum, a professional clown. He and his wife, Shirlee, fostered thirty-seven children over a thirty-one-year period.

The movie opens with Thum performing at the children's ward of a Chicago hospital. One of the doctors, who we later learn is his personal physician, looks on and laughs along with the kids. Thum begins to cough during his routine, and the doctor looks concerned. The clown goes back to a large closet that serves as his dressing room, where he begins removing his makeup. The doctor wants to see him for a checkup, but Thum claims to be too busy just then.

He is still coughing as he climbs the stairs to his apartment and has to stop and catch his breath. He goes into his apartment and is greeted by his wife, Shirlee (Anne Jackson), and an apartment full of foster children. As soon as he settles into his chair, he lights up a cigarette, begins to complain that his work is drying up, and blames it on TV, saying it has ruined kids. He then adds, "Maybe I'm just not funny anymore."

Cooper has surrounded Rooney with many other great character actors, like Allen Garfield as Thum's physician Dr. Abrahms, and Elisha Cook, Jr., as Jetter, a bartender who is a retired clown and a friend of Thum's. William Windom, who was a fixture in American films and television for half a century, plays the successful clown Smiley Jenkins. Mickey manages to shine through because, for one of the few times in his later career, the project is built around his performance.

When Thum gets the news from his doctor that he is dying, he tries to process his feelings. He slowly arrives at the realization that he will have to go in for surgery and that he won't be able to work for two months. He tells his doctor that he *has* to keep working; he is a freelance performer, after all. In an attempt to find work, Thum begins to make calls to everyone he knows so that he can have some money set aside when he is hospitalized. He becomes angrier and angrier as everyone tells him that they just don't have any work for him at the time. He finally storms out of the house, causing Shirlee to wonder what is wrong. He goes to see Jenkins, who is the last of his old buddies to still be in the Big Time. We suspect that Thum is there to borrow money, but he can't bring himself to ask. He heads over to the bar to talk to Jetter. It is nearly closing time and Thum convinces his pal to tie one on with him. They get more and more inebriated as they talk about old times.

When Shirlee shows up, she shakes her head at the spectacle before her. She takes the bartender aside and asks what is troubling her husband. He refuses to tell her at first and then trembles as he finally admits, "Your old man has a bad lung. The doctor wants to take it out." (Everyone is wonderful in the scene, but Rooney's vulnerability in his sad drunken state is nothing short of magnificent.)

Thum doesn't have health insurance, but his care at the hospital is taken care of because he donated thirty years of performances for the children's ward. His older foster kids get jobs to help out. He continues to entertain the kids during his own hospital stay and there is a great scene when Shirlee is applying his makeup for him. (Jackson and Rooney have a wonderful, easy rapport in their roles.)

After Jack undergoes surgery, it is revealed that the situation is terminal; he has only six to twelve months to live. Naturally depressed, he tells Shirlee, "Lying here thinking about my life. It's all been pointless."

Shirlee goes to Jetter with her concerns and they decide to contact all the kids that the Thums have fostered throughout the years. Dozens of people show up at their small apartment to tell Jack how much they care about him. There are grown foster kids with their own children. Jack realizes that his life *has* had some purpose.

John J. O'Connor, in the *New York Times*, wrote:

> "Leave 'em Laughing" is that old-fashioned theatrical commodity: a vehicle for a star. The chief product is a bravura performance surrounded by a good deal of capable but not distracting support. In this instance, the star is Mickey Rooney and, despite some uneven moments, he delivers the emotional goods.

Another great characterization for TV occurred in an episode of *The Dick Powell Show* for NBC, on November 7, 1961. This program, directed by Arthur Hiller, was called "Somebody's Waiting." It was written by Adrian Spies and co-starred Susan Oliver, Tige Andrews, Warren Oates, and—in a minor role—future director Paul Mazursky. The story is about a lonely merchant seaman named Augie Miller (Rooney), who tries too hard to make friends, thereby pushing people away. Miller and a group of merchant seamen have just arrived in San Pedro, California, and go to a local bar. Miller, as usual, is trying to be the life of the party. He runs afoul of two young punks who try to sell the seamen a bottle of booze. He starts yelling at the punks for overcharging his buddies for the bottle. His friends don't like this because they already agreed on a price, and the hoods become angry at Augie for screwing up the deal. Everybody heads their separate ways, with Miller going to see some relatives who live nearby. It turns out that the relatives can't stand him either, and as soon as he arrives they have to leave for a "prior engagement." Carla (Oliver), a lonely young blonde woman from next door, has witnessed the encounter from her window. A sympathetic individual, she introduces herself and listens to his sad life story. Carla invites him over to her house to meet her mom, with whom she lives. He notices all their books and tells them he belongs to the Book of the Month Club.

The young punks find out where Miller's relatives live and show up in the neighborhood, looking for him. Meanwhile, Miller and Carla are taking a stroll in a park, observing the families gathered there. Carla actually enjoys Augie's one-sided conversation, which is a new experience for him. She is very shy and likes the fact that she doesn't have to talk much with him around. He continues to talk about himself in the third person, about a guy who presses too much, and she does the same thing by telling about a girl she knows who had an affair with a married man at her workplace. Carla and her mom invite him to stay for dinner. He accepts the invitation, but insists on going out and purchasing a bottle of wine for the occasion.

The punks spot Miller heading for the liquor store and corner him in an alley, where they beat him mercilessly; he is stabbed with a knife and left for dead. A little boy finds the bleeding man and Miller tells him to go get help. The kid just stares at him. Finally, he pleads with the boy: "I don't want to die. Somebody's waiting!"

Carla is indeed waiting for him and he has been gone a long time. Carla's mother tells her she shouldn't have told him about the mess with the married man—maybe she scared him off. His friends are walking along the street and begin to feel bad about having given their friend the brush-off. They walk by the alley where he is lying but don't see him. Miller thinks he saw his friends but then realizes they would never have come back for him. Carla shows up and cradles him in her arms after calling for help. His fellow seamen show up as the ambulance arrives.

Rooney received an Emmy nomination for *Somebody's Waiting* and, not unlike the situation with *Leave 'em Laughing* and *Bill*, the performances were so close together on the broadcast schedule that one of the performances—in this case the *Naked City* episode—got overlooked.

Another fine, albeit completely different, Rooney performance could be seen on an episode of *Kraft Suspense Theatre*, called "The Hunt" (1963). Robert Altman co-wrote the story and began directing the episode but was

Mickey Rooney was nominated for an Emmy for his portrayal of the lonely merchant seaman Augie Miller in an episode of *The Dick Powell Show* called "Somebody's Waiting" (1961).

told that he had to recast the role of Rick Peterson, a black character, with a white actor. Altman became angry and quit, saying that *Kraft Suspense Theatre* was "as bland as their cheese."

Peterson (now played by James Caan) is a surfer bum who wanders into a small Southern town when his car breaks down. Sheriff Williams (Rooney) is a redneck, power-hungry bastard who runs his town like a little fiefdom. He puts anybody in jail that he doesn't like then sets them up to be hunted by letting them get out so he can run them down with his dogs and kill them. It is clear that Altman wanted the story to be about racism. For Rooney's part, he has the Southern accent down and he is completely believable as a ruthless, conniving megalomaniacal lawman. Bruce Dern, who seemed to make a career out of playing loathsome characters, portrays one of the sheriff's deputies. If the episode had been given the context Altman intended, it would have made a much greater impact and Rooney's completely believable performance as the menacing sheriff would have received much more attention.

Despite his success in television dramas, Rooney clearly wanted to be back up on the big screen. TV work, it seemed, was just his way of making his alimony payments. Once someone has been a motion picture star, particularly in the Golden Age of Hollywood, everything else seems inferior. This is indicated by the short shrift he gives his television performances in his memoirs. *Leave 'Em Laughing*, for instance, rates only three lines in his autobiography; "Ooftus Goofus" and "Somebody's Waiting" are not mentioned at all.

Of course, one portrayal that Mickey Rooney essayed on the small screen—that of the mentally challenged real-life individual Bill Sackter—is a modern-day classic which deserves a chapter of its own.

CHAPTER THIRTEEN

Bill

> Special thanks to Mickey Rooney. He said, "Kid, when the time comes to deliver, I'll deliver," and he sure did.
> —writer Corey Blechman, from his Emmy acceptance speech for his original screenplay, *Bill*, 1982

When an aging actor is fortunate enough to experience a resurgence, one of the happy side effects is that he is suddenly being offered better scripts. One script to reach Mickey's agent was entitled "Bill." Written by first-time writer Corey Blechman, who was being mentored by Alan Landsberg, the head of a large production company, "Bill" is the sensitive true story of an intellectually challenged adult named Bill Sackter. Since the age of seven, Sackter has been living in a dreary institution, where he had been placed by his parents. Now in his sixties, Sackter makes the difficult, yet ultimately rewarding, challenge of transitioning into society. He is taken in by a kind couple, filmmaker Barry Morrow and his wife, Bev. (In writing about *Bill*, the author was fortunate to secure interviews with Corey Blechman and Rob Morrow; their quotes herein are exclusive to this book.)

After completing the treatment, Blechman traveled to Iowa to meet with Sackter and the Morrows. Barry Morrow was intimately aware of Sackter's endearing way of communicating; he had recorded hours of his conversations for a documentary he made about this exceptional human being. Once they approved the script, the CBS network greenlit the project as a prime-time two-hour TV-movie, an extremely popular genre in the late '70s and early '80s. Mel Stuart, of Landsburg Productions, was assigned to produce the teleplay.

When tossing out names of sixty-something actors, Jackie Gleason was suggested. (Gleason had starred as a slow-witted deaf-mute in the 1962 film *Gigot*.) Apparently, the Great One was either unavailable or uninterested, which prompted someone to mention Mickey Rooney, who was then starring on Broadway in *Sugar Babies*. Rooney liked the script and expressed interest in the project, but giving eight live performances a week left him little time to essay the role. The producers, realizing he would be the ideal actor for their film, promised to build the production around Rooney's busy schedule. He agreed.

Not unlike Gleason, Rooney hated to rehearse; in addition, his time constraints prevented his having more than one read-through before shooting commenced. The read-through would be held on a Friday, with production to begin the following Monday. As writer Blechman explained to this author:

> Mickey came in and he sat in a room full of people, executives from CBS, [British TV and film director] Anthony Page, of course, Mel Stuart, Alan Landsburg I'm sure was there, and I was there. I didn't say a word, as it was Anthony Page's ballgame at this point. But, you probably know these stories. No one was happy.... It was just not … these creative endeavors are fraught with personality conflicts and egos, and who does what. Creative issues. So there was not a lot of happiness at the read-through. We read it through and, as I said, Anthony was in charge, and he was doing the best he could to keep everyone in the same boat.

Rooney, of course, was a notorious ad-libber, paying little attention to any writer's actual dialogue (unless, of course, that writer was the Bard of Avon himself). Although one might assume that such a role would benefit from Rooney's verbal imagination, Blechman disagreed. "Bear in mind that there was a real Bill Sackter. Was Bill in New York? I don't think so, but Barry was certainly in New York off and on during the week leading up to the production. Bill was back in Iowa. So there was a real Bill and people had met him and so in that situation, for better or worse, there is a template, there is the person himself, like a historical figure, like someone alive, like someone who is a celebrity."

Although there was logic in this statement, it remained a fact that the public at large was unaware of how Sackter spoke.

"Good point," agreed Blechman,

> Exactly … And Bill has all kinds of communication problems himself, yes, exactly… In any case, there were not a lot of people happy through the weekend. Monday morning the production started. So Monday morning there was a huge crisis on the set. I think it started with the executives at CBS saying, "Boy oh boy, I don't know what we got here." That's how it started, and then it came down to Anthony, and then Mel, who was the producer. Then I got an emergency phone call that they were sending a limo for me and I was on my way out of town, I was

Thirteen. Bill

heading back to L.A. Usually they just as soon get writers out of the picture (no pun intended) because [the director, technicians, and actors] are going to do the "serious" work of making a film. So I went out and I stood in the back and, you know, Mickey was … he was working his way toward the performance. He was working intuitively. He was working from the inside out. And that was his genius. There was a ton of pressure and finally they said to me, "We want you to sit in a room with Mickey and tell him what you think" (laughs). And so they set that up. I found myself in a room and they brought in Mickey. He was hugely unhappy. He didn't like all the pressure and thought it was way out of proportion. We sat there a little bit and he wanted to know what my credentials were and what I had written and how long I had been in the film business, that kind of stuff. I didn't have anything to tell him, other than I told him what I felt. I told him that he needed to pay more attention to the real Bill. I told him that there were big, big problems in interpretation at this point. The *real* Bill, even though he was not a person that most people would know, was charming in his ability to talk with you. He had that kind of singsong, kind of up and down—he would repeat things, he would meet your gaze and then he would kind of look away, and he was charming. He had wonderful little sayings he would say.

Everybody started to pay a lot more attention … give Mickey a lot of credit. The first afternoon Mickey came over and sat with me a little bit and we'd chat some more and Anthony is doing his thing, and holding everything together. Then they decided the first day of production. Productions are expensive, everyone is making money and they decided to throw out the first day and start over on the second day, and Mickey started rising to the challenge. He was a great, great actor!

Barry Morrow recalls the early stages of the project with less nostalgia. An Oscar recipient for co-writing the screenplay for *Rain Man* (featuring the memorable character Raymond Babbitt, based on an autistic savant Morrow met named Kim Peek), Morrow knew ahead of time the problems he would face in getting the television movie produced.

Fred [Landsberg] called and said, "You know, we need to get a screenwriter," he said. I wasn't a screenwriter and they told me they found a writer and he was going to be coming to interview us, and then they called and said he wasn't because he had cancer and died. A lot of time went by because of some additional problems with preproduction. When it came time to sign this contract with the production company, I had never seen a contract like this where they have rights to your life story in perpetuity. I said, "This is all well and good but where does it say in here that you're not going to make fools of Bill or me or any of the people that I love who would be in the story?" They said, "What do you mean?" and I said just what I said, "Where are our protections for our portrayal?" They said, "It's not customary to have these things in the contract, don't you trust us?" I said, "I would like to trust you, and I'm willing to trust you with your portrayal of me or my friends or anyone else involved because I could talk to them and I'm sure they'll say yes, but I can't let you do whatever you want with Bill, because I care for him." I was his conservator. So I have to have something in the language that protects him, and they basically said that was a deal breaker. They said they've never done this before and won't do it now and so, thank you, and goodbye.

Several months later they called back and asked if I had changed my mind and I said no; in fact, Bill and I were just getting ready to start our own documentary. And they said, "Look, we'll put the language in," and offered [us] less money. So, in other words, I had to buy insurance. Bill and I ended up getting, for the rights to our life stories, $12,500. Then I got $5,000 for the story. It turned out that Bill couldn't even get his money because it threatened his receiving his Medicaid. Bill didn't care about anything like that, though. It wasn't a lot of money, obviously. It was, like, peanuts. But it was all about doing the story right, getting Bill [portrayed] right. I'll never forget the day when I heard that they picked Mickey Rooney to play the part of Bill. I picked Bill up at work and on the way home I told him the news and I'll bet you out of a thousand actors' names, Bill would have only known Mickey Rooney. Because, you know, in the institution, they showed his films to the patients.

Here we go into the drama of making this movie. They didn't seem to want me around. They were shooting in Yonkers, New York. Prior to that they asked me what materials I could send them about Bill, so Mickey could look at it. I sent them big chunks of a documentary film, I sent them Bill's audio tapes, I sent them everything I could and packaged it up as professionally as I could afford to do. Then they told me Mickey wouldn't look at it. So when I went to New York I was hoping, somehow, because I brought more material with me in my suitcase in a condensed version, that I could have a minute or two with Mickey to talk to him about Bill, to tell him what he was about. I was told that Mickey didn't want to do that. I don't know if that's true or not, but that's what I was told. I was invited to come to one of the readings, one of the rehearsals, and Mickey blew in a little bit late. Anthony Page, the director, begins the rehearsal. Mickey won't sit down; he's got to be moving. I was kind of in the back, just observing, like a fly on the wall. Mickey starts doing a scene from the movie and he sounded like this [imitates a twisted voice]; he was simultaneously using spastic movements with his hands and wrists. I've been around people with disabilities for forty-some years and Mickey was throwing all the spaghetti at the wall. He had cerebral palsy, he had a lisp, he had a twitch, his jaw was set to the side, his eyes rolling around, I'm telling you, it was just short of Quasimodo.

Anthony says, "Ah, Mickey"—he's a fairly effete Brit—"Mickey, uh, can we ..." and then they would talk a little bit. Meanwhile, Anthony Page is sort of glancing at me then eventually there is a little break and he takes me out in the hallway and says, "Barry, I saw the blood drain from your face." And he proceeds to reassure me that this is what actors do. It's clay, he's molding and shaping and, believe me, when we start shooting on Wednesday, "everything will be fine." I went back to my hotel, just sick to my stomach. I just prayed that everything would be fine. I saw the dailies from the first day of shooting and I saw Mickey lurching down the sidewalk in the dark, which is still the opening scene in the movie. It was one of the few things they were able to save. It was shot at night, and he looks drunk. You kind of think, here's the beginning of the movie and this guy is staggering down

Thirteen. Bill

the street, he looks drunk, you think this Bill must be an alcoholic—at least that's how *I* saw it. It was just raw footage too, there's no music, words, and then I see a few more scenes. The next day I took my briefcase that I only brought because I wanted to look like I was a grown-up. I didn't have anything in it except for this little four-page contract. There was some language in that contract that I insisted they put in there to protect Bill against ridicule and humiliation. I set the bar pretty high. I felt that Mickey had cleared it easily. I called my wife and she wanted to know how things were going, and I told her it's not going very well. So I took a cab to CBS headquarters. In those days you could just walk into one of these skyscrapers and take an elevator to the top floor, which is what I did. So I just walked into one of the offices and there was an executive there by a desk and I introduced myself. He said, "Oh, yes we're shooting that right now." I told him the problem I was having with it and told him that I have a contract here that I think has been breached. He looked at it and made a copy. The executive said that he would contact me at the hotel where I was staying. The next thing I know they've shut down the production. The executives from Hollywood are flying back to New York. Then there is all this drama. I can feel it, I can hear certain things, but they're not telling me what is going on. Then Corey [Blechman] and I met and he told me that they had put him in a room with Mickey to talk to him—which is like throwing a Christian to the lion. Corey didn't have a prayer. Mickey is a very sweet guy, but....

And here Morrow made a stunning admission: "I'll be honest with you. I don't think Anthony Page got the performance; I think Mickey Rooney got the performance out of desperation." He continues:

I think most of us working in the arts work best when there is a little fear behind it. We had to shut the whole thing down. The production company for two or three days on a twenty-one-day shoot, the margin of profit is in, can you bring it in on time or a day ahead? When you lose three days it almost becomes a losing proposition economically.

Well, I went back to the set. All I can say is that Mickey was given an ultimatum to either reinvent this or we're not going to do it. Mickey was on Broadway then doing *Sugar Babies* and all that, so it wasn't like he didn't have a gig, but he needed this. He may have come back and said, "I'm going to give them the least I can give them." Maybe that was part of it. You gotta believe, I mean, you have to agree that there is something about this performance that is different from anything else he'd done before. I think this hurt him because he never had anybody tell him before that we will kill this picture rather than accommodate you, Mister Biggest Star in the World for Three Years. I think something ... and then it could've been, too, that someone asked me for the book of photos of Bill and I gave it to them, and I always assumed they showed them to Mickey or he asked for it, but it didn't have any spoken words by Bill, or anything else.

Mickey, more than any other actor, was able to maintain that connection to his childhood. It probably hurt him in his personal life, but as an actor, that sparks ... it's the physicality of it. The fact that the way he moves, the way he sits, it's like a child. You've got to have a special connection to that inner child that most people lose that he somehow hung on to. I guess you could say he never went through the maturation process.

Here's what I love to say about … to summarize it. It was very painful to go through it. I was terrified that I was going to go back home and this movie is going to come out and everybody is going to say, "Barry, you sold Bill right down the river." Everybody assumed I was going to get rich on this thing. So I had to drop the hammer and they then dropped it on Mickey.

I went back for one more day of shooting. He went into a kind of rant that was directed at me, but he wasn't looking at me. It was about "I don't do impersonations, I do interpretations." He was angry, he hated me, and he was ticked off at me, at Corey, the whole production. It's like, *he's* Mickey Rooney and I'm there trying to tell *him* how to do something. When I went to rehearsal one day he marched into the room and the director, Anthony Page, tried to talk to him about the scene or something and he said, "I don't need to know. Where's my mark?" That's *all* he wanted to know. He just comes in and stands where the tape is on the floor and he's ready to go. He was in the scene, I could tell, and he was just going to wing it. They did a few takes and then there was a break and then he kind of looked at the script and he kind of cobbled it together. The thing is, all an actor needs out of fifteen to twenty takes is one good one. Mickey wouldn't give you the same thing with nuance; he was giving you completely different things. Then the editors had to really kind of scramble to find continuity for the character and what the best take and scene was. You could tell sometimes that there is, you know, greater relief in his role than with a lot of other actors. Essentially when he absolutely nails those moments in *Bill*. There are some that are just so resonant you wonder where that came from.

Remarkably enough, Morrow's candor about his unhappiness with Rooney's initial "interpretation" may have been the catalyst to the veteran actor giving one of his most acclaimed performances. If that is the case, Morrow isn't one to take credit for it.

It was something totally inadvertent on my part. I was protecting my own honor by protecting Bill's. Here's the crazy thing. Mickey is right! He didn't do an impersonation of Bill. What he did was, once he got rid of all the gimmicks, then that kid [inside him], that child was naked right in front of us. I have to tell you, as hard as some of the movie was for some of us to watch because it was so far from what the reality was, there are moments in that movie where I, to this day, because I've seen it so many times, where I can't speak, I … I … it's just so emotional. It's not Bill, it's something else. It's not even Mickey Rooney.

Is there any particular scene that stands out in Morrow's mind?

One of my favorite scenes is when he is trying to call Barry [played by Dennis Quaid]. He can't communicate with the operator and he's trying to remember the phone number, you can see the pain on his face, he can't remember the numbers and when he's defeated and can't complete the call, he hangs up the phone and his entire body sags. I mean, you can't teach that.

Thirteen. Bill

There is a scene early in the movie when Morrow, who is doing a documentary on the real-life story of Sackter, a mentally handicapped man who was warehoused with schizophrenics and people with every manner of mental impairment for forty-six years, has foolishly taken him back to Granville to see how he would react. When Barry goes on a tour of the institution he leaves Bill with one of the patients he remembers from his decades there. Bill soon misses Barry and wanders off to try and find him. Barry becomes concerned when he comes back and finds him missing. He eventually locates Bill hiding in a corner and comforts him. Bill is frightened out of his wits and rushes back to Barry's car. On the drive home Bill is sure he sees his sister, Sara, walking down the street and forces Barry to stop the car. Bill gets out and approaches the woman, who runs away from him. Bill follows her, calling "Sara! Sara!" He finally catches up to her and she tells him she is *not* Sara, that her name is Ida. The look of terror on Rooney's (Bill's) face is reminiscent, in its total anguish, of Munch's *The Scream*. People talk about the actor's mask; nowhere has it been more compelling than in that scene.

One of the most remarkable things about Mickey Rooney was how he was able to maintain an almost childlike emotional connection to performing. Film critic Thomson called it an almost "psychic identification with fantasy." Nowhere is this childlike sensibility more evident than in his performance as Sackter. He plays the character as if he is a child with very adult problems. We see this quality in the way he moves, walks, sits, and talks. There is a scene of Bill sitting on the floor with Barry's young son, Clay, playing with a toy. Bill's posture is that of a kid, with short legs out-

For what may be the greatest performance of his ninety-one-year career, Rooney won an Emmy and a Golden Globe (and the hearts of the television-viewing audience) for his sympathetic portrayal of the mentally challenged man Bill Sackter, in *Bill* (1981) (courtesy of Lane Wyrick).

stretched on the floor. He pulls the string on the talking toy and bends toward Clay so they can both hear the message.

But Bill is not a child. He is an adult with severe limitations. When Barry and his wife have to move away to take another job, leaving Bill essentially where they found him, he is alone again. Bill walks with a limp because he has an ulcerated leg that was not taken care of at Granville. His gait is slow and then quickens like a kid who doesn't quite know what he wants to do—and then suddenly remembers. He is hesitant when he speaks, so self-conscious is he about his lack of communication skills. But his words pour out quickly when he gets excited and feels secure with the person to whom he is talking. Rooney used all the skills he had acquired as an actor to, in essence, play a child.

Anthony Page was at the helm of *Bill*. Page's background had been largely in the theatre, but here he directs Rooney to a marvelously restrained performance that does justice to the real-life story of Sackter. The film made its debut on the CBS television network on December 22,

Mickey Rooney is pictured in costume on the set of *Bill: On His Own* (1983), with writer Barry Morrow (right, facing Rooney) and the real Bill Sackter (left). Sackter died the year the sequel aired. This was also the year Rooney received his honorary Academy Award (courtesy of Lane Wyrick).

Thirteen. Bill

1981, to instant acclaim. Mickey Rooney deservedly won an Emmy and a Golden Globe for this, the greatest performance of his career. He went on to receive another Emmy nomination for the sequel, *Bill: On His Own* (1983).

In his interview for The Archives of American Television, he is asked to speak about his work in *Bill*, but he finds it difficult. Beyond giving the outline of the story and saying that he played the role "to the best of my ability," he is reluctant to talk about the issue of institutionalizing the mentally handicapped, just saying, "He was an impaired man. How do you talk about that?" It's as if Rooney felt sorry for the real Bill Sackter and didn't want to tarnish his memory (Bill died in 1983) by discussing him. He was a completely instinctive actor. It is highly doubtful that he did much analyzing of his work either before or after a performance. He just did it without thinking about it and, for him, that approach worked magnificently. About Bill, he complained that everyone was telling him how to play the part of a mentally challenged man, but "I told them to shut up"—he pounds his chest, indicating his heart—"I'll do it from *here*." When he was asked by the Archives of American TV site to talk about his role as Bill, he was all but inarticulate. But, unlike actors who can expound on the techniques attributed to Stanislavski and never make an impact on the public, Mickey Rooney delivered the goods time and time again.

Chapter Fourteen

The Long Exit

> Mickey was a working guy. If he wasn't working, he wasn't happy.
> —Tim Farley

The 1980s was a time when seeing screen icons from the Golden Age of Hollywood on television was a common experience—and not just on *The Late, Late Show*. Often sporting face lifts, capped teeth, and sometimes unconvincing hairpieces, these former stars showed their generation of fans that they still had what it takes. Elizabeth Taylor, Bette Davis, Fred Astaire, James Stewart, Loretta Young, James Cagney, and Katharine Hepburn starred in TV-movies. Jane Wyman, Lana Turner, Ava Gardner, Howard Duff, Barbara Bell Geddes, Donna Reed, Charlton Heston, Barbara Stanwyck, Joan Collins, John Forsythe, and Rock Hudson acted on nighttime soap operas. And just about every contract player—from Jane Powell to Lassie—guest starred, at one time or another, on Aaron Spelling's Saturday night guilty pleasures, *Love Boat* and *Fantasy Island*. The producers, writers, and make-up artists did their best to present these beloved former stars to their aging demographic in the most favorable light. For the first time in decades, it didn't seem to hurt an actor's chances of being hired if they were over sixty (or even seventy) and had films like *National Velvet* or *King's Row* on their résumés. One such former actor, Ronald Reagan, was even the leader of the Free World, reminiscing on a daily basis with his personal barber about his days as a contract player for Warner Brothers. During his first term as president, he invited the number-one star from 1939, '40, and '41 and his eighth wife to dinner at the White House.

"Damn it!" Mickey responded. "It's always when I'm working, but thank goodness that I am."

President Reagan replied:

Fourteen. The Long Exit

May 31, 1985
Mr. and Mrs. Mickey Rooney
Hollywood, California

Dear Jan and Mickey,

Sorry you can't make it June 12th but you have an ongoing rain check. While we'll miss you we're happy you are working 'cause that means pleasure for a lot of people. Mickey, I'll bet you don't remember the first time we met. The year was 1937 or thereabouts. I was new in Hollywood living in the Montecito apartments. Someone had run over a dog in the street outside. You came in to look for a phone book so you could find the nearest veterinarian and take the dog to him. I figured this had to be a nice guy and I was right.

Nancy sends her best, and so do I.

Sincerely,
Ronald Reagan

Live theatrical shows also catered to the Greatest Generation, featuring tried-and-true musicals with recognizable names from a better time. Rooney could be seen in the Kern-Hammerstein musical extravaganza *Show Boat* (in which he played Captain Andy, gently encouraging his daughter to sing "After the Ball" to a group of unruly patrons), Neil Simon's *The Odd Couple* (for which he essayed the role of Oscar Madison opposite the future Felix Unger of TV fame, Tony Randall), and *The Sunshine Boys* (in which he was the cranky ex-vaudevillian Willie Clark bickering endlessly with his former onstage partner, Al Lewis, played in one production by fellow MGM alumnus Donald O'Connor). Rooney and O'Connor had such a lively rapport that they reunited in a touring program of songs, dances, and patter called *Two for the Show*. Rooney even had another successful stint on Broadway, this time with *The Will Rogers Follies* from 1991 to 1993. Clive Barnes gave him a rave review in the *New York Times*: "Go! The great Mickey Rooney is touching, rhythmic and quite brilliant." There would also be a sold-out run at Madison Square Garden of *The Wizard of Oz* in which Rooney (who had missed the chance to appear in the 1939 classic) was cast as the mysterious man behind the curtain.

But with an 8:00 p.m. Sunday night time slot on CBS for years, *Murder, She Wrote*, starring Angela Lansbury and produced by her husband, writer Peter Fischer, Rooney's guest appearance was probably viewed by more people than all of his stage shows combined. The episode, "Bloodlines," which originally aired on November 9, 1993, marked the two hundredth entry in the non-violent crime detective show. Rooney plays Matt Cleveland, the owner of a racetrack who is murdered before he can expose a fraud. It is one of the series' better episodes, and features some top-notch production values. The publicity connected with the telecast, not surprisingly, played up the fact that this would be the first time Lansbury and Rooney had acted together since *National Velvet*, fifty years earlier. In that landmark MGM film, Lansbury played Velvet Brown's older sister Edwina. She had an incredible career of her own that included other classic films like *Gaslight* (1944), for which she received an Academy Award nomination as Best Supporting Actress, and *The Manchurian Candidate* (1962), in which she is the incestuous mother of political hopeful Raymond Shaw (Laurence Harvey). Lansbury also had a string of Broadway successes that included a Tony Award for her star turn in Jerry Herman's 1966 musical adaptation of *Mame*, and her unapologetically ghoulish role as Nellie Lovett in the original production of Stephen Sondheim's *Sweeney Todd: The Demon Barber of Fleet Street*, which made its debut in 1979, the same year that Mickey and *Sugar Babies* took Broadway by storm. Speaking of that major career booster, Rooney and Ann Miller toured with the show for years. The play ran for three years on Broadway and he toured with it all over America and had a successful run in London in 1988.

His longest-running live show, however—approximately twenty years—was with his wife, Jan. They toured all over the U.S. and indeed, around the world, in a show of song and remembrance, called *One Man, One Wife* (a.k.a. *Let's Put On a Show*). This author was fortunate enough to see one of their presentations, in Clearwater, Florida. The act consisted of a little marital comedy patter, then Rooney did a few impressions, and Jan belted out some Patsy Cline songs. They also showed film clips from Mickey's screen career.

The fact that Mickey and Jan had such a long relationship made it seem that he had finally settled down with the right woman and that there was a happy ending to his tumultuous and, at times, sordid personal life. The fact that they stayed together for so long, working together in professional venues, made it appear to be a feel-good story. But it was destined for a sad ending.

Toward the end of his life Rooney filed a lawsuit against his stepson, Chris Aber, claiming that Aber had stolen millions of dollars from him and that he had also been the victim of emotional and physical abuse by Jan, as well as Aber's wife, Christina. Rooney moved out of the house to live with his other stepson, Mark, and his wife Charlene, in 2012; they were appointed his caregivers in 2011. Chris Aber later admitted in court that

Fourteen. The Long Exit

he had siphoned off almost $3 million when he took over the actor's financial affairs and forced Rooney to sign documents without his reading them. It is disturbing to think of what Rooney might have gone through, but we simply can't know what actually happened because one side of the Aber clan was blaming the other, and the biological family had not been in the picture for the last several years of Rooney's life.

On March 2, 2011, Rooney appeared before Congress addressing the Senate Special Committee on Aging and gave emotionally wrenching testimony about the helplessness and terror he felt in his own home: "For years I suffered silently. I didn't want to tell anybody. I couldn't muster the courage, and you have to have courage…. I needed help and I knew I needed it. Even when I tried to speak up, I was told to shut up."

His appearance caused quite a stir and it was widely covered on the network and cable news outlets. Attorney General Eric Holder even presented him with a Special Courage Award in the spring of 2012 for his speaking out on this sensitive topic.

Charlene Rooney talked about all the care the actor required at this stage in his life. She mentioned that he would sit and watch TV for twelve hours a day unless they tried to engage him in some activities. She said that they got him into a health club and that he was enjoying the exercise and interacting with the other members in the club. She seemed to be very caring about his health and well-being. Fred Roos, the producer of *The Black Stallion*, mentioned to this writer that he had seen Mark assisting Mickey urinate in a public restroom, and remembered hoping that Rooney was being treated well at that late stage of his life.

No doubt Rooney wanted to work, but one has to question the wisdom of putting him before the public when his health was in such steep decline. For instance, Rooney was to appear in late 2012 at an event called "An Evening with Mickey Rooney," at Lyons English Grille in Palm Springs. Attendees reported that many in the audience were brought to tears as the former raconteur began rambling on about nothing. The audience was expecting a pleasant meet-and-greet for which they had each paid $65 a plate and, instead, encountered a very weak and sad man who didn't even know why he was there. In early 2013, he was part of the Turner Classic Movies boat cruise, an immensely popular event for film buffs to get to see and chat with former movie stars. But when Rooney was introduced to the crowd of enthusiasts, he began to ramble on about politics or something and at least one of the fans said he had to avert his eyes in embarrassment. Rooney may have had his good days, even at this late stage in life. Still, an ailing ninety-three-year-old man who had worked continuously for ninety-one years deserves some rest.

That rest finally came to him, in his sleep, on April 6, 2014.

Jan, his wife of thirty-five years, found out about her husband's death on the Internet. The Abers were angry with Charlene and Mark Rooney, who were his caregivers at the end, for not notifying them when he died. They were also furious that Rooney had updated his will just a month before he died, leaving everything to Mark. Some sources hinted that Rooney felt his biological children were sufficiently well off that they didn't need anything. There were reports that, at the end, Charlene and Mark and Mickey's other stepson, Chris, along with his wife, Christina, and of course Jan, prevented his biological children from having access to him for the final five or so years of his life.

There were no Hollywood luminaries invited to deliver eulogies, but Mark did run into Mickey Rourke a few days prior to Rooney's death. The actor told him that Rooney had sent him a fan letter when he was just starting out and that it had meant a lot to him. A meeting was set up between the two, but Rooney died before they could get together. Rourke decided he owed it to the screen legend to at least attend his viewing.

"It was a pathetic sight to see him in what looked like a fuckin' eighty-five-dollar polyester gray suit, with his little hands folded, looking so tiny and all alone," Rourke recalls sadly. "I thought to myself, Wow, after all he accomplished, all he did, the effort that he put forward …" Told that Rooney's favorite wine was kosher Manischewitz, Rourke brought along a bottle, took a slug, and left it beside the body. "I kissed him on the forehead, thanked him for the letter and held his hand," says Rourke. "It was cold."

There was even haggling over Rooney's burial by warring factions of the family. Two separate funeral services were held, with Jan, Mark, and Charlene at the first (Chris Aber and his wife were denied admittance), and the biological children and their families at the second. After much debate, it was determined that he would be buried in Hollywood Forever Cemetery (formerly Hollywood Memorial Park, the final resting place of such legends as Douglas Fairbanks, Sr., Rudolph Valentino, and Cecil B. DeMille). The Rooney estate was a meager $18,000, not enough to pay for his burial and some outstanding taxes and medical bills. There was a trust set up to accept donations to pay off the debts that Rooney had at the time of his passing.

Fourteen. The Long Exit

As saddening as his passing was to the Hollywood community, the outpouring of love, affection, and respect from the public and his peers was truly remarkable. No one would have enjoyed all the fuss that was being made about his life and career more than Rooney. Tributes poured in from young and old alike, all of whom were reminded of a man who had the greatest career in terms of longevity and breadth of experience, more than anyone else in the history of show business. His death and a recapping of his career were covered on national television, and there were countless columns of appreciation for this little man with the big talent. Of the hundreds of remarks on Twitter and TV, the most appropriate, quite possibly, was by Billy Crystal, who said, "Mickey Rooney was barely five feet tall and everyone in Hollywood looked up to him."

Mickey Rooney's life spanned seventeen U.S. presidents, from Woodrow Wilson to Barack Obama; his career ranged from vaudeville to Broadway, radio to television, silent movies to CGI. In the words of Hamlet (Act 1, Scene 2), "He was a man, take him for all in all. [We] shall not look upon his like again."

Appendix A

Those Interviewed for This Book

Carroll Ballard was born on October 14, 1937, in Los Angeles, California. He was a classmate of Francis Ford Coppola at UCLA film school. He began his career as a documentary filmmaker, with films like *Beyond This Winter's Wheat* (1965) and *Harvest* (1967), which was produced for the U.S. Information Agency. *Harvest* went on to receive an Oscar nomination. A very filmic documentary called *Rodeo* (1970) was shot like an action movie and covered the National Finals Rodeo in Oklahoma City in 1968. He worked for another film school alum when he was second-unit director on *Star Wars* (1977). Ballard's first feature was the breathtakingly beautiful *The Black Stallion* (1979), which was produced by his film school friend Coppola. The movie was nominated for two Oscars, including one for Rooney as Best Supporting Actor for his portrayal of the kind and enthusiastic former jockey who trains the young Alec to ride The Black to victory. In addition to the nod to Rooney, Robert Dalva was nominated for Best Film Editing, and Alan Splet was given a Special Achievement Award for Sound Editing. In 2002, the Library of Congress added *The Black Stallion* to the National Film Registry.

Ballard went on to direct *Never Cry Wolf* (1983), another beautiful study of man and animal, this time the wolves of the Arctic Circle. The movie is based on Farley Mowat's book of the same name and stars Charley Martin Smith as the biologist braving the arctic winter to study these magnificent animals. He also directed *Fly Away Home* (1996) about a lonely young girl who finds some goose eggs left behind when a construction crew destroys a small wilderness area. When they hatch, the little girl, in a sense, becomes their mother and must teach them to fly home or they will have their wings clipped by the local game warden. Amy, played by Anna Paquin, and her father, played by Jeff Daniels, teach these Canadian geese to fly south for the winter. Ballard also directed *Duma* (2005), a story about an orphaned cheetah that becomes the pet of a young South African boy. These films, along with his acclaimed documentaries, make him one of our most talented filmmakers.

Appendix A

Corey Blechman is a writer-producer-director who was born in the state of Washington and grew up in the Seattle-Tacoma area. He attended the University of Maryland and has several relatives and friends in the Baltimore area. He is a huge Baltimore Orioles baseball fan. Blechman moved out to Southern California in 1976 and began scriptwriting. He landed work with Alan Landsburg Productions and it was there that he was commissioned to write the script for *Bill* in 1980. He would go on to win an Emmy for his script and later worked in films as a writer-director. He wrote the screenplay for *Dominick and Eugene* (1988), starring fraternal twins Tom Hulce and Ray Liotta. Dominick is slow-witted because of a childhood accident and works as a sanitation engineer to help put his brother Eugene through medical school. Blechman would also write *Free Willy* (1993) about the rescue of an aquarium whale, and the sequel *Free Willy 2: The Adventure Home* (1995). He has also directed TV-movies, including *Prince for a Day* (1995), a modern version of *The Prince and the Pauper*.

Roger Corman was born April 5, 1926, in Detroit, Michigan. He moved with his family to Los Angeles in his teens and graduated from Beverly Hills High School. He attended Stanford as an industrial engineering student. While attending college he entered the V-12 Navy College Training Program, then returned to finish his degree at Stanford after the war. He began directing movies in the mid–1950s, cranking out about nine quickies a year, including *Swamp Women* (1955). An early success was *The Little Shop of Horrors* (1960) that included in its cast a young actor by the name of Jack Nicholson who hilariously played a masochistic dental patient. *Horrors* was shot in two days and one night; over twenty years later would become the basis of a rock musical of the same title and, in 1986, a successful film directed by Frank Oz.

Corman's most successful work as a director was in the early 1960s. This was the series of American-International Pictures based on the works of Edgar Allan Poe. *House of Usher* (1960), *The Pit and the Pendulum* (1961), *The Premature Burial* (1962), *Tales of Terror* (1962), *The Raven* (1963), *The Masque of the Red Death* (1964), and *The Tomb of Ligeia* (1964) did well with audiences and critics alike. All of these films (with the sole exception of *The Premature Burial*, with Ray Milland) starred Vincent Price. It was during this period that Corman directed a World War II movie called *The Secret Invasion* (1964), which served almost as a blueprint for Robert Aldrich's *The Dirty Dozen* (1967). Rooney is one of the stars of *Invasion*, along with Stewart Granger and Raf Valone, as part of a group of war criminals offered a chance at a pardon if they can rescue an imprisoned Italian general sympathetic to the Allies. Rooney plays Terence Scanlon, a demo-

Those Interviewed for This Book

litions expert from the Irish Republican Army, with gusto and a totally convincing Irish accent. The film itself overcomes its low budget and is a solid action picture that made a lot of money and received some favorable reviews.

Tim Farley is the son of Walter Farley (1915-1989), who was the author of *The Black Stallion* books, beginning in 1941. Tim has a photography degree from Brooks Institute in Santa Barbara, California, and right after graduation he went to work on the film *The Black Stallion* as a production assistant. "Production assistant" was his screen credit, but the entire crew consisted of only thirty people, so he had to do a little bit of everything on set. He is president and creator of TheBlackStallion.com and is co-founder of the HorseTales.org literacy program. He continues his photographic pursuits and lives in Florida, but spends a lot of time in New Mexico as well.

Barry Morrow was born June 12, 1948, in Austin, Minnesota. He went to St. Olaf College in Northfield, Minnesota. He is best known as the Emmy Award-winning producer of the TV-movie *Bill*. The story of Bill Sackter was a personal one for Morrow. He befriended the mentally challenged Sackter and made a documentary about his experiences trying to adjust to a new world after spending forty-six years warehoused in an institution. The CBS network became interested in doing a TV-movie based on the documentary, and the touching story of Sackter's triumph over adversity reached an audience of millions. Morrow, along with scriptwriter Blechman, received Emmys for the writing, and Rooney won his only major competitive acting award when he received an Emmy for his touching and sensitive portrayal of Sackter. Morrow went on to co-write (with Ronald Bass) the story of an autistic savant for Barry Levinson's film *Rain Man* (1988), receiving an Oscar for his work. The film also received the Best Picture Oscar and Dustin Hoffman won for his virtuoso performance as Raymond Babbitt, an autistic savant being cared for by his brother, Charlie (Tom Cruise). *Bill* and *Rain Man* have a similar theme: "Am I my brother's keeper?" Morrow gave his Oscar statuette to Kim Peek, the real-life Raymond Babbitt.

Morrow began his career as an actor in summer stock and toured Hawaii with a children's theatre group before turning to documentary filmmaking. He also taught media studies and filmmaking at the University of Iowa, where he met Sackter and began his friendship and the documentary that eventually brought him to Hollywood. Many of his early documentaries focused on people with disabilities; he has received a Lifetime Achievement Award from the National Society of Social Workers. Morrow went on to write the sequel to *Bill*, called *Bill: On His Own* (1983). He also penned the script for the TV-movies *Christmas on Division Street* (1991), which starred

Fred Savage and Hume Cronyn, and *The Karen Carpenter Story* (1989). He continues to write and produce for both TV and film.

Carl Reiner is a genuine show business legend. He was born March 20, 1922, in the Bronx, New York City. His parents were Jewish immigrants, his father from Romania and his mother from Austria. His career as an actor began on Broadway with the lead role in a musical called *Call Me Mister*. His comedy career began in 1950 when he became part of an ensemble of actors and writers who created, along with the incredible Sid Caesar, *Your Show of Shows*. Reiner was featured in sketches with Caesar, Imogene Coca, Howie Morris, and others, but he was also part of the writing staff that included Mel Brooks, Neil Simon, Larry Gelbart, Aaron Reuben, and, later, a very young Woody Allen.

In 1961, Reiner teamed with Mel Brooks for a comedy skit known as "The 2000-Year-Old Man." The hilariously imaginative duo put out several highly successful comedy albums, with Reiner feeding Brooks questions that only a two-thousand-year-old man could answer.

Reiner followed the advice that every young writer gets and proceeded to write about what he knew; in his case, that meant writers trying to write a comedy show. This eventually became the TV classic *Dick Van Dyke Show*. He not only wrote most of the early episodes but also played the vain and difficult star of *The Alan Brady Show* that the writers—played by comedians Morey Amsterdam, Rose Marie, and Dick Van Dyke—were trying to please in order to keep their jobs. Reiner and his excellent cast ended up creating one of TV's iconic sitcoms that audiences have been enjoying for half a century. He won a slew of Emmys as the writer-creator of the show and so did Van Dyke and Mary Tyler Moore for their performances as Rob and Laura Petrie. He went on to a prolific career directing films including *The Comic* (1969) that co-starred Rooney, and *The Jerk* (1979), which brought Steve Martin to the big screen.

Kelly Reno was born on a cattle ranch in Pueblo, Colorado, on June 15, 1966. He began riding horses almost from the time he could walk. A friend of the family saw an ad in the local newspaper about a nationwide search for a boy who could ride horses for a new film being planned, based on the classic Walter Farley book *The Black Stallion*. Reno's mom thought it might be a good idea for him to try out for the part. He went to the first open audition and was instructed to come for a second, and then a third. It was a long process, as he detailed in our interview, but he got the part and as long as the casting process was, the shoot was even longer. He went on to reprise his role as Alec Ramsey in the sequel *The Black Stallion Returns* (1983) and followed that with *Hosszu vagata* (1984), a war movie with John

Those Interviewed for This Book

Savage of *The Deer Hunter* (1978) fame. He followed that with a role in the TV series *Amazing Stories* (1984). Reno wanted to continue his career but was derailed when the pickup truck he was driving was hit by an 18-wheeler and he suffered several severe injuries. He recalled that he lost two immediate acting jobs because he was out of action for almost a year with the injuries. As he later commented in an interview, "Hollywood forgets you fast." Once the acting work dried up he had to find other employment; he worked as a cattle rancher for fifteen years before getting his trucking license. He lives in Wisconsin now with his wife, Dawn.

Fred Roos was born in Santa Monica, California, on May 22, 1934. He has been in movies and TV for more than half a century. He started his career as a casting director for *The Andy Griffith Show*. For those of us who are huge fans of that iconic sitcom, it is impossible to think of any other actors for the leads than Andy Griffith, Don Knotts, Francis Bavier, and Ron Howard as the central characters. But the secondary characters also represent perfect casting, like Howard McNear as Floyd the barber, and Jim Nabors as Gomer Pyle. There were also wonderful guest performers, including *Your Show of Shows* alum Howard Morris as the backwoods crazy Ernest T. Bass, and Denver Pyle as the head of the Darling family.

Roos moved from television to film and was largely responsible for putting together the casts for *Five Easy Pieces* (1970) for Bob Rafelson, *American Graffiti* (1973) for George Lucas, and *The Godfather* (1972) for Francis Ford Coppola, among many others. Roos received an Oscar for his work as co-producer on *The Godfather: Part II* (1974). He has produced all of Sofia Coppola's movies to date, including, of course, *Lost in Translation* (2003), starring Bill Murray. Among the many great films he has produced, one of his proudest accomplishments is Carroll Ballard's *The Black Stallion*. More recently, he produced another Bill Murray vehicle, *St. Vincent* (2014). Francis Ford Coppola said in 2004, "There's no doubt in my mind that Fred is one of the greatest casting talents in the last forty years of American movies."

Appendix B

Mickey Rooney's Credits

The following is a list of films, television programs, and theatrical performances, with the date and the name of the character Rooney played.

Movies

Year	Title	Character
1927	Orchids and Ermine	uncredited
1932	The Beast of the City	Mickey Fitzpatrick
1932	Sin's Pay Day	Chubby Dennis
1932	High Speed	Buddy Whipple
1932	Fast Companions	Midge
1932	My Pal, the King	King Charles V
1932	Officer Thirteen	Buddy Malone
1933	The Big Cage	Jimmy O'Hara
1933	The Life of Jimmy Dolan	Freckles
1933	The Big Chance	Arthur Wilson
1933	Broadway to Hollywood	Ted Hackett III as a child
1933	The Chief	Willie
1933	The World Changes	Otto Peterson, as a child
1934	Beloved	Tommy
1934	The Lost Jungle	Mickey
1934	I Like It That Way	Messenger Boy
1934	Manhattan Melodrama	Blackie as a boy
1934	Love Birds	Gladwyn Tootle
1934	Half a Sinner	Willie Clark
1934	Hide-Out	William "Willie" Miller
1934	Chained	Boy Shipboard Swimmer
1934	Blind Date	Freddie
1934	Death on the Diamond	Mickey
1935	The County Chairman	Freckles
1935	Reckless	Eddie
1935	The Healer	Jimmy
1935	A Midsummer Night's Dream	Puck, or Robin Goodfellow
1935	Rendezvous	Country Boy
1935	Ah, Wilderness!	Tommy

APPENDIX B

1936	*Riffraff*	Jimmy
1936	*Little Lord Fauntleroy*	Dick
1936	*Down the Stretch*	"Snapper" Sinclair
1936	*The Devil Is a Sissy*	"Gig" Stevens
1937	*A Family Affair*	Andy Hardy
1937	*Captains Courageous*	Dan Troop
1937	*Slave Ship*	Swifty
1937	*Hoosier Schoolboy*	Shockey Carter
1937	*Live, Love and Learn*	Jerry Crump
1937	*Thoroughbreds Don't Cry*	Timmie Donovan
1937	*You're Only Young Once*	Andrew "Andy" Hardy
1938	*Love Is a Headache*	Mike O'Toole
1938	*Judge Hardy's Children*	Andy Hardy
1938	*Hold That Kiss*	Chick Evans
1938	*Lord Jeff*	Terry O'Mulvaney
1938	*Love Finds Andy Hardy*	Andrew Hardy
1938	*Boys Town*	Whitey Marsh
1938	*Stablemates*	Michael "Mickey"
1938	*Out West with the Hardys*	Andy Hardy
1939	*The Adventures of Huckleberry Finn*	Huckleberry Finn
1939	*The Hardys Ride High*	Andy Hardy
1939	*Andy Hardy Gets Spring Fever*	Andy Hardy
1939	*Babes in Arms*	Mickey Moran
1939	*Judge Hardy and Son*	Andy Hardy
1940	*Young Tom Edison*	Thomas Alva "Tom" Edison
1940	*Andy Hardy Meets Debutante*	Andy Hardy
1940	*Strike Up the Band*	Jimmy Connors
1941	*Andy Hardy's Private Secretary*	Andy Hardy
1941	*Men of Boys Town*	Whitey Marsh
1941	*Life Begins for Andy Hardy*	Andy Hardy
1941	*Babes on Broadway*	Tommy Williams
1942	*The Courtship of Andy Hardy*	Andy Hardy
1942	*A Yank at Eton*	Timothy Dennis
1942	*Andy Hardy's Double Life*	Andy Hardy
1943	*The Human Comedy*	Homer Macauley
1943	*Thousands Cheer*	Emcee at the show
1943	*Girl Crazy*	Danny Churchill, Jr.
1944	*Andy Hardy's Blonde Trouble*	Andy Hardy
1944	*National Velvet*	Mi Taylor
1946	*Love Laughs at Andy Hardy*	Andy Hardy
1947	*Killer McCoy*	Tommy McCoy/Killer McCoy
1948	*Summer Holiday*	Richard Miller

1948	*Words and Music*	Lorenz Hart
1949	*The Big Wheel*	Billy Coy
1950	*Quicksand*	Dan
1950	*The Fireball*	Johnny Casar
1950	*He's a Cockeyed Wonder*	Freddie Frisby
1951	*My Outlaw Brother*	J. Dennis "Denny" O'Moore
1951	*The Strip*	Stanley Maxton
1952	*Sound Off*	Mike Donnelly
1953	*Off Limits*	Herbert Tuttle
1953	*All Ashore*	Francis "Moby" Dickerson
1953	*A Slight Case of Larceny*	Augustus "Geechy" Cheevers
1954	*Drive a Crooked Road*	Eddie Shannon
1954	*The Atomic Kid*	Barnaby "Blix" Waterberry
1955	*The Bridges at Toko-Ri*	Mike Forney
1955	*The Twinkle in God's Eye*	Rev. William Macklin II
1956	*The Bold and the Brave*	Dooley
1956	*Francis in the Haunted House*	David Prescott
1956	*Magnificent Roughnecks*	Frank Sommers
1957	*Operation Mad Ball*	MSgt. Yancy Skibo
1957	*Baby Face Nelson*	Lester M. "Baby Face Nelson" Gillis
1958	*A Nice Little Bank That Should Be Robbed*	Gus Harris
1958	*Andy Hardy Comes Home*	Andy Hardy
1959	*The Big Operator*	Little Joe Braun
1959	*The Last Mile*	"Killer" Mears
1960	*Platinum High School*	Steven Conway
1960	*The Private Lives of Adam and Eve*	Nick Lewis / The Devil
1961	*King of the Roaring '20s— The Story of Arnold Rothstein*	Johnny Burke
1961	*Everything's Ducky*	Kermit "Beetle" McKay
1961	*Breakfast at Tiffany's*	Mr. Yunioshi
1962	*Requiem for a Heavyweight*	Army
1963	*It's a Mad, Mad, Mad, Mad World*	Ding Bell
1964	*The Secret Invasion*	Terence Scanlon, Demolition
1965	*Twenty-Four Hours to Kill*	Norman Jones
1965	*How to Stuff a Wild Bikini*	Peachy Keane
1966	*The Devil in Love*	Adramalek
1966	*Ambush Bay*	Sgt. Ernest Wartell
1968	*Skidoo*	George "Blue Chips" Packard

Appendix B

Year	Title	Role
1969	The Extraordinary Seaman	Cook 3 / C. W. J. Oglethorpe
1969	The Comic	Martin "Cockeye" Van Buren
1969	80 Steps to Jonah	Wilfred Bashford
1970	Cockeyed Cowboys of Calico County	Indian Tom
1970	Santa Claus Is Comin' to Town	Kris Kringle\Santa Claus (Voice only)
1971	Mooch Goes to Hollywood	Himself
1971	The Manipulator	B. J. Lang
1972	Evil Roy Slade	Nelson Stool
1972	Richard	Guardian Angel
1972	Pulp	Preston Gilbert
1973	The Godmothers	Rocky Mastrasso
1974	Thunder County	Gas Station Attendant
1974	Journey Back to Oz	Scarecrow (Voice only)
1974	The Year Without a Santa Claus	Santa Claus (Voice only)
1974	That's Entertainment!	Himself. Co-Host / Narrator / Clips from *Babes in Arms*, *Girl Crazy*, and *Babes on Broadway*
1975	Rachel's Man	Laban
1975	Ace of Hearts	Papa Joe
1975	From Hong Kong with Love	Marty
1976	Find the Lady	Trigger
1977	The Domino Principle	Spiventa
1977	Pete's Dragon	Lampie
1978	The Magic of Lassie	Gus
1979	The Black Stallion	Henry Dailey
1979	Arabian Adventure	Daad El Shur
1979	Rudolph and Frosty's Christmas in July	Santa Claus (Voice only)
1981	The Fox and the Hound	Tod (Voice only)
1982	The Emperor of Peru/Odyssey of the Pacific	The Railway Engineer
1985	The Care Bears Movie	Mr. Cherrywood (Voice only)
1986	Lightning, the White Stallion	Barney Ingram
1988	Bluegrass	John Paul Jones
1989	Erik the Viking	Erik's Grandfather
1989	Little Nemo: Adventures in Slumberland	Flip (Voice only)
1990	Home for Christmas	Elmer
1991	My Heroes Have Always Been Cowboys	Junion (Jesse's roommate at Retirement Home)

Mickey Rooney's Credit

1992	*Sweet Justice*	Zeke
1992	*Silent Night, Deadly Night 5: The Toy Maker*	Joe Petto
1992	*Maximum Force*	Chief of Police
1993	*The Legend of Wolf Mountain*	Pat Jensen
1993	*The Milky Life*	Barry Reilly
1993	*The Magic Voyage*	Narrator
1994	*Revenge of the Red Baron*	Grandpa Spencer
1994	*The Outlaws: The Legend of O. B. Taggart*	O. B. Taggart
1994	*Making Waves*	Gabriel
1994	*The Gambler Returns: Luck of the Draw*	The Director
1997	*Killing Midnight*	Professor Mort Sang
1998	*Babe: Pig in the City*	Fugly Floom
1998	*The Face on the Barroom Floor*	
1998	*Animals and the Tollkeeper*	Tollkeeper
1998	*Michael Kael vs. the World News Company*	Griffith
1998	*The Snow Queen*	Ol Dreamy
1998	*Sinbad: The Battle of the Dark Knights*	Sage
1999	*Holy Hollywood*	
1999	*The First of May*	Boss Ed
2000	*Internet Love*	Himself
2000	*Phantom of the Megaplex*	Movie Mason
2001	*Lady and the Tramp II: Scamp's Adventure*	Sparkey (Voice only)
2002	*Topa Topa Bluffs*	Prospector
2003	*Paradise*	Simon / Henry Sr.
2005	*Strike the Tent*	David McCord
2005	*The Happy Elf*	Santa
2005	*A Christmas Too Many*	Grandpa
2006	*The Thirsting*	Savy
2006	*To Kill a Mockumentary*	Max
2006	*Night at the Museum*	Gus
2007	*The Yesterday Pool*	Trobadar
2007	*Bamboo Shark*	Brooks
2008	*Lost Stallions: The Journey Home*	Chief
2008	*A Miser Brothers' Christmas*	Santa Claus (Voice only)
2009	*Night at the Museum: Battle of the Smithsonian*	Gus (Deleted scene only)
2009	*Saddle Up with Dick Wrangler & Injun Joe*	Owen Blumenkrantz
2010	*Gerald*	The Doctor
2010	*Now Here*	Swifty

Appendix B

Year	Title		
2011	Night Club		Jerry Sherman
2011	The Muppets		Elderly Smalltown Resident
2012	Last Will and Embezzlement		Himself
2012	Driving Me Crazy		Mr. Cohen
2012	The Voices from Beyond		Johnny O'Hara
2012	The Woods		Lester
2014	Night at the Museum: Secret of the Tomb		Gus
2015	Dr. Jekyll and Mr. Hyde		Mr. Louis

Short Subjects

Year	Title
1926	Not to Be Trusted
1927	Mickey's Circus
	Mickey's Pals
	Mickey's Eleven
	Mickey's Battles
1928	Mickey's Parade
	Mickey in School
	Mickey's Nine
	Mickey's Little Eva
	Mickey's Wild West
	Mickey in Love
	Mickey's Triumph
	Mickey's Babies
	Mickey's Movies
	Mickey's Rivals
	Mickey the Detective
	Mickey's Athletes
	Mickey's Big Game Hunt
1929	Mickey's Great Idea
	Mickey's Menagerie
	Mickey's Last Chance
	Mickey's Brown Derby
	Mickey's Northwest Mounted
	Mickey's Initiation
	Mickey's Midnite Follies
	Mickey's Surprise
	Mickey's Mix-Up
	Mickey's Big Moment

Year	Title
	Mickey's Strategy
1930	Mickey's Champs
	Mickey's Explorers
	Mickey's Master Mind
	Mickey's Luck
	Mickey's Whirlwinds
	Mickey's Warriors
	Mickey the Romeo
	Mickey's Merry Men
	Mickey's Winners
	Screen Snapshots Series 9, No. 24
	Mickey's Musketeers
	Mickey's Bargain
1931	Mickey's Stampede
	Mickey's Crusaders
	Mickey's Rebellion
	Mickey's Diplomacy
	Mickey's Wildcats
	Mickey's Thrill Hunters
	Mickey's Helping Hand
	Mickey's Sideline
1932	Mickey's Busy Day
	Mickey's Travels
	Mickey's Holiday
	Mickey's Big Business
	Mickey's Golden Rule
	Mickey's Charity
1933	Mickey's Ape Man

Mickey Rooney's Credit

Year	Title	Role
1992	Sweet Justice	Zeke
1992	Silent Night, Deadly Night 5: The Toy Maker	Joe Petto
1992	Maximum Force	Chief of Police
1993	The Legend of Wolf Mountain	Pat Jensen
1993	The Milky Life	Barry Reilly
1993	The Magic Voyage	Narrator
1994	Revenge of the Red Baron	Grandpa Spencer
1994	The Outlaws: The Legend of O. B. Taggart	O. B. Taggart
1994	Making Waves	Gabriel
1994	The Gambler Returns: Luck of the Draw	The Director
1997	Killing Midnight	Professor Mort Sang
1998	Babe: Pig in the City	Fugly Floom
1998	The Face on the Barroom Floor	
1998	Animals and the Tollkeeper	Tollkeeper
1998	Michael Kael vs. the World News Company	Griffith
1998	The Snow Queen	Ol Dreamy
1998	Sinbad: The Battle of the Dark Knights	Sage
1999	Holy Hollywood	
1999	The First of May	Boss Ed
2000	Internet Love	Himself
2000	Phantom of the Megaplex	Movie Mason
2001	Lady and the Tramp II: Scamp's Adventure	Sparkey (Voice only)
2002	Topa Topa Bluffs	Prospector
2003	Paradise	Simon / Henry Sr.
2005	Strike the Tent	David McCord
2005	The Happy Elf	Santa
2005	A Christmas Too Many	Grandpa
2006	The Thirsting	Savy
2006	To Kill a Mockumentary	Max
2006	Night at the Museum	Gus
2007	The Yesterday Pool	Trobadar
2007	Bamboo Shark	Brooks
2008	Lost Stallions: The Journey Home	Chief
2008	A Miser Brothers' Christmas	Santa Claus (Voice only)
2009	Night at the Museum: Battle of the Smithsonian	Gus (Deleted scene only)
2009	Saddle Up with Dick Wrangler & Injun Joe	Owen Blumenkrantz
2010	Gerald	The Doctor
2010	Now Here	Swifty

Year	Title		Role
2011	Night Club		Jerry Sherman
2011	The Muppets		Elderly Smalltown Resident
2012	Last Will and Embezzlement		Himself
2012	Driving Me Crazy		Mr. Cohen
2012	The Voices from Beyond		Johnny O'Hara
2012	The Woods		Lester
2014	Night at the Museum: Secret of the Tomb		Gus
2015	Dr. Jekyll and Mr. Hyde		Mr. Louis

Short Subjects

Year	Title	Year	Title
1926	Not to Be Trusted		Mickey's Strategy
1927	Mickey's Circus	1930	Mickey's Champs
	Mickey's Pals		Mickey's Explorers
	Mickey's Eleven		Mickey's Master Mind
	Mickey's Battles		Mickey's Luck
1928	Mickey's Parade		Mickey's Whirlwinds
	Mickey in School		Mickey's Warriors
	Mickey's Nine		Mickey the Romeo
	Mickey's Little Eva		Mickey's Merry Men
	Mickey's Wild West		Mickey's Winners
	Mickey in Love		Screen Snapshots Series 9, No. 24
	Mickey's Triumph		
	Mickey's Babies		Mickey's Musketeers
	Mickey's Movies		Mickey's Bargain
	Mickey's Rivals	1931	Mickey's Stampede
	Mickey the Detective		Mickey's Crusaders
	Mickey's Athletes		Mickey's Rebellion
	Mickey's Big Game Hunt		Mickey's Diplomacy
1929	Mickey's Great Idea		Mickey's Wildcats
	Mickey's Menagerie		Mickey's Thrill Hunters
	Mickey's Last Chance		Mickey's Helping Hand
	Mickey's Brown Derby		Mickey's Sideline
	Mickey's Northwest Mounted	1932	Mickey's Busy Day
			Mickey's Travels
	Mickey's Initiation		Mickey's Holiday
	Mickey's Midnite Follies		Mickey's Big Business
	Mickey's Surprise		Mickey's Golden Rule
	Mickey's Mix-Up		Mickey's Charity
	Mickey's Big Moment	1933	Mickey's Ape Man

Mickey Rooney's Credit

Year	Title	Year	Title
	Mickey's Race	1941	*Meet the Stars #4: Variety Reel #2*
	Mickey's Big Broadcast		
	Mickey's Disguises	1943	*Show Business at War*
	Mickey's Touchdown	1947	*Screen Snapshots: Out of This World Series*
	Mickey's Tent Show		
	Mickey's Covered Wagon	1953	*Screen Snapshots: Mickey Rooney—Then and Now*
1934	*Mickey's Minstrels*		
	Mickey's Rescue	1958	*Screen Snapshots: Glamorous Hollywood*
	Mickey's Medicine Man		
1935	*Pirate Party on Catalina Isle*	1968	*Vienna*
		1974	*Just One More Time*
1937	*Cinema Circus*	1975	*The Lion Roars Again*
1938	*Andy Hardy's Dilemma*	2008	*Wreck the Halls*
1940	*Rodeo Dough*		

Television Appearances

(List of performances and the name of the character. Selected titles have more complete production credits and author's comments.)

The Milton Berle Show
- Season 8, Episode 12 (May/19/1956)—As Himself
- Season 7, Episode 1 (Sep/21/1954)—As Himself
- Season 6, Episode 16 (Mar/02/1954)—As Himself
- Season 4, Episode 28 (Mar/25/1952)—As Himself

Hey, Mulligan (1954)—As Mickey Mulligan

The Colgate Comedy Hour
- Mickey Rooney, George Raft (Dec/18/1955)—As Himself [Guest Hosts]
- GALA FOOTBALL REVUE (Oct/23/1955)—As Himself [Guest Hosts]

Schlitz Playhouse of Stars
- The Lady Was a Flop (Jan/04/1957)—As Red McGivney

The Steve Allen Show (1956)
- Season 5, Episode 8 (Nov/23/1959)—As Himself
- Season 2, Episode 27 (Apr/21/1957)—As Himself
- Season 2, Episode 3 (Sep/30/1956)—As Himself

Playhouse 90
- Season 1, Episode 20, The Comedian (February 14, 1957)—As Sammy Hogarth
- Season 1, Episode 19, The Miracle Worker (Feb/07/1957)—As Host

The Mickey Rooney Show
- December Bride (Apr/14/1958)—As Himself

Appendix B

Alcoa Theatre (TV Series)
- Eddie (1958)—As Eddie

What's My Line? (U.S.)
- Episode #799 (Jan/16/1966)—As Mystery Guest #2
- Episode #533 (Oct/02/1960)—As Mystery Guest #4
- Episode #397 (Jan/12/1958)—As Guest Panelist

Ford Startime
- The Dean Martin Show (Nov/03/1959)—As Himself

This Is Your Life
- Billy Barty (Mar/30/1960)—As Himself

General Electric Theatre
- The Money Driver (Dec/18/1960)—As Al Roberts

Wagon Train
- Wagons Ho! (Sep/28/1960)—As Samuel T. Evans [Special Guest Stars]
- The Greenhorn Story (Oct/07/1959)—As Samuel T. Evans [Special Guest Stars]

The Dick Powell Theatre (TV Series)
- Who Killed Julie Greer? (Sep/26/1961)—As Sampini
- Somebody's Waiting (Nov/7/1961)—As Augie Miller

The Dick Powell Show
- Special Assignment (Sep/25/1962)—As Putt-Putt Higgins

Pete and Gladys
- The Top Banana (Apr/16/1962)—As Himself

The Jack Benny Program
- Modern Prison Sketch (Apr/15/1962)—As Himself [Special Guest Stars]

The Investigators
- I Thee Kill (Oct/26/1961)—As Jack Daley

Naked City (TV Series)
- Ooftus Goofus (1961)—As George Bick

Combat! (1962)
- Silver Service (Oct/13/1964)—As Harry White [Special Guest Stars]

The Ed Sullivan Show
- Burt Lancaster, Mickey Rooney (Jan/24/1965)—As Himself
- Mickey Rooney, Patti Page (Jan/14/1962)—As Himself
- Mickey Rooney, Bob Newhart (Oct/02/1960)—As Himself
- The "West Side Story" Cast, Mickey Rooney (Sep/14/1958)—As Himself

Kraft Suspense Theatre (TV Series)
- The Hunt (1963)—As Sheriff Williams

Mickey Rooney's Credit

The Twilight Zone
- The Last Night of a Jockey (Oct/25/1963)—As Grady

Alcoa Premiere (TV Series)
  Five, Six, Pick Up Sticks (1963)—As Babe Simms

Mickey (1964)—As: Mickey Grady

Rawhide
- Incident of the Odyssey (Mar/26/1964)—As Pan Macropolous [Special Guest Stars]

Burke's Law
- Who Killed His Royal Highness? (Feb/21/1964)—As Archie Lido

Arrest and Trial
- Funny Man with a Monkey (Jan/05/1964)—As Hoagy Blair

The Dean Martin Show (1965)
- Kate Smith, Barbara Eden, Mickey Rooney, Les Brown (Mar/20/1969)—As Himself
- Keely Smith / Mickey Rooney / Minnie Pearl / Don Cherry (Feb/22/1968)—As Himself
- Mickey Rooney / Kate Smith / Tammy Grimes / Corbett Monica (Nov/11/1965)—As Himself

The Red Skelton Show
- Mickey Rooney / Martha Raye (Mar/07/1967)—As Himself
- Mickey Rooney / Simon and Garfunkel (Sep/20/1966)—As Himself
- Mickey Rooney / U.S. Marine Drum & Bugle Team (Sep/28/1965)—As Himself
- Mickey Rooney / Jackie Coogan / The Snobs (May/05/1964)—As Himself

The Hollywood Palace
- Host: Sammy Davis, Jr. (Feb/11/1967)—As Himself
- Host: Bing Crosby (Jan/04/1964)—As Himself

The Lucy Show (TV Series)
- Lucy Meets Mickey Rooney (1966)—As Himself

The Fugitive
- This'll Kill You (Jan/18/1966)—As Charlie Paris

The Carol Burnett Show (1967)
- with Mickey Rooney, Nancy Wilson, Emmaline Henry, Roland Winters (Dec/30/1968)—As Himself
- with Mickey Rooney, John Davidson (Dec/11/1967)—As Himself

The Smothers Brothers Comedy Hour
- Show #22 (Sep/17/1967)—As Himself

Rowan & Martin's Laugh-In (1968)
- Episode #65 (Mar/09/1970)—As Himself

Appendix B

Santa Claus Is Comin' to Town (1970)—As Kris Kringle/Santa Claus (Voice)
The Tonight Show Starring Johnny Carson
- 720517 (May/17/1972)—As Himself

Night Gallery (TV Series)
- Rare Objects (1972)—As August Kolodney

The Year Without a Santa Claus (1974)—As Santa Claus (Voice)
The Wonderful World of Disney
- Donovan's Kid (2) (Jan/14/1979)—As Old Bailey
- Donovan's Kid (1) (Jan/07/1979)—As Old Bailey

Rudolph and Frosty's Christmas in July (1979)—As Santa Claus (Voice)
Leave 'em Laughing (1981)—As Jack Thum
Bill (1981)—As Bill Sackter
One of the Boys (1982)—As Oliver Nugent
Bill: On His Own (1983)—As Bill Sackter
It Came Upon the Midnight Clear (1984)—As Mike Halligan
The Golden Girls
- Larceny and Old Lace (Feb/27/1988)—As Rocco

This Is Your Life (UK)
- Mickey Rooney (Oct/19/1988)—As Himself

The Adventures of the Black Stallion (1990)—As Henry Dailey
Jack's Place
- Solo (Jun/16/1992)—As Harry Burton

MGM: When the Lion Roars (1992)—As Himself (interviewed)
Full House
- Arrest Ye Merry Gentlemen (Dec/13/1994)—As Mr. Dreghorn

The Simpsons
- Radioactive Man (Sep/24/1995)—Voiced Himself

Kung Fu: The Legend Continues
- A Shaolin Treasure (Oct/30/1996)—As Harold Lang

Conan
- The Heart of the Elephant (1) (Sep/22/1997)—As Grobe

Mike Hammer, Private Eye
- Lucky in Love (May/03/1998)—As Lucius

ER
- Exodus (Feb/26/1998)—As George Bikel

E! True Hollywood Story
- The Last Days of Judy Garland (Jan/14/2001)—As Himself
- Elizabeth Taylor (Nov/29/1998)—As Himself

Norm
- Retribution (Mar/08/2000)—As Himself

Chicken Soup for the Soul (TV Series)
- Goodbye, My Friend (1999)—As Old Man

Kleo the Misfit Unicorn (2002)—As Talbut (Voice)

Biography
- Mickey Rooney (2005)—As Himself

Above the Line (2008)—As Mickey

Celebrity Ghost Stories
- Mickey Rooney, Brande Roderick, Eric Mabius, Kim Coles (Nov/26/2011)—As Himself

The Tonight Show with Jay Leno
- Sandra Bullock, Blake Shelton, Vintage Trouble (Feb/05/2014)—As Himself (in the audience)

American Dad! (TV Series) (2015)
- A Star Is Reborn (2015) ... Short Producer (voice)

Producer (7 credits)

1951   *My Outlaw Brother* (executive producer)
1954   *The Atomic Kid* (producer)
1954–1955 *The Mickey Rooney Show* (TV series) (executive producer—twenty episodes)
1955   *The Twinkle in God's Eye* (producer)
1956   *Jaguar* (associate producer)
2007   *The Yesterday Pool* (Short) (producer)
2012   *The Martini Shot* (executive producer)

Director (5 credits)

1951   *My True Story*
1956   *The Bold and the Brave* (uncredited)
1960   *The Private Lives of Adam and Eve*
1960   *Happy* (TV Series)
1966   *The Jean Arthur Show* (TV Series) (1 episode)
—Did Clarence Darrow Start This Way?

Writer (2 credits)

1975   The Godmothers
1994   Outlaws: The Legend of O. B. Taggart

Stage Work

1934   *A Midsummer Night's Dream*
1951   *Sailor Beware*

Appendix B

1963   *The Tunnel of Love*
1965   *A Funny Thing Happened on the Way to the Forum*
1967   *The Odd Couple*
1969–70   *George M!*
1971   *Three Goats and a Blanket*
1971   *Hide and Seek*
1971   *W. C.* (closed on the road)
1972–74   *See How They Run*
1973   *A Midsummer Night's Dream*
1975   *Goodnight Ladies*
1975   *Sugar*
1976   *Alimony*
1979–82, 1983–88   *Sugar Babies*
1983   *Show Boat*
1986   *The Laugh's On Me*
1987   *A Funny Thing Happened on the Way to the Forum*
1989   *Two for the Show*
1990   *The Sunshine Boys*
1991–1993   *The Will Rogers Follies*
1993   *Lend Me a Tenor*
1994   *The Mind with the Naughty Man*
1995   *Crazy for You*
1997–1999   *The Wizard of Oz*
2000   *Hollywood Goes Classical*
2003   *Singular Sensations*

Appendix C

Awards and Honors

Year	Award	Result
1938	Academy Awards, Academy Juvenile Award (with Deanna Durbin) "For their significant contribution in bringing to the screen the spirit and personification of youth, and as juvenile players setting a high standard of ability and achievement."	**Honored**
1939	Best Actor in a Leading Role, *Babes in Arms*	**Nominated**
1943	Best Actor in a Leading Role, *The Human Comedy*	**Nominated**
1956	Best Actor in a Supporting Role, *The Bold and the Brave*	**Nominated**
1957	Emmy Awards, Best Single Performance in a Leading or Supporting Role, *The Comedian*, episode of Playhouse 90	**Nominated**
1958	Best Single Performance in a Leading or Supporting Role, Alcoa Theatre: *Eddie*	**Nominated**
1961	Emmy Awards, Best Single Performance in a Leading or Supporting Role, "Somebody's Waiting," episode of *The Dick Powell Show*	**Nominated**
1964	Golden Globe Awards, Best Television Star—Male *Mickey*	**Won**
1980	Academy Awards, Best Actor in a Supporting Role, *The Black Stallion*	**Nominated**
1980	Tony Awards, Best Performance by a Leading Actor in a Musical, *Sugar Babies*	**Nominated**
1980	Drama Desk Awards, Outstanding Actor in a Musical, *Sugar Babies*	**Nominated**
1981	Emmy Awards, Outstanding Lead Actor in a Limited Series or Special, *Bill*	**Won**
1981	Golden Globe Awards, Best Actor in a Television Mini-Series or Motion Picture, *Bill*	**Won**
1983	Academy Awards, Academy Honorary Award "In recognition of his 50 years of versatility in a variety of memorable film performances."	**Honored**
1983	Emmy Awards, Outstanding Lead Actor in a Limited Series or a Special, *Bill: On His Own*	**Nominated**

Appendix C

1991	Gemini Awards, Best Performance by an Actor in a Continuing Leading Dramatic Role *The Adventures of the Black Stallion*	**Nominated**
1991	Young Artist Awards, Former Child Star Award for lifetime achievement as a child star (Subsequently renamed "The Mickey Rooney Award")	**Honored**
1996	Giffoni Film Festival François Truffaut Award	**Honored**
2004	Pocono Mountains Film Festival	**Lifetime Achievement Award**
2005	Telluride Film Festival	**Silver Medallion Award**

On February 8, 1960, Rooney was initiated into the Hollywood Walk of Fame with a star heralding his work in motion pictures, located at 1718 Vine Street, one for his television career located at 6541 Hollywood Boulevard, and a third dedicated to his work in radio, located at 6372 Hollywood Boulevard. On March 29, 1984, he received a fourth star, this one for his live performances, located at 6211 Hollywood Boulevard.

Bibliography

Agee, James. *Agee on Film*. New York: Modern Library, 2000.
Baby Face Nelson. DVD. Directed by Don Siegel. 1957. Saskatoon, SK, Canada: Roberts Hard to Find Videos.
Basinger, Jeanine. *The Star Machine*. New York: Alfred A. Knopf, 2007.
Bill/Bill: On His Own. DVD. Directed by Anthony Page. 1981; Westlake Village, CA: Brentwood Home Video, 2007.
The Black Stallion. DVD. Directed by Carroll Ballard. 1979. New York: The Criterion Collection, 2015.
The Bold and the Brave. DVD. Directed by Lewis R. Foster. 1956. London, UK: Optimum Releasing LTD.
Boys Town. DVD. Directed by Norman Taurog. 1938. Burbank, CA: Warner Home Video, 2005.
Brady, John. *Frank & Ava: In Love and War*. New York: Thomas Dunne Books, 2015.
The Comedian. DVD. Directed by John Frankenheimer. 1957. New York: The Golden Age of Television, Criterion Collection, 2009.
The Comic. DVD. Directed by Carl Reiner. 1969. Culver City, CA: SPE, 2013.
Considine, David M. *The Cinema of Adolescence*. Jefferson, NC: McFarland, 1985.
Crowther, Bosley. *Hollywood Rajah*. New York: Holt, Rhinehart and Winston, 1960.
Drive a Crooked Road/Columbia Pictures Film Noir Classis III. DVD. Directed by Richard Quine. 1957. Atlanta: TCM, 2012.
Evans, Peter, and Ava Gardner. *Ava Gardner: The Secret Conversations*. New York: Simon & Schuster, 2013.
A Friend Indeed: The Bill Sackter Story. DVD. Directed by Lane Wyrick. 2008. Iowa City, IA: XAP Interactive, Inc. 2009.
Gardner, Ava. *Ava: My Story*. New York: Bantam Books, 1990.
Gilbert, Douglas. *American Vaudeville: Its Life and Times*. New York: Dover Publications, 1963.
The Golden Age of Television: The Comedian. DVD. Directed by John Frankenheimer. 1957. New York: The Criterion Collection, 2009.
Groebel, Lawrence. *Conversations with Ava Gardner*. CreateSpace Independent Publishing Platform (September 5, 2014).
Hannsberry, Karen Burroughs. *Bad Boys: The Actors of Film Noir*. Jefferson, NC: McFarland, 2003.
Higham, Charles. *Ava: A Life Story*. New York: Delacorte, 1974.
Hirsch, Foster. *Acting Hollywood Style*. New York: Harry N. Abrams, 1991.
Kahn, Roger. *Into My Own*. New York: Thomas Dunn, 2006.
Killer McCoy. DVD. Directed by Roy Rowland. 1947. Beverly Hills, CA: MGM, 2009.
"Last Night of a Jockey"/ *The Twilight Zone*. VHS tape. Directed by Joseph M. Newman. 1963. Los Angeles: CBS Video Library, 1988.
Leave 'Em Laughing. DVD. Directed by Jackie Cooper. 1981. Hollywood, CA: First Home Video, 1990.
Lovell, Allan. *Don Siegel: American Cinema*. London: British Film Institute, 1975.
"Lucy Meets Mickey Rooney"/*The Lucy Show*. DVD. Directed by Maury Thompson. 1966. Los Angeles: Paramount, 2011.

Bibliography

Maltin, Leonard. *The Great Movie Shorts*. New York: Crown, 1972.

Marill, Alvin H. *Mickey Rooney: His Films, Television Appearances, Radio Work, Stage Shows, and Recordings*. Jefferson, NC: McFarland, 2005.

Marx, Arthur. *The Nine Lives of Mickey Rooney*. New York: Stein and Day, 1986.

The Mickey Rooney & Judy Garland Collection (Babes in Arms/Babes on Broadway/ Girl Crazy/ Strike Up the Band). Directed by Busby Berkeley. 1939-1941. Burbank, CA: Warner Home Video, 2007.

The Mickey Rooney Show: Hey, Mulligan. DVD. Produced by Mickey Rooney Enterprises. 1955. Timeless Media Group, 2007.

A Midsummer Night's Dream. Directed by Max Reinhardt and William Dieterle. 1935. Burbank, CA: Warner Home Video, 2007.

Miller, Don. *B Movies*. New York: Ballantine Books, 1973.

National Velvet. DVD. Directed by Clarence Brown. 1944. Burbank, CA: Warner Home Video, 2004.

"Ooftus Goofus"/*The Naked City*. DVD. Directed by Arthur Hiller. 1961. Chatsworth, CA: Image Entertainment, 2013.

Operation Mad Ball. DVD. Directed by Richard Quine. 1959. Culver City, CA: Sony Pictures Home Entertainment, 2011.

Private Screenings: Mickey Rooney. DVD. Directed by Tony Barbon. 1997. Atlanta: Turner Entertainment Networks, Inc. 2000.

Reagan, Ronald. *Reagan: A Life in Letters*. New York: Free Press, 2003.

Requiem for a Heavyweight. DVD. Directed by Ralph Nelson. 1962. Culver City, CA: Sony Pictures Home Entertainment, 2002.

Rooney, Mickey. *I.E.: An Autobiography*. New York: Putnam, 1965.

_____. *Life Is Too Short*. New York: Ballantine Books, 1991.

Schatz, Thomas. *Boom and Bust: The American Cinema in the 1940's*. New York: Charles Scribner's Sons, 1997.

_____. *The Genius of the System: Hollywood Filmmaking in the Studio Era*. Minneapolis: University of Minnesota Press, 2010.

Server, Lee. *Ava Gardner: Love is Nothing*. New York: St. Martin's Griffin, 2007.

Siegel, Don. *A Siegel Film: An Autobiography*. London: Faber & Faber, 1993.

Sobel, Bernard. *A Pictorial History of Burlesque*. New York: G.P. Putnam's Sons, 1956.

_____. *A Pictorial History of Vaudeville*. New York: The Citadel Press, 1961.

The Strip. DVD. Directed by Laszlo Kardos. 1951. Los Angeles: MGM.

That's Entertainment. DVD. Directed by Jack Haley Jr. 1974; Burbank, CA: Warner Home Video, 2004.

Thomson, David. *The New Biographical Dictionary of Film*. New York: Alfred A. Knopf, 2010.

Trav, S.D. *No Applause—Just Throw Money: The Book That Made Vaudeville Famous*. New York: Faber and Faber, 2005.

Vaudeville. DVD. Directed by Greg Palmer. 1997. New York: American Masters Production, Winstar TV & Video, 2000.

Vidal, Gore. *Screening History*. Cambridge, MA: Harvard University Press, 1992.

Wagner, Walter. *You Must Remember This: Oral Reminiscences of the Real Hollywood*. New York: Putnam, 1975.

Wayne, Jane Ellen. *Ava's Men*. New York: St. Martin's Press, 1990.

Woodside, Judy B. "Advantages of an Arrested Development: The Onscreen Adolescence of Mickey Rooney." Ph.D. dissertation, Pennsylvania State University. Ann Arbor: ProQuest/UMI, 2004 (Publication No. 3140095).

Young Tom Edison. DVD. Directed by Norman Taurog. 1940. Burbank, CA: Warner Brothers Studio, 2009.

Index

Numbers in **_bold italics_** indicate pages with photographs.

Abbott, Norman 133
Abbott and Costello 44
ABC 151–152, 159
Aber, Chris 129, 178–180
Aber, Christina 178, 180
Above the Line 199
Academy Awards 29, 55, 101, 174, 178, 201; see also Oscars
Ace of Hearts 192
The Addams Family 65
The Adventures of Huckleberry Finn 190
The Adventures of the Black Stallion 46–47, 146, 198, 202
Agee, James 46
Ah, Wilderness! 30–31, 50, 96, 189
The Alan Brady Show 186
Albee, Edward Franklin 6
Alcoa Premiere 197
Alcoa Theatre **_155_**, 156, 196, 201
Aldrich, Robert 184
Alexander, Van 69
Ali, Muhammad 74; see also Clay, Cassius
Alimony 200
All Ashore 104, 191
Allen, Ralph 129–131, 133
Allen, Woody 186
Altman, Al 84
Altman, Robert 165–166
Amazing Stories 187
Ambush Bay 115, 191
American Dad! 199
American Masters 9
Amorde, Todd 137
Amos 'n' Andy Show 5
Amsterdam, Morey 186
Anchors Aweigh 104
Andrews, Anthony 146
Andrews, Tige 164
The Andy Griffith Show 187
Andy Hardy Comes Home 109, 191
Andy Hardy Gets Spring Fever 190
Andy Hardy Meets Debutante 190
Andy Hardy's Blonde Trouble 190
Andy Hardy's Double Life 190
Andy Hardy's Private Secretary 190
Animals and the Tollkeeper 193
Apocalypse Now 143
Arabian Adventure 192
Armstrong, Louis 61
Arnold, Philip 26
Arrest and Trial 197
Astaire, Fred 9, 23, 36, 42, 143, 176
The Atomic Kid 109, 191, 199
Autry, Gene 44
Axton, Hoyt 138, 145
Ayars, Ann **_41_**

Babe: Pig in the City 193
Babes in Arms 41–42, 190, 192, 201
Babes on Broadway 41, **_43_**, 82, 190, 192
Baby Face Nelson 59, 63–**_66_**, 67–69, 72, 79, 81, 108, 191
Bacall, Lauren 99
Baker, Buddy 99
Ball, Lucy 153–154
Ballard, Carroll 138–**_142_**, 144–145, 147–148, 183, 187
Bamboo Shark 193
Bancroft, Anne 121
Bancroft, George **44**
The Barefoot Contessa 92
Barker, Bobby 7
Barry, Red 116
Barrymore, John 23
Barrymore, Lionel 30–32
Bartholomew, Freddy 31, 49
Bass, Ronald 185
Bavier, Francis 187
The Beast of the City 189
Beery, Wallace 23, 30, 44, 47, 50–51
Bela Lugosi Meets a Brooklyn Gorilla 107
Bell, Mark Russell 136–137
Beloved 189
Benny, Jack 7
Bergen, Candice 128
Bergman, Ingmar 2
Berkeley, Busby 42, 81
Berkeley, Martin 55

205

Index

Berle, Milton 13, 35, 154
Best, Willie 47
The Best of Burlesque 133
Beyond This Winter's Wheat 183
The Big Bluff 102
The Big Cage 21, 189
The Big Chance 189
The Big House 50
The Big Operator 59, 69, 72, 191
The Big Sleep 99
The Big Wheel 100, 191
Bill 149, 162, 165, 167, 172–175, 184–185, 198, 201
Bill: On His Own 174–175, 185, 198, 201
Biography 199
Black, David 130–131
The Black Stallion 46–47, 51, 54, 138–139, **140**, 141–142, **143**, 144, 146–148, 179, 183, 185–187, 192, 201
The Black Stallion Returns 146, 186
Blechman, Corey 167–168, 171–172, 184–185
Blind Date 189
"Bloodlines" 177
Bluegrass 146, 192
Blythe, Ann 96
Bogart, Humphrey 79, 99
The Bold and the Brave 108, 191, 199, 201
Bond, Ward 156
Boys Town 39, **40**, 129, 190
Bracken, Eddie 124
Brando, Marlon 2
Breakfast at Tiffany's 191
Breakston, George P. 38
Brenner, Alfred 156
Breslin, Patricia 110
The Bridges at Toko-Ri 108, 191
Broadway to Hollywood 21, 189
Brooks, Mel 148, 186
Brown, Clarence 30, 51, 81
Brown, Joe E. 26
Burke, Paul 159
Burke's Law 197
burlesque 3, 7–9, 12, 34–35, 123, 129, 131, 133–134, 149, 154
Burns & Allen 7
Bushman, Francis X. 34
Byington, Spring 31

Caan, James 166
Caesar, Sid 186
Cagney, James 26, 29, 42, 44, 79, 159, **160**, 176
Cagney, Jeanne 60
Caine, Michael 78
Call Me Mister 186
Candid Camera 154
Cantor, Eddie 7
Capra, Frank 140
Captains Courageous 190
The Care Bears Movie 192
Carlton, Claire 149
Carmine, Al 130
The Carol Burnett Show 132, 197
Carson, Johnny 128
Carter, Nell 6–8, 13–15, 18–21, 23, 25, 28, 86, **87**, 88, 100
Carvey, Dana 152
Catania, Wilma 116
CBS 152, 167–168, 171, 174, 177, 185
Celebrity Ghost Stories 199
Chained 189
Chamberlin, Jan 128–129, 131, 136–137, 177–178, 180
The Champ 50–51
Chandler, Raymond 59
Chaplin, Charlie 23, 153
Charlie's Angels 146
Chase, Borden 55
Chayevsky, Paddy 80
Chicken Soup for the Soul 199
The Chief 189
Christie's Minstrels 6
Christman, George 15
Christmas on Division Street 185
A Christmas Too Many 193
Clark, Dane 99
Clay, Cassius 74; *see also* Ali, Muhammad
Clemens, William 47
Cline, Patsy 178
Coca, Imogene 186
Cochran, Steve 11
Cockeyed Cowboys of Calico County 192
Cohan, George M. 30, 130, 159
The Colgate Comedy Hour 195
Collins, Joan 176
Columbia Pictures 61, 104, 132
Combat! 1, 156, 196
The Comedian 2, 80, 157, 201
The Comic 119, **120**, 186, 192
Conan 198
Connolly, Walter 26
Coogan, Jackie 153, 197
Cook, Elisha, Jr. 48, 163
Cooke, Sam 99
Cooper, Gary 23, 44, 126
Cooper, Jackie 20, 50–51, 162–163
Coppola, Carmine 138, 140
Coppola, Francis Ford 138–139, **140**, 142–143, 183, 187
Coppola, Sofia 187
Corman, Roger 110, 114, 184
The County Chairman 189
The Courtship of Andy Hardy 190
Cox, Richard Ian 146–147

Index

Cox, Wally 108
Craig, James 61
Crawford, Joan 23
Crazy for You 200
Crisp, Donald 53
Crockett, Dick 104
Cronyn, Hume 186
Crosby, Bing 44, 69, 197
The Crowd Roars 96
Cruise, Tom 185
The Cry Baby Killer 110, 114
Crystal, Billy 181

Daddy Mack 16
Daltrey, Roger 156
Dalva, Robert 183
Damone, Vic 61
Daniels, Jeff 183
Darin, Bobby 99
Darmour, Larry 18–20
Daughty, Hershel 157
David, Clifford 70
Davis, Bette 44, 155–156, 176
Davis, Sammy, Jr. 92, 154, 197
Dawson, Ralph 29
Day, Doris 69
The Dean Martin Show 196–197
Death on the Diamond 189
de Corsia, Ted 64
The Deer Hunter 187
DeHaven, Gloria 96
de Havilland, Olivia 23, 26, 29
DeMille, Cecil B. 180
Dempsey, Jack 76
Dern, Bruce 166
Deschanel, Caleb 141–142, 147
Deutsch, Milton 125
The Devil in Love 191
The Devil Is a Sissy 190
Devry, Elaine Mahnken 104–106, 109–113
Dick, Peggy Chantler 162
The Dick Powell Show 164–165, 196, 201
The Dick Powell Theatre 196
The Dick Van Dyke Show 152, 186
Dieterle, William 26, 28
Dillinger, John 22, 66, 68
The Dirty Dozen 184
Dirty Harry 64
Disney, Walt 137
Dittman, Dean 126
Dobkin, Lawrence 159
Dr. Jekyll and Mr. Hyde 194
Doff, Red 116, 119
Dominguin, Luis Miguel 92
Dominick and Eugene 184
The Domino Principle 128, 192
Donlevy, Brian 96

Down the Stretch 46–47, **48**, 148, 190
Drake, Tom 91, 96
Drive a Crooked Road 59, 61–**63**, 72, 81, 104, 191
Driving Me Crazy 194
Dubin, Al 134
Ducich, Dan 104–105
Duff, Howard 176
Duggan, Tom 127
Duke, Maurice 106–109, 151
Duma 147, 183
Durgan, Bullets 152

E! True Hollywood Story
Eastwood, Clint 64
Ebert, Roger 139
The Ed Sullivan Show 154, 196
Edison, the Man 45
Edwards, Blake 61, 81, 104, 109, 149
80 Steps to Jonah 192
Ellis, Patricia 47
Emmy Awards 69, 73, 149, 156, 165, 167, 173, 175, 184–186, 201
The Emperor of Peru 192; see also *Odyssey of the Pacific*
ER 156, 198
Erik the Viking 192
Everything's Ducky 191
Evil Roy Slade 192
The Extraordinary Seaman 192

The Face on the Barroom Floor 193
Fairbanks, Douglas, Sr. 180
A Family Affair 31–32, 190
Fantasy Island 176
Farley, Tim 138, 142–143, 145, 176, 185
Farley, Walter 138, 147, 185–186
Fast Companions 21, 189; see also *The Information Kid*
Faulkner, William 99
Faye, Alice 44
Fields, Dorothy 134
Fields, W.C. 23, 130
Film Booking Offices of America (FBO) 18, 20
film noir 1, 59–62, 69–70, 72–73, 78–79, 81, 99–100
Find the Lady 192
Finian's Rainbow 143
The Fireball 102, 191
The First of May 193
Fischer, Peter 177
Fitzgerald, Ella 69
Five Easy Pieces 187
Flatt, Ernest 132–134
Fleming, Victor 21, 81
Flint, Helen 30

207

Index

Flynn, Errol 44, 50
Fly Away Home 147, 183
Ford Startime 196
Forman, Joey 108, 150, 154
Forrest, Sally 61
Forsythe, John 176
Foster, Dianne 62
Foster, Preston 70
Four Fast Guns 103
Fox, Fontaine 18, 20–21
The Fox and the Hound 192
Francis in the Haunted House 191
Frankenheimer, John 157–159
Free Willy 184
Free Willy 2: The Adventure Home 184
Frolich, Sig 112, 116, 129
From Hong Kong with Love 192
Froug, William 156
The Fugitive 197
Full House 198
A Funny Thing Happened on the Way to the Forum 200

Gable, Clark 21–23, 44, 50, 85, 126
The Gambler Returns: Luck of the Draw 193
Garbo, Greta 23, 86
Gardner, Ava 2, 51, 82, **83**, 84–86, 88–89, **90**, 91–93, 95, 103, 127, **135**, 176
Gardner, Bill 110, 118
Gardner, Mollie 89
Garfield, Allen 163
Garland, Judy 20, **37**, 38, 41–42, **43**, 44, 47–**49**, 85, 97, 105, 128, 198
Garr, Teri 138
Garrett, Betty 97
Gaslight 178
Geddes, Barbara Bell 176
Gelbart, Larry 186
General Electric Theatre 196
George, Susan 146
George M! 130, 200
Gerald 193
Gershwin, George and Ira 81
Gigot 167
Gilbert, John 86
Girl Crazy 42, 190, 192
"Glasgow Belongs to Me" 8
Gleason, Jackie 73, **75**–76, 78, 151, 167–168
The Godfather 187
The Godfather: Part II 187
The Godmothers 192, 199
The Golden Girls 198
Goldwyn, Samuel 34
Gone with the Wind 21
Goodman, Ralph 133
Goodnight Ladies 200
Gordon, Gale 153

Gordon, Leo **66**
Gould, Sid 10, 12
Granger, Stewart 184
Grayson, Kathryn 33, 125
The Great Secret 34
Grey, Joel 130
Griffin, Eleanore 39
Griffith, Andy 187

Haas, Charles 72
Hackman, Gene 128
Half a Sinner 189
Hannsberry, Karen Burroughs 59, 67
Happy 199
The Happy Elf 193
Harding, Pat 149
Hardwicke, Sir Cedric 66, 68
Hardy, Andy (character) 2, 31–36, **37**, 38–39, 49–50, 71, 78, 96–97, 102, 105, 110, 128
The Hardy Family (radio program) 102
The Hardys Ride High 190
Harlow, Jean 31
Harris, Julie 73, 75, 77–78
Hart, Lorenz 96–97
Hartung, Philip T. 63
Harvest 183
Harvey, Laurence 178
Hawks, Howard 55, 99
Hayden, Sara 32, 110
Haymes, Dick 104
The Healer 189
Hemingway, Ernest 92
Henie, Sonja 44
Hepburn, Katharine 176
Herbert, Hugh 26
Herman, Al 19
Herman, Jerry 178
He's a Cockeyed Wonder 102, 191
Heston, Charlton 176
Hey, Mulligan 149, 195
Hide and Seek 200
Hide-Out 189
High School Confidential 69
High Speed 189
Higham, Charles 87
Hillard, Robert J. 124
Hiller, Arthur 159, 164
Hines, Earl "Fatha" 61
Hitchcock, Alfred 21
Hockett, Carolyn 123–125
Hodges, Mike 78
Hoffman, Dustin 185
Hogarth, Sammy 2
Hold That Kiss 190
Holden, Fay 32, 109
Holden, William 108
Holder, Eric 179

Index

Holloway, Jean 156–157
Holloway, Sterling 26
Hollywood Blue 123
Hollywood Goes Classical 200
The Hollywood Palace 154, 197
Hollywood Squares 126
Holy Hollywood 193
Home for Christmas 192
Hoosier Schoolboy 190
Hope, Bob 12, 44, 94
Hopper, Hedda 35
Hosszu vagata 186
Houdini, Harry 7
House of Usher 184
House Un-American Activities Committee (HUAC) 48
How Green Was My Valley 53
How to Stuff a Wild Bikini 191
Howard, Ron 187
Hudson, Rock 176
Hughes, Howard 92
Hughes, Ken 156
Hulce, Tom 184
The Human Comedy 30, 39–40, **41**, 190, 201
"The Hunt" 165
Hunter, Kim 73, 157
Huston, John 59
Huston, Walter 23
Hyde, Johnny 100

I Am a Fugitive from a Chain Gang 33
I Like It That Way 189
The Incredible Shrinking Man 69
The Information Kid 21; see also *Fast Companions*
Internet Love 193
Invasion of the Body Snatchers 69
The Investigators 196
It Came Upon the Midnight Clear 198
It's a Mad, Mad, Mad, Mad World 112, 191

The Jack Benny Program 196
Jack Reid's Record Breakers 3, 7
The Jackie Gleason Show 151
Jackson, Anne 162–163
Jack's Place 198
Jacobs, William 47
Jaguar 199
The Jean Arthur Show 199
The Jerk 186
Jessel, George 7
jockey 46–47, **48**, 51, 54–57, 91, 138–139, 141, 145, 183
Jolson, Al 7
Jones, Carolyn 65, 68–69
Jory, Victor 26
Joseph Hart Vaudeville Co. **4**

Journey Back to Oz 192
Judge Hardy and Son 190
Judge Hardy's Children 190
The Judy Garland Show 154

Kahn, Roger 114, 117
The Karen Carpenter Story 186
Keaton, Buster 6, 9, 121
Keith, Benjamin Franklin 6
Kelly, Grace 108
Kelly, Jack 62, **63**
Kessel, Barney 99
Killer McCoy 2, 71, 96, 190
Killing Midnight 193
King, Woody 124
King of the Roaring '20s—The Story of Arnold Rothstein 191
King's Row 176
Kleo the Misfit Unicorn 199
Knotts, Don 187
Korngold, Erich Wolfgang 26, 29
Kraft Suspense Theatre 165–166, 196
Kramer, Stanley 112, 128
Kramer, Terry Allen 130–132, 136
Kung Fu: The Legend Continues 198

Ladd, Cheryl 146
Ladd, Diane 146
Lady and the Tramp II: Scamp's Adventure 193
"The Lady Was a Flop" 46–47, 55
Lahr, Bert 9
Lahr, John 9, 13
Lamour, Dorothy 125
Landsburg, Alan 167–169
Lane, Marge 115–116, 118–119
Lane, Nathan 152–153
Lang, Fritz 59, 81
Lansbury, Angela 177–178
The Last Mile 59, 69–71, **72**, 191
"The Last Night of a Jockey" 46–47, **56**, 57, 80, 196
Last Will and Embezzlement 194
The Late, Late Show 176
The Late Show with David Letterman 127–128
The Laugh's On Me 200
Lawlor, Ma 20
Lear, Norman 137
Leave 'Em Laughing 162, 165–166, 198
Leavey, William A. 146
Lee, Peggy 69
Leeds, Peter 134
The Legend of Wolf Mountain 192
Lehman, Ernest 157
Lend Me a Tenor 200
LeRoy, Mervyn 18

INDEX

Letterman, David 128
Levinson, Barry 185
Life Begins for Andy Hardy 190
The Life of Jimmy Dolan 189
Lightning, The White Stallion 146, 192
Linden, Eric 30
Liotta, Ray 184
Little Caesar 33
Little Lord Fauntleroy 31, 190
Little Nemo: Adventures in Slumberland 192
The Little Shop of Horrors 184
Live, Love and Learn 190
Loew, Marcus 34
Lonesome Dove 146
Long, Dermont 114
Lorca, Isabel Garcia 146
Lord Jeff 190
Lorre, Peter 81
Lost in Translation 187
The Lost Jungle 189
Lost Stallions: The Journey Home 193
Louise, Anita 26
Love Birds 189
Love Boat 176
Love Finds Andy Hardy **37**, 190
Love Is a Headache 190
Love Laughs at Andy Hardy 94–95, 190
Love Story 159
Loy, Myrna 22–23
The Lucy Show 153, 197
Ludwig, William 37
Lumet, Sidney 159
Lupino, Ida 99
Lyles, A.C. 100

M 81
Macauley, Homer 2
Madame Spivy 74
The Magic of Lassie 192
The Magic Voyage 193
Magnificent Roughnecks 191
Mahan, Larry 147
Mahnken, Fred 105–106
Maibaum, Richard 51
Mainwaring, Daniel 68
Making Waves 193
Malvin, Arthur 132
Mame 178
Mamoulian, Rouben 81, 96
The Man I Love 99
The Manchurian Candidate 178
Mandelberg, Cynthia 162
Manhattan Melodrama 22, 66, 189
The Manipulator 192
Marie, Rose 186
Marquis, Margaret 31
Marsh, Whitey (character) 2, 39, **40**

Martin, Steve 186
The Martini Shot 199
Marx, Arthur: *The Nine Lives of Mickey Rooney* 26, 40, 94, 98, 106, 109, 126, 130–131, 133, 151–152
Marx, Groucho 9, 151
The Marx Bros. 6
Mason, James 127
The Masque of the Red Death 184
Massey, Raymond 80
Matheson, Melissa 138
Maximum Force 193
Mayer, Louis B. 21–22, 33–36, 86–88, 96, 98
Mazursky, Paul 164
McCarthy, Kevin 62
McDonald, Ray 104
McGuire, Mickey 2, 16, 18–21
McHugh, Frank 26
McHugh, Jimmy 131–132, 134
McMahon, Horace 159
McMurtry, Larry 146
McNear, Howard 187
McPherson, Aimee Semple 7
Men of Boys Town 190
Merrill, Dina 151–152
The Merv Griffin Show 126
Metro-Goldwyn Mayer (MGM) 2, 9, 21–22, 31–36, 40, 42, 50, 55, 59, 81, 83–84, 87–88, 91, 96–98, 104, 128, 131, 154, 177–178
Metro Pictures Corporation 34
Metropolis 81
MGM: When the Lion Roars 198
Michael Kael vs. the World News Company 193
Michener, James 107–108
Mickey 151–152, 197, 201
Mickey Mouse 2
Mickey Rooney Enterprises 149
The Mickey Rooney Show 1, 149, 195, 199
A Midsummer Night's Dream 23, **24**, **27**, 29–30, 124, 134, 153, 189, 199–200
Mike Hammer, Private Eye 198
The Milky Life 193
Milland, Ray 184
Miller, Ann 126, 131, **132**, 133–134, **135**, 178
Miller's Maidens 6
The Millionaire 103
Milosevic, Milos 115–117
The Milton Berle Show 195
The Mind with the Naughty Man 200
Minelli, Vincente 43
minstrelsy 3–6
Miranda, Carmen 82, 85
A Miser Brothers' Christmas 193
Mr. Broadway 159
Mitchell, Carolyn 110, **115**; *see also* Thomason, Barbara Ann

210

Index

Mitchell, Duke 107
Mitchelson, Marvin 124
Mix, Tom 14, 21
Mohr, Hal 29
Monroe, Marilyn 126
Monti, Carlotta 130
Mooch Goes to Hollywood 192
Moon, Keith 155–156
Moore, Colleen 18
Moore, Dennis 47
Moore, Mary Tyler 186
Moran, Mickey 2
Morris, Howard 186–187
Morrow, Barry 167, 169, 171–173, **174**, 185
Mowat, Farley 183
Muir, Jean **24**
Muni, Paul 159
The Muppets 194
Murder, She Wrote 177
Murray, Bill 187
Murrow, Edward R. 106
Muse, Clarence 140
My Heroes Have Always Been Cowboys 192
My Outlaw Brother 191, 199
My Pal, the King 21, 189
My True Story 199

Nabors, Jim 187
Naked City 159, 165, 196
Nation, Carrie 7
National Velvet 30, 46–47, 51–**52**, 53–54, 93, 176, 178, 190
NBC 151–152, 164
NBC Follies 154
Nelson, Ralph 73, 77
Never Cry Wolf 147, 183
A Nice Little Bank That Should Be Robbed 191
Nicholson, Jack 110, 184
Night at the Museum 193
Night at the Museum: Battle of the Smithsonian 193
Night at the Museum: Secret of the Tomb 194
Night Club 194
Night Gallery 79–80, 198
Nijinska, Bronislava 26
Norm 198
Not to Be Trusted 17
Now Here 193

Oates, Warren 164
Obama, Barack 181
O'Brien, Edmund 157, 159
O'Connor, Donald 125, 177
The Odd Couple 177, 200
Odyssey of the Pacific 192; see also *The Emperor of Peru*

Off Limits 191
Officer Thirteen 189
Oklahoma! 37
Oliver, Susan 164
Olivier, Laurence 1, 2, 151
One Man, One Wife 178
One of the Boys 152, 198
On the Town 104, 125
On the Waterfront 72
O'Neill, Eugene 2, 30, 81, 96
"Ooftus Gooftus" 159, 166, 196
Operation Mad Ball 191
Oppenheimer, George 35
Orchids and Ermine 18, 189
Osborne, Robert 33, 76, 95, 154
Oscars (awards) 27, 39–40, 50, 53, 77, 82, 108, 125, 136, 149, 159, 169, 183, 185, 187; see also Academy Awards
Our Gang 14–15, 21
Out West with the Hardys 190
The Outlaws: The Legend of O.B. Taggart 193, 199
Overton, Frank 70
Oz, Frank 184

Paar, Jack 126–127
Pagano, Jo 159
Page, Anthony 168–170, 172, 174
"Pal o' My Cradle Days" 13
Palance, Jack 73
Pankey, Fred 88, 100
Paquin, Anna 183
Paradise 193
Parker, Cecilia 30, 32, **37**, 110
Parsons, Louella 35
Pastor, Tony 6
Pat White and His Gaiety Girls 8
Peck, Ed 122
Peek, Kim 169, 185
Perry Mason 103
Pete and Gladys 196
Peters, Bernadette 130
Peterson, Les 35, 87–89
Pete's Dragon 128, 192
Petrillo, Sammy 107
Phantom of the Megaplex 193
Phillips, Betty Jane 93–94, 98–100, 103, 113
Pichel, Irving 81
Pickford, Mary 23
The Pit and the Pendulum 184
Platinum High School 70, 191
Playhouse 90 73, 157, 195, 201
Poe, Edgar Allan 184
Pompian, Paul 133
Powell, Dick 26
Powell, Jane 176
Powell, William 22

INDEX

Power, Tyrone 44
Praskins, Leonard 51
The Premature Burial 184
Presley, Elvis 42, 99
Price, Vincent 184
Prince for a Day 184
The Private Lives of Adam and Eve 70, 191, 199
Proctor, Frederick Freeman 6
Public Enemy 33
Puck (character) 23, **24**, 25–26, **27**, 28–30, 153, 189
Pulp 78–80, 192
Pyle, Denver 187

Quaid, Dennis 172
Quicksand 59–60, 62, 81, 100, 191
Quine, Richard 61, 81, 101, 103–104, 149
Quinn, Anthony 73, **75**–76, 78

Rachel's Man 192
Rafelson, Bob 187
Rain Man 169, 185
Randall, Tony 177
"Rare Objects" 79–80, 198
The Raven 184
Rawhide 197
Raye, Martha 126
Reagan, Ronald 176–177
Rebecca 21
The Rebel 103
Reckless 189
Red River 55
The Red Skelton Show 197
Reddy, Helen 128
Reed, Donna 176
Reeve, Birdie 9
Reiner, Carl 119, 121, 186
Reinhardt, Max 23–26, 28–29
Rendezvous 189
Reno, Kelly 47, 138, **143**, 144–146, 186–187
Requiem for a Heavyweight 73, **75**–76, 80, 151, 191
Reuben, Aaron 186
Revenge of the Red Baron 193
Revere, Anne 53
Reynolds, Gene 37
Rice, Thomas D. 3–4, 6
Richard 192
Riffraff 31, 190
Rigby, Harry 129–133, 137
Riot in Cell Block 11 64
Roach, Hall 14–15, 18
Rockwell, Norman 36
Rodeo 147, 183
Rodgers, Richard 96
Rodman, Howard 159

Rogers, Ginger 36, 42
Rogers, Will 7
Rogers, William 32
Rojas, Manuel 102
Rooney, Charlene 178–180
Rooney, Mark 178–180
Rooney, Michael 117
Rooney, Pat 21
Roos, Fred 54, 138–139, 179, 187
Roosevelt, Franklin Delano 89
Rose, Reginald 80
Rosenberg, Jeanne 138
Rosenthal, Larry 130
Rourke, Mickey 180
Rouverol, Aurania 31
Rowan & Martin's Laugh-In 197
Rowland, Roy 96
Ruben, Aaron 119
Rudolph and Frosty's Christmas in July 192, 198
The Russians Are Coming! The Russians Are Coming! 115
Ruth, Babe 7
Rutherford, Ann 32, **37**, 110
Ryan, Meg 152

Sackter, Bill 2, 166–173, **174**, 175, 185, 198
Saddle Up with Dick Wrangler & Injun Joe 193
Sailor Beware 199
St. Vincent 187
The Sandow Trocadero Vaudevilles **11**
Santa Claus Is Comin' to Town 192, 198
Santell, Alfred 18
Saroyan, William 40, 81
Savage, Fred 186
Savage, John 186–187
Scarlet Street 81
Schary, Dore 39, 96
Schatz, Thomas: *The Genius of the System: Hollywood Filmmaking in the Studio Era* 32
Schlitz Playhouse of Stars 46, 55, 195
Scott, Lizabeth 79
Seaton, George 108
The Secret Invasion 114, 184, 191
See How They Run 200
Seitz, George B. 32
Selznick, David O. 21–22, 31, 34
Sennett, Mack 50
Serling, Rod 73, 75, 80–81, 157
Servano, Nick 107
Shakespeare, William 2, 23, **24**, 25, 28–29, 158
Shaw, Artie 92
Shore, Dinah 69
Shorty Bell, Cub Reporter 102

Index

Show Boat 92, 177, 200
Shulman, Irving 68
Siegel, Don 64–65, 68–69, 81, 108
Silent Night, Deadly Night 5: The Toy Maker 193
Simon, Neil 177, 186
The Simpsons 198
Sinatra, Frank 86, 92, 99
Sinbad: The Battle of the Dark Knights 193
Sinclair, Ronald **49**
Singular Sensations 200
Sin's Pay Day 189
Sirk, Douglas 69
Skidding 31
Skidoo 191
Slave Ship 190
The Slaves of New York 3
A Slight Case of Larceny 124, 191
Smight, Jack 156
Smith, Al 13
Smith, Charley Martin 183
The Smothers Brothers Comedy Hour 154, 197
The Snow Queen 193
The Snows of Kilimanjaro 92
"Somebody's Waiting" 164–166
Sondheim, Stephen 178
Sonny 8, 10, 12–19
Sound Off 103–104, 191
Spelling, Aaron 176
Sperling, Milton 130
Spies, Adrian 164
Splet, Alan 183
Stablemates 46–47, 50–51, 190
Stander, Lionel 79
Stanwyck, Barbara 176
Stapleton, Maureen 161
Star Wars 183
Sternberg, Tom 138
The Steve Allen Show 195
Stewart, James 100, 176
Stiefel, Sam 59–60, 81, 97–98, 100
Stone, Lewis 32, 102, 109
Strike the Tent 193
Strike Up the Band 42, 190
The Strip 59, 61, 191
Stuart, Mel 167–168
Sugar Babies 123, 131, **132**, 133–134, **135**, 136–137, 149, 152, 168, 171, 178, 200–201
Summer Holiday 190
Sunset Boulevard 50
The Sunshine Boys 177, 200
Susskind, David 73
Swamp Women 184
Swanson, Gloria 50
Sweeney Todd: The Demon Barber of Fleet Street 178

Sweet Justice 193
"Sweet Rosie O'Grady" 12, 16, 25

Tales of Terror 184
Taps, Jonie 104
Taurog, Norman 97
Taylor, Elizabeth 47, 51–**52**, 176, 198
Taylor, Robert 50, 96
Teagarden, Jack 61
Teddy at the Throttle 50
Temple, Shirley 44
The Texaco Star Theatre 154
Thalberg, Irving 34
That Way with Women 99
That's Entertainment! 192
Theilade, Nini 26
The Thirsting 193
This Is Your Life 196, 198
Thomas, Frankie 31
Thomason, Barbara Ann 110–111, 114, **115**, 116–117, 119, 123, 127; *see also* Mitchell, Carolyn
Thoroughbreds Don't Cry 46–**49**, 190
Thousands Cheer 190
Three Goats and a Blanket 124, 200
Thum, Jack 162–163
Thunder County 192
To Kill a Mockumentary 193
The Tomb of Ligeia 184
The Tonight Show 126–127
The Tonight Show Starring Johnny Carson 128, 198
The Tonight Show with Jay Leno 199
Toomey, Regis 149
"Toonerville Folks" 18
"The Toonerville Trolley That Meets All the Trains" 18
top banana 8, 130–131, 136, 196
Topa Topa Bluffs 193
Tormé, Mel 157–158
Touch of Evil 69
Townsend, Pete 156
Tracy, Spencer 31, **40**, 44–45, 50, 70–71
Travolta, John 42
Treacher, Arthur 26
Tronto, Rudy 133–134
Trumbo, Dalton 48
Tucker, Sophie 7, 49
The Tunnel of Love 200
Turner, Lana 33, **37**, 38, 84, 176
Twain, Mark 41
Twenty-Four Hours to Kill 191
The Twilight Zone 46, **56**–57, 80, 196
The Twinkle in God's Eye 191, 199
Two for the Show 177, 200

United Artists 71, 100

Index

Valentino, Rudolph 180
Valone, Raf 184
Van, Bobby 118, 154
Van Doren, Mamie 69, 72–73
Van Dyke, Dick **120**, 121–122, 186
Van Dyke, W. S. 22
Van Riper, Kay 32
vaudeville 1, 3, 5–10, 12–13, 16, **17**, 19, 21, 25, 42, 73, 103, 106, 144, 154, 177, 181
Venable, Evelyn 26
Vickers, Martha (Mart) **99**, 100–103, 113
Vidal, Gore 80
The Voices from Beyond 194
The Volunteer Organist 3

Wagon Train 1, 156, 196
Walsh, Raoul 99
Wannamaker, Ted 130
Warner, Jack 28
Warner Brothers 18, 24, 26, 28–29, 33, 176
Waterman, Sam 147
Watson, Bob **40**
Wayne, John 55
W.C. 130, 133, 200
Webb, Chick 69
Webb, Ruth 125–126, 128, 136
Weidler, Virginia **44**
Weinstein, Arnold 130
Weissberger, Felix 24–25
Welbeck, Peter 146
Welles, Orson 59, 69
Wexley, John 70–71
What's My Line? 196
White, Pat 8, 13
The Who 155
Wilder, Billy 59

The Will Rogers Follies 177, 200
Williams, Esther 33
Williams, Tennessee 2
Wilson, Carey 32, 34–35
Wilson, Woodrow 181
Wincer, Simon 146
Windom, William 163
Windust, Bretaigne 156
Witliff, William D. 138
The Wizard of Oz 9, 177, 200
Wolf, George 141
The Wonderful World of Disney 198
Wood, Sam 51
The Woods 194
Woodside, Judy B.: "Advantages of an Arrested Development: The Onscreen Adolescence of Mickey Rooney": 36, 39, 41
Words and Music 96, 191
The World Changes 189
Written on the Wind 69
Wyman, Jane 176
Wynn, Ed 73
Wynn, Keenan 73

A Yank at Eton 190
The Year Without a Santa Claus 192, 198
The Yesterday Pool 193, 199
Young, Gig 125
Young, Loretta 176
Young Tom Edison **44**, 45, 190
Your Show of Shows 186–187
You're Only Young Once 31–32, 190
Yule, Joe, Jr. 2, 16, **17**, 20–21, 130
Yule, Joe, Sr. 3, 7–8, 13, 88, 102, 143

Zugsmith, Albert 69–70, 72